THE COST OF COOL

KENNETH E. MONTAGUE SERIES

IN OIL AND BUSINESS HISTORY

Jon Roberts

WITH CONTRIBUTIONS BY

Tracye McDaniel

Elsie L. Echeverri-Carroll

Evan Johnston

Jennifer Todd-Goynes

TEXAS A&M UNIVERSITY PRESS

COLLEGE STATION

First edition

∞ This paper meets the requirements of ANSI/NISO Z39.48-1992 (Permanence of Paper).
Binding materials have been chosen for durability.
Manufactured in the United States of America.

Library of Congress Cataloging-in-Publication Data
Names: Roberts, Jon (Corporate director), author.
Title: The cost of cool: Austin's tech growth and the people left behind / Jon Roberts; with contributions by Tracye McDaniel, Elsie L. Echeverri-Carroll, Evan Johnston, and Jennifer Todd-Goynes.
Other titles: Kenneth E. Montague series in oil and business history.
Description: First edition. | College Station: Texas A&M University Press, [2026] | Series: Kenneth E. Montague series in oil and business history | Includes bibliographical references and index.
Identifiers: LCCN 2025039500 (print) | LCCN 2025039501 (ebook) | ISBN 9781648433832 (paperback) | ISBN 9781648433849 (ebook)
Subjects: LCSH: High technology industries–Texas–Austin. | Economic development–Social aspects–Texas–Austin. | Entrepreneurship–Texas–Austin. | Austin (Tex.)–Economic policy.
Classification: LCC HC108.A95 R63 2026 (print) | LCC HC108.A95 (ebook)
LC record available at https://lccn.loc.gov/2025039500
LC ebook record available at https://lccn.loc.gov/2025039501

Published by Texas A&M University Press
John H. Lindsey Building, Lewis Street
College Station, TX 77843
www.tamupress.com

This book complies with the EU General Product Safety Regulation (GPSR) (Regulation (EU) 2023/988). For regulatory inquiries and product safety matters within the EU, contact our authorized representative:
Mare Nostrum Group B.V.
Mauritskade 21D
1091 GC Amsterdam
The Netherlands
Email: gpsr@mare-nostrum.co.uk
Website: https://mngbookshop.co.uk/

This publication has undergone a risk assessment and meets applicable safety standards. Traceability identifiers: ISBN, batch number, and publisher contact details are provided for compliance. No hazardous materials or components are included in this product.

CONTENTS

vii Preface

One
1 Visions of Austin

Two
29 Something in the Water

Three
47 Why Capital Matters

Four
63 An Open Society

Five
77 Austin's Tech Entrepreneurial Ecosystem
by Elsie L. Echeverri-Carroll and Evan Johnston

Six
107 Ambition, Exclusion, and the Erasure of Black Culture
by Tracye McDaniel

Seven
135 Upsetting the Apple Cart: Innovation and Disruption

Eight
155 According to Plan
by Jennifer Todd-Goynes

Nine
169 The Future of Jobs

Ten
185 The Future of Austin

193 Afterword

195 Acknowledgments

197 Notes

205 Bibliography

229 Index

PREFACE

n the January 2023 issue of *Texas Monthly*, Austin was given the magazine's annual "Bum Steer" award. The subhead read: "How a funky little college town became the unbearable-traffic, unaffordable-real-estate, insufferable-tech-bro, inanely-precious-restaurant, expensive-BBQ capital of the world!"

To read the article is like listening to a spurned lover's lament. Your ideal mate turns out to have become a different person, someone who has moved beyond you. To grouse about the fact that Austin is no longer the city it was ten years ago is, in fact, a decennial event both predictable and comical. Complaints about Austin no longer being Austin (the Austin *you* moved to) date back well over fifty years. This latest jeremiad follows in those footsteps. The reality, of course, is that *change* is in the very nature of the city. Unlike many communities across the nation, Austin is defined by its near-constant evolution, its metamorphosis from one state of being to another. When newcomers are the antithesis of who we thought we were (whether they are "hippies" or "Californians" or "tech bros"), our city no longer feels like it belongs to us.

None of this is to say that Austin is not facing enormous problems associated with growth. No city in the United States has experienced the same consistent level of population increases as has Austin. So yes, the challenge is not just to answer our question—the question of how Austin became Austin—but also to go further and wager guesses at how Austin can *remain* Austin.

When I first entertained the notion of writing about Austin, I imagined a relatively simple task. I wanted to update the work done by authors who had chronicled the city's emergence as a technology center, since technology is the dominant engine responsible for Austin's rapid growth. What I quickly discovered, however, was that explaining that history would require much more than chronicling the new companies and investments that had occurred over the last twenty years or so. While it should have been obvious from the outset, you can't talk about tech and progress without talking about people and place. Few had taken a broad perspective on the city's economic growth. So, what began with a seemingly straightforward project soon blossomed into something far more massive. It was also a project I could no longer tackle on my own. Joining me in this exploration are several important contributors. The first of these is Tracye McDaniel.

Tracye has led economic development under five governors as well as for the Greater Houston Partnership. She is currently the president of TIP Strategies. And most relevant to this book, she was the first president of the Greater Austin Black Chamber of Commerce. The story of Austin cannot be told from one perspective. What does tech growth mean for all residents of a city? Does increased wealth flow equitably across the community? Or—and this thought is still heretical in many circles—does it widen the gap and leave the Black and Hispanic population less well off? Of course, this question is not restricted to Austin, but Austin does serve as a unique test case for this debate.

In addition to Tracye's contribution, Professor Elsie L. Echeverri-Carroll and Evan Johnston tackle the role of entrepreneurship in Austin's growth. Elsie has long been associated with the IC² Institute of the University of Texas and has done extensive research on entrepreneurial ecosystems. Knowing how Austin has capitalized on entrepreneurship and how vital it is to tech growth is a pressing issue for communities everywhere. Evan has researched entrepreneurship at the IC² Institute and is a senior analyst at TIP. Their research sheds new light on this topic.

Then there is the troubling concern highlighted by *Texas Monthly*. Has Austin's growth come at the expense of the city's identity? Central to this debate is the role that planning has played. And finally, Jennifer Todd-Goynes, a former principal planner with the City of Austin before becoming a senior consultant at TIP Strategies, weighs in on urban planning. Her intimate knowledge of the city's planning efforts, both those that succeeded as well as those that failed, are crucial to an understanding of how Austin became Austin.

There are, of course, many other perspectives to be taken on Austin. Some we do little more than acknowledge in passing. Music. Festivals. Sports. And, of course, politics. Any one of these could fill entire shelves.

What this book is ultimately about, however, is the challenge that technology poses for the soul of a city—a challenge that, if met creatively, can be transformative.

Nowhere is that more obvious than in the challenge posed by artificial intelligence (AI). It would be too glib to say that this is just another phase in the steady progress of technology into our lives. Yes, the telephone was a radical departure from the way we communicated after that first Alexander Graham Bell call in 1876 ("Mr. Watson, come here, I want to see you.") And the widespread use of the internet continues to dominate our lives. AI, however, is different. While we may have worried about what jobs would look like in previous tech advances, we are now being forced to ask whether *any* job will require human participation. This is not a topic we explore here, but it looms large in the future we are facing. What sounds like science fiction today could be the norm tomorrow.

For those in the professional classes, COVID-19 ushered in changes in where we can work and how we can work. Virtual collaboration became commonplace. As radical as this transition was, however, it didn't challenge the *concept* of work. AI does. What if the job you trained for, and the companies you hoped to be part of, simply don't need your skills? What if the work you do can be done by generative AI? Then what? Chapter 9 of this book, "The Future of Jobs," addresses the very concept of what a "job" is. AI heightens that philosophical question into something very practical. If humans aren't necessary for production, what is the meaning of a job? There are answers to this question, but they are fraught with social and economic implications we will have to work out—individually and collectively. What we do know is that we will continue to live together, in cities, and the future of those cities is ours to determine.

THE COST OF COOL

CHAPTER ONE

Visions of Austin

"This should be the seat of an empire." Austin's first vision statement, uttered on a hilltop in 1838 by the new Texas republic's first vice president, Mirabeau Lamar, was, quite frankly, insane. By any century's standards. Standing on a ridge of Mount Bonnell, minutes away from Austin's present-day downtown, Lamar made this bold pronouncement as he took in his first view of Texas' Colorado River, winding around gentle bends through the emerald-green Hill Country. This oasis of flowing water and rolling greenery bewitched Lamar, as it does today's first-time visitors, who are often taken aback by the incongruence between what is expected of Texas—dry, flat, dusty—and the lush panorama that greets them. For Lamar, the expansive vista was more than an invitation to think about the charm of the wilderness spread out before him—it was a challenge to create and to grow. To birth an empire.

Lamar's proclamation must have sounded like wishful thinking to the local scouts who accompanied him on what had begun as a buffalo hunt. In reality, this territory was anything but a likely site for the seat of an empire, let alone a flourishing city. Waterloo, as Austin was called at the time, was a tiny village sparsely populated by European Americans who began arriving in the early 1830s. Yes, these settlers saw promise in this beautiful spot at a bend in the Colorado River near natural springs (e.g., Barton Springs, named after settler William "Uncle Billy" Barton). But natural charms notwithstanding, Central Texas was a dangerous place to settle, vulnerable to kidnappings by the fierce and unrelenting Comanches. The simplest errands could end in a hail of arrows.

The Comanche, however, were not the only source of resistance to a new seat of the republic's empire. The thriving Gulf Coast city of Houston was already laying claim to that title. Named after the republic's first president, Sam Houston, the city was the de facto capital in many people's minds. Waterloo, by contrast, was far-flung and vulnerable to attacks from both Mexicans and Native Americans whose claim to the land predated those of more recent settlers. The Tonkawa and Comanche, who'd long inhabited the area and the hallowed springs, were far from reconciled to the region's newest residents. European Americans' expansionist ambitions, of course, often came at a high and deadly cost to Native Americans, who were ultimately killed en masse or mercilessly driven from their land. (For a meticulously researched and well-written account of these events, I recommend *Seat of Empire* by Jeffrey Stuart Kerr.)

Despite these drawbacks, Lamar remained transfixed by his vision of Austin. This vision of an expansive empire, an empire whose definition would gradually change entirely, is still deeply ingrained in us.

Two hundred years later, gazing out the window of a Southwest Airlines jet coming over the parched West Texas plains, a present-day visitor will see the same stunning vista Lamar saw. The small shadow of the plane glides over the Texas Colorado River as it pools into seven glistening lakes. And further out is the sharp rise of the *balcón*—the escarpment that defines the eastern border of Texas' Hill Country. The river snakes through a city of both high-rises and narrow green swaths visible even from a mile up. As the plane touches down, there are no dusty, cattle-filled plains to greet the visitor. What emerges instead is a city more green than brown, more Pacific Northwest than barren oil town.

Geography constitutes the DNA of cities. The urban landscape changes, but the hills and the river define both origins and outcomes. It is no great stretch to see how this geography, this setting, would have inspired any explorer. It still inspires the first-time visitor. Lamar was willing to take a gamble on Waterloo. And what is a vision if not a gamble? He imagined an empire that would one day stretch all the way to the Pacific. Now, Austin holds the promise of a vision that stretches across the entire country, and internationally as well. Lamar's commitment to a singular bold vision, despite its huge risks and the high price others had to pay for it, would set in motion not only the events that would shape the state's capital but define its character, and its idiosyncrasies, for decades to come.

Lamar was soon to be elected the republic's second president that same year, and his commitment to Austin as Texas' new capital would be more easily realized. Several cities had already served as the young nation's seat of power—an itinerant strategy intended to evade capture by Mexico. In 1839, however, the Texas Congress appointed a commission to select a permanent home, the first of many site-selection efforts that would eventually choose Austin. Like the technology companies that would begin flocking here a century and a half later, and like Lamar himself on his famous buffalo hunt, the selection commission, steered by Lamar, recognized something special and auspicious about Waterloo—the beauty of the land, the promise of the river, the charm of the springs, the potential of its inhabitants and their own desire for growth and prosperity—and recommended it as the capital. That same year, 7,735 acres were purchased to serve as the site.

Lessons in Economic Development: Site Selection and Vision

To economic developers, the successful outcome of a site-selection process is akin to grasping the holy grail. The question of what determined the outcome—why a particular site was chosen—is the subject of intense analysis. There are a host of considerations that make a particular site advantageous for businesses these days. At the top of that list, two factors have dominated in recent years for metro regions. The first is the availability of an accessible workforce—the talent equation. The other is transportation access. Certainly other factors matter, too: infrastructure, business climate, and a dizzying array of additional metrics. Most confounding, however, has been the "quality of life" element. It appears high on every chamber of commerce list of desirable features while remaining notoriously vague.

While a business and a city are vastly different, the idea of selecting a site for either has overlapping considerations. And as is often the case, cost factors and a detailed analysis of all the pros and cons can quickly give way to less tangible influences. In the case of Austin—and of certain high-profile corporations—the choice of a particular site is sometimes driven by the desire to make a statement. In short, it is driven by a vision for what could be, not just what makes the most financial sense. That was most certainly the case with the site selection team led by Lamar.

Unsurprisingly, not everyone's vision of the city's future was shared. Shortly after Lamar christened Waterloo the republic's capital—now renamed after the "Father of Texas," Stephen F. Austin—Sam Houston attempted to move the capitol to his eponymous city, which had served as the capital before Waterloo. In *Seat of Empire*, Kerr masterfully tells the story of the struggle between these two iconic Texas figures: Houston, colorful and flamboyant, never to be reconciled to the fact that his namesake city was not to become the permanent capital; and Lamar, more reserved, but no less determined to argue the case for a vulnerable and still remote settlement in the wilderness.

Houston spent several years plotting a capital coup. In 1841, he succeeded Lamar and again became president. The following year he initiated a heist. His men were ordered to reclaim the archives, documents deeply symbolic to the republic. Wherever the archives were, the thinking went, the capital would follow.

Unfortunately for Houston, Lamar's vision of Austin as the seat of government had taken a deep hold on its residents. Austinites, among them innkeeper Angelina Eberly, did not sit back idly. She spied Houston's men approaching, rolled out a cannon, and fired, threatening to blast the looters all the way to Mexico. The short-lived Texas Archives War had begun. She and Austin held firm, and prevailed. How much of this story stands up to historical scrutiny, and how much is apocryphal, is up for debate. Today, however, a bronze statue of Eberly, bracing herself against the wind, her hand perched over the cannon fuse, graces Congress Avenue in downtown Austin. Visions require myths, and we have them in abundance.

The archives remained, and in 1845 Anson Jones, the fourth and final president of the Republic of Texas, reluctantly conceded that the capital should indeed be Austin. Texas was annexed by the United States the same year. Finally, a statewide vote in 1872 settled the matter once and for all.

The Challenge of Crafting a Vision

"Vision" is a concept that bedevils every leader and every community. It is a challenge to politicians from the president down to the mayor of a small town. In the private sector, corporations struggle with it as well. Does a company need a "vision statement"? And how does a vision statement tie to slogans and taglines? Nike's vision statement is: *To bring inspiration and innovation to every athlete* in the world. *If you have a body, you are an athlete.*

The tagline, as we all know, is "Just do it." The "it" for Nike, is the transformation of every person into an "athlete." And it's a compelling vision. But it's easier for corporations to declare a vision than it is for a community. The success of a company is easier to measure than what counts as success in a community. And this is precisely why community vision statements bog down. It is also why Mirabeau Lamar's vision held firm. He did not convene a committee to craft a statement. He saw the future—and he made that future compelling to everyone he encountered.

Crisis after crisis, Mirabeau Lamar held fast to the vision he had formed on his first visit to Austin, a vision compelling enough to outlast Native American raids, disillusioned settlers, and the political machinations of Sam Houston. And it was inspirational enough to get buy-in from the community, giving it traction and strength in numbers. It was a vision that proved itself successful over time and that endures even if we no longer quote it. Today, Austin is indeed a seat of an empire—culturally and commercially. With its burgeoning software sector, vibrant startup community (the city was ranked no. 1 in the Kauffman Index for startup activity in 2015 and 2016), intellectual property (IP) emerging from the University of Texas (UT), and international draws, such as South by Southwest (SXSW), Austin can lay claim to being a dominant power player in the tech space, as well as a pacesetter in emerging sectors such as AI.

"Seat of an empire" would not resonate today. And it would certainly not be adopted by a chamber of commerce. When we speak of the "vision" for a city, we typically mean something quite different than one man's over-the-top and futuristic dream—and something far less interesting and far less passionate. Regional leaders and economic developers know that if a city wants to thrive in the twenty-first century, it must attract new business, new investment, and new people, and must not hemorrhage them. So, vision statements are often created with this checklist of measurable factors in mind. This makes sense, but it invariably results in the most trite of pronouncements.

Over the years, I've sat in countless meetings with people from all parts of the country and from different sectors (government, corporate business, nonprofit) and can say confidently that vision matters. Just as we respond to corporate visions and the taglines they generate, businesses are attentive to the vision a community sets out for itself.

Most often, however, efforts to craft a vision statement go sideways. Not only is the result anemic, it is in no way unique or compelling. Some variation of wanting a community to be "a great place to live, work, and play" has become the norm. It is entirely typical of committee work—acceptable to everyone, deeply appealing to none.

How can economic developers avoid the blandness that often springs from vision-by-committee? One way to put a vision statement to the test is to ask what it commits us to. What do we have to risk? What do we have to sacrifice? Lamar's vision "statement" was certainly high-stakes. It was anything but one of the lifeless varieties drafted by committee. Angelina Eberly inherited his vision, consciously or not; she was so convinced Austin should be the state capital that she chased off Houston's men with cannon fire. She wasn't looking for a city that would be "a great place to live, work, and play"—that could have been had elsewhere. She knew that she lived in the rightful capital of Texas, a seat of empire, and she was ready to fight for that belief.

Another way many vision statements miss the mark: They tend to be deficient in narrative, in plot, in the throughline that connects a community's past with its present and future. In Austin's case, its successes of the twentieth and twenty-first centuries rest solidly on its origin story. Today's empire—however you want to define it—was made possible by Lamar's singular vision and the community's commitment to it. While it's easy to read too much into events that stretch back centuries, there really was something in the ambition and determination of those early inhabitants that has persevered through the decades, that we can recognize in Austin's successive vision statements (more on that shortly) and meteoric growth over the last fifty years. Yes, competing visions of Austin continue to chafe against each other—our generation has its own Lamars and Houstons—but the impassioned notion that this is a city with a great destiny, no matter the odds, still prevails. This is the thread that connects the Waterloo of 1840 with the Austin of the 2020s—the willingness to risk and to sacrifice for a singular vision, however tenuous, that is deeply and passionately held to.

So, what makes a vision stick? What makes it compelling? Yes, boldness matters. And a sense of what makes the community *unique*. It would be wrong to assume that it has to spring full-blown from a single individual, but it is true that "vision by committee" is unlikely to evoke passion. What is more often the case is that the vision for a community is already latent in the people who live there, though not in ways easily appreciated by civic leaders who are looking to smooth the edges of controversy. Nothing tells this story better than Austin's current tagline (and de facto vision): Keep Austin Weird.

Weirdness: Music and Culture

For footloose individuals in the 1970s seeking like-minded young people—as I was when I first visited Austin—there weren't many places that could meet that promise. San Francisco's Haight-Ashbury, yes, and Manhattan's Greenwich Village. Or Austin, Texas, where music and a counterculture vibe were always at hand. And where being "weird" was a welcome trait.

The free-spirited renaissance that defined the 1960s arrived a little late to Austin, which embraced it more wholeheartedly in the early 1970s. Live music venues were everywhere—including the Armadillo World Headquarters, housed in a former National Guard armory on South First Street and Barton Springs Road, and Soap Creek Saloon out west, on Bee Caves Road. Hippies and rednecks alike mingled here, an unlikely fellowship that helped birth progressive country, the "cosmic cowboy" sound epitomized by Jerry Jeff Walker and Willie Nelson, who, like Angelina Eberly, are immortalized in bronze here. Marijuana and psychedelics were plentiful.

The city's weirdness was precisely this mix of the counterculture with cowboy culture—something that didn't fit anyone's conception of what could (or should) work. Local personalities with an affinity for the unconventional helped solidify the alternative culture vibe in Austin. John Aielli, who launched a public radio show in 1966 called *Eklektikos*—which highlighted the best of music from *all* genres ("eklektikos" means "to gather" in Greek), from folk to rock to Indian classical to Tuvan throat singers—broadcast his eclectic worldview to listeners until 2020. His show, a medley of music, interviews with writers, and musings on topics as diverse as the color pink (!), was so beloved that the City of Austin proclaimed September 16, 2016, as "John Aielli Day." He even got his own infamous Twitter handle: @shitjohnaiellisays. I was fortunate enough to know John personally—we'd gone to high school together in Killeen, Texas—and in 1965 I hitchhiked down from San Francisco to visit him. In retrospect, having John as my guide for my inaugural visit was like getting a tour of Oz from the Wizard himself. Seen through John's kaleidoscope glasses, the city made a huge impression on me. Not unlike Mirabeau Lamar, I responded viscerally to Austin's captivating blend of geography and people. Thirty years later, with an offer from the Ann Richards administration to work on economic development in Texas, I didn't hesitate to leave the Pacific Northwest.

In 2000, several years after my arrival, Austin's countercultural brand finally became codified when local community college librarian Red Wassenich called into KOOP, a community radio station, to make a donation. The host asked him why he was donating. "I don't know," Wassenich replied. "It helps keep Austin weird." What could have been a throwaway comment caught on like wildfire. Austin already had a history of similar designations. Stickers proclaiming, "Keep Austin Austin," an imperative likely designed to differentiate the town from Dallas or Houston, had festooned car bumpers as early as 1982. Soon "Keep Austin Weird"—an against-the-grain phrase that encapsulated that distinctive but hard to classify spirit born in the 1970s—blanketed the city, adorning T-shirts, graffiti, and laptop stickers.

The sentiment behind the tagline took many forms, direct and indirect. On my way to Starbucks at Sixth and Congress every morning, I was greeted by Leslie Cochran, a high-heel-wearing, thong-sporting homeless man. He was the most unlikely of icons, a living embodiment of keeping Austin weird. When he got sick, the city chipped in to give him medical treatment. His death in 2012 was met with citywide remembrances. March 8 has been Leslie Day ever since.

The slogan became so ubiquitous, in fact, and so synonymous with Austin's counterculture, that other communities would eventually want to either claim it their own (Portland, Oregon) or disclaim it. Round Rock, a suburban community just to Austin's north, cheekily urges its residents to keep their own hometown "mildly unusual," and Austin's neighbor to the south embraces its less-hip status with "Keep San Antonio Lame." In any case, the spread of "Keep Austin Weird" can be largely attributed to small, locally owned businesses, including Waterloo Records and BookPeople. BookPeople is the city's largest independent bookstore and hosted a talk and book-signing by Wassenich himself in 2016. The phrase has also become a rallying cry against chain stores moving to town. The "Keep Austin Weird" message was clear: Our downtown will not, or should not, look like every other. The city's growth since Wassenich's consequential KOOP phone call in 2000 has challenged that vision over and over again, but the sentiment behind it remains strong—and vocal, especially when new corporate residents consider making Austin their new home. Walking around present-day downtown, despite the proliferation of new high-rises, you are hard-pressed to find more than a handful of national chain outlets (an Anthropologie here, a Starbucks there). Locally owned shops still thrive, despite the loss of iconic venues such as Las Manitas. The city's longstanding (and formal) strategy for prioritizing residential buildings over corporate retail has helped make that possible. The stores that do thrive downtown largely serve those living in or near its heart.

Despite its origins, the "Keep Austin Weird" campaign represents more than mere nostalgia or local-business boosterism. It reflects the openness and tolerance that has been part of the city's identity in the decades since the counterculture revolution. "Weird," after all, is the opposite of "mainstream," "exclusionary," or "closed-minded." While some may be tempted to ascribe Austin's openness to good ol' Texan friendliness—or as Lyle Lovett puts it, "That's right you're not from Texas, but Texas wants you anyway"—it's more than that.

Culturally speaking, Austin has—in its best moments since its 1970s awakening—embodied a concept I was introduced to as a grad student, that of Viennese philosopher Karl Popper's "open society." Inclusiveness, individuality, and openness are closely aligned with that philosophy. Newcomers and new ideas are not just tolerated, they are welcomed. They are critical not only in establishing a city's charm and sense of place but also to its economic success. Individuality and openness are central to experimentation, experimentation is central to lasting growth, and an experimentation ethos is central to Popper's ideas. Openness, in other words, means growth, and not only for residents of those cities but for the cities themselves. Put more directly: Openness is a prerequisite for creativity, one of the main ingredients that allows a city like Austin to become—and continue to be—Austin.

Of course, any discussion of openness would be remiss without acknowledging that not everyone has equal access to its economic benefits, and not all aspects of a city's economy are truly inclusive of all residents. In this regard, Austin is no different from the rest of the nation. We explore that topic in chapter 6, written by Tracye McDaniel. The east-west division of the city by Interstate 35 followed a pattern sadly common even to this day—displacement and a loss of opportunity following in its wake.

Despite the link between "weirdness" and an "open society" on the one hand, and growth on the other, it's doubtful that "Keep Austin Weird" would have been endorsed as the long-term vision for the city's future. City committees default to traditional values, and "weirdness" and conventionality are not comfortable bedfellows. The same can be said of "Live Music Capital of the World." It's not obvious how you would measure it and whether it's true in the first place, but it has stuck, and the city claims it. Ultimately, visions and taglines reinforce the values of the people. When they succeed, they resonate. When they don't, they quickly become irrelevant.

At the core of Austin's vision statements, from the exalted to the quirky, a welcoming and forward-looking vibe is deeply embedded. In this regard, not all cities are as welcoming of newcomers, regardless of how progressive or forward-thinking they may be. When I lived in the Pacific Northwest, I would occasionally get the uncomfortable sense that people were waiting for me to fail. When I later heard about the "Seattle chill," I instinctively understood its meaning, that of being frozen out of certain circles. In Austin, on the other hand, I've always felt the opposite: People wanted me to succeed. I never felt there were circles from which I'd be excluded.

I once brought up this dichotomy to Tim McClure, who cofounded GSD&M in 1971. The company was eventually to become one of the country's top marketing and advertising agencies. I'd met Tim through my work in the late 1990s. Tim was the genius behind the "Don't Mess with Texas" slogan, an antilitter campaign that reached well beyond its original message and has a uniquely defiant and assertive tone. He knew immediately what I meant. "We started the company right out of college," he told me. People in the advertising industry, he recalled, said, "You guys are out of your mind. You either have to be in New York or California or Chicago. You don't start an advertising agency in Austin." Austinites, on the other hand, encouraged and supported him. A friend of McClure's anonymously gave him $5,000 so he and his cofounders could build credit with local TV stations, and that friend, that benefactor, remained anonymous until decades later, when he told Tim, "You believed in yourself, so I believed in you."

John Mackey, the founder of Whole Foods, has a similar story to tell. Despite being turned down by venture capitalists and not being able to convince lenders that this quirky grocery store that sold only organic products could succeed, he persisted. His vision was tightly intertwined with Austin's weirdness. Organic and natural food was far from mainstream at that time, associated more with a small and insignificant counterculture community. But Mackey believed in the core vision behind his retail model. Despite the flood of 1981 that inundated the little store, and despite initial resistance from traditional finance sources, Mackey never wavered. The result, as we all know, is an international chain of over five hundred stores and ninety thousand employees and an eventual sale to Amazon for $13.7 billion.

Many who move to Austin or build careers in the city can relate to Mackey and McClure and dozens of others. When I first met the legendary Pike Powers, an early and forceful architect of Austin's technology landscape, he made a point of encouraging me to become part of the tech scene and made it clear that he would do all he could to help me succeed. My venture capital background and successful track record helped, but Pike was supportive long before he knew any of that.

Understanding what breeds this culture of openness is important, even if we can't establish exactly where it comes from. Certainly a large churn of university students plays a role—a fresh, annual crop of young learners (nearly fifty-four thousand students enrolled in the University of Texas at Austin the fall of 2024) can certainly inject a place with an excitement for the new and different—but other communities have large campuses as well. The difference: Austin is notable for keeping its students, both those who graduate and those who drop out. John Mackey was one of those dropouts, as was Michael Dell, founder of Dell Technologies, one of the globe's most successful technology companies. Both stayed in the city. And both are still proud residents in addition to being very, very wealthy. In fact, the (cringeworthy) term Dellionaires was created to describe the many Dell employees who profited handsomely from stock sales. That wealth, in turn, fueled not only the housing market but also a host of new startup companies.

Austin's uniqueness begins precisely from within this same vision—the desire to be unique. It is a dynamic that appeals to the young, talented citizens who serve as an economic engine for any major metro area. Creative, open, and yes, weird: This is Austin's DNA.

The Technopolis and the Consequences of Growth

When I first set out to capture what made Austin so important, both to me and to the economic development profession of which I am a part, it was entirely within the context of the city's technology boom. Tech, perhaps more than any other factor (barring the live music scene and the now supersized South by Southwest festival), put Austin on the national and international map.

The fact that Austin is now one of the country's dominant tech hubs was not a fortuitous accident. The city's technology story was crafted by design, the result of decades of planning and collaborations between individuals and institutions. And one man in particular led the charge, a modern-day Lamar with an outsize vision for what Austin's tech role could be: George Kozmetsky and his vision of Austin as a "technopolis." While that term may bring to mind *The Jetsons*, the space-age 1960s cartoon featuring dad George Jetson zipping off on his flying saucer to his mind-numbing job at Spacely's Space Sprockets, the real-life George was very much grounded in reality.

Kozmetsky, the son of Russian Jewish immigrants, joined UT Austin as dean of the School of Business Administration in 1966, arriving with an impressive entrepreneurial resume from California, where he cofounded the technology-industrial conglomerate Teledyne. Kozmetsky not only possessed an evangelical belief in "tech as king" but an astute and prescient understanding of what was needed to seed and feed a robust tech environment—a triad partnership between private, government, and academic institutions. His vision took its first big step in 1977 when he founded IC^2 (Institute of Constructive Capitalism) at UT Austin. IC^2 was—and still is—a think-and-do tank focused on how public-private collaborations can drive technological and economic advancements in ways that benefit regional communities. That's a mouthful, but essentially, IC^2 was the academic spoke of George's "technopolis wheel," which he envisioned would fuel Austin's economic growth. Incubators, chambers of commerce, and professional organizations would serve as supporting spokes, keeping it all spinning forward.

George got more done at the start of the day than most Austinites got done by the end of it. That was what I had heard long before I arrived for our first predawn coffee over twenty years ago at a West Austin restaurant now long gone.[1] I was still new to the city, so to have George be willing to meet me for breakfast surprised me. I'd recently heard him speak at the University of Texas, and I had left his talk mesmerized. He was larger than life, intellectually voluminous, prolific. The only other time I'd heard anyone like George was when Marshall McLuhan—whose concept of a globally connected world of instantly accessible media prefigured the internet—visited the University of Hawaii while I was there in the late '60s.[2] Like McLuhan, George was someone who saw things no one else did, as if he had come from the future to tell us about it. This was how a visionary thought. When cities could scarcely time traffic lights, George was painting a portrait of metropolitan areas fully connected—centers of high-tech innovation. What was more, he charted a path toward that future, where corporations were in partnership with community planners, and where university research was immediately put to the benefit of the people living in the community, including underserved populations. George's vision was not science fiction any more than Marshall McLuhan's was. He was seeing the underlying structures of what the future would have to be. I heard him talk about "smart cities" before it was a term on every urban planner and economic developer's lips. And when in 2005 Bill Clinton, through his foundation, persuaded Cisco Systems to spend $25 million and five years of research on making cities "smart," I'd bet that his Rose Garden encounter with George over ten years earlier, when the president had presented Kozmetsky his technology-achievement medal, had crossed his mind.

The kind of collaboration envisioned by Kozmetsky centered on tech transfer—"transferring" intellectual property from the engineering and sciences departments to private companies. This process was intended to provide cutting-edge technology to those corporations—and entrepreneurs—who could quickly commercialize that technology and directly benefit the communities in which it originated. While with the Oregon Technology Corporation, I pursued a similar course with Oregon State University. And though it was never an easy process, it was a way of thinking about collaboration that remains active and successful today. We would be remiss in not tracing the practice of technology transfer back to Silicon Valley and the relationship between Stanford University's Office of Technology Licensing and a host of now globally recognized companies—Sun, Cisco, Yahoo, and Google. George Kozmetsky, however, was outlining this strategy as early as 1971.

It was clear to George, and to an increasing number of companies and creative individuals, that the capital available to fund the transfer of technology would follow quickly. And it was also clear to George that implicit in this broader collaboration was an underlying commitment to "openness." This openness meant a steady elimination of the barriers that were typically erected between the public and private sectors, and those of academia.

Of course, "tech" was already a part of the Austin landscape when Kozmetsky launched his visionary IC^2 Institute. The defense electronics company Tracor (1962) was headquartered here; Dallas-based Texas Instruments (1969) had opened up a large campus; and national companies, such as IBM (1967) and Motorola (1974), stationed offices here. The technology sector had been growing since the 1950s, encouraged by the Austin Area Economic Development Foundation, and Austin had indeed already been dubbed a "miniature Silicon Valley" by some. In addition, the J. J. Pickle Research Campus played a major role in Austin's tech growth. Not only is this University of Texas campus associated with a who's who of established technology firms, but it has also helped incubate local companies such as Tracor and Radian. US Representative J. J. Pickle, who worked tirelessly in support of what was originally called the Balcones Research Center, had the campus named after him in 1994.

The technopolis vision that was carried into the 1980s became ever more ambitious. That is, technology would no longer be a piece of an overall economic development puzzle, but rather the very image that emerges upon the puzzle's completion. And that image was of an Austin built not on high-tech equipment manufacturing alone, a downstream delta, but on high-tech ideas, a fountainhead. I, and others who have chronicled Austin's tech history, consider the launching of IC^2 as the next major chapter in Austin's tech ascendancy. With the founding of IC^2 things accelerated, influencing new and exciting startup growth.

MCC and the Era of the Semiconductor

Nowhere was the technopolis vision more clearly realized than with the announcement in 1983 that Austin would soon be the headquarters of the Microelectronics and Computer Technology Corporation (MCC), the vanguard assembled to fight the looming specter of Asian technological supremacy. MCC was the first for-profit research consortium in the United States. It brought together a number of microelectronics firms to challenge Japan's growing prominence. Driving MCC's formation was, in part, the sense that Japan and its rapidly industrializing Pacific neighbors weren't playing fair, that they were gaining ground not solely on their own merits but rather by infringing upon US companies' intellectual property. Tolerated at first, when Japan wasn't seen as an economic threat, this would no longer fly. A "knowledge economy" overtaking traditional manufacturing—a prediction made since the mid-twentieth century, most notably by Peter Drucker, the father of modern management—had by the early 1980s moved out of the realm of abstraction. It was happening, it depended heavily on intellectual property, and Japan in particular was a threat in its growing microchip dominance. MCC, composed of over a dozen high-tech companies—including Motorola, Advanced Micro Devices, and RCA—would serve as the United States' central command against the would-be usurper. The warlike metaphor might have seemed overwrought if Bobby Inman—an admiral, former head of the National Security Agency, and onetime deputy director of the CIA—hadn't been the one leading MCC's charge, with the blessing of the Defense and Justice departments. US decision-makers feared that East Asia's modus operandi would lead to military, as well as economic, asymmetry. The threat was considered existential in some quarters, so much so that MCC effectively sidestepped a century's worth of US antitrust law to neutralize it. (You can read more about MCC's role in Austin's entrepreneurial arc in chapter 5, authored by Elsie L. Echeverri-Carroll and Evan Johnston.)

The question many asked at the time (and which may be on the mind of economic developers reading this) was: Why was Austin chosen as the base for the US government's first international information-knowledge showdown? How did Austin beat out established high-tech heavyweights such as the University of California's various campuses, North Carolina's Research Triangle, and Boston's Route 128? It had much to do with the city's own evolving technopolis vision, as well as the determination of both the City of Austin and the State of Texas. "A large potential employee base" and "overall cost of operation" (a criterion tied, naturally, to financial incentives) certainly came into play. Yet on this last point, despite some of the losing cities' suspicions, financial incentives were not MCC's driving attraction, at least not directly. "Most of the financial incentives," Everett

Rogers and David Gibson wrote in their landmark book, *R&D Collaboration on Trial: The Microelectronics and Computer Technology Corporation (MCC),* "were raised by the private sector and they went to Texas' two flagship universities," the University of Texas at Austin among them. (*R&D Collaboration on Trial* is an exhaustive academic study—ten years in the making—of Austin's technology history and, despite being published in 1994, is still the benchmark for understanding Austin's emergence as an economic powerhouse. Gibson is still a senior research scientist at IC^2 and consults globally on innovation and technology. Everett Rogers, who passed in 2004, was a professor of communications at University of New Mexico and renowned sociologist.) Austinites and Texans made great efforts, for instance, to recruit top-notch university personnel—$15 million, a third of it privately raised, was earmarked to endow academic positions and dozens of high-tech faculty positions.

However, another significant attraction for MCC—and the hundreds of tech companies that followed—was Austin's quality of place, namely, the green space and waterways. As I was researching the MCC site selection process, a detail in Gibson and Rogers's MCC chronicle struck me, something a site-selector for the technology consortium said: "Most of us who had not been to Texas had the image that most people had. You go to Dallas or to Houston, and . . . you think that's the state. [Yet,] in the brochure that Austin's Chamber of Commerce had prepared to sell the city, there is water in every scene. It's a picture of Town Lake, or it's a picture of Lake Travis. . . . When I took the helicopter ride over Austin, I looked down at Lake Travis, and I thought, 'Boy . . . beautiful place.'" Not only had this MCC individual's first impression been flipped, but he had also recognized the same land that Austin's first mayor, Edwin Waller, called "naturally most beautiful" when describing the geography in 1841—as had Lamar and his contemporaries, even if in their time the Colorado River had not yet been tamed. MCC had become as entranced as anyone with it all. Austin's water, among its other natural bounties, had beguiled again.

Austin's site win for MCC, however deserved, was truly a gift from the tech gods, and it rang in an era of semiconductor proliferation. On MCC's heels followed SEMATECH (Semiconductor Manufacturing & Technology Institute), a nonprofit research consortium of thirteen semiconductor manufacturing companies (Austin was chosen over eleven other sites nationwide); and then Samsung Semiconductor—which opened its flash memory production facilities (the first in the US) in Austin in 1998. Samsung Semiconductor was the biggest new business opportunity since MCC. The fact that it was not Dallas or Houston or San Antonio that won this prize had less to do with incentives or workforce availability than with, yes, *vision*. Firstly, Kozmetsky's vision of private-public-academic collaboration and tech transfer. The University of Texas was an important consideration in Samsung's decision. It was a connection that I pushed vigorously in the Ann Richards administration.

When I moved to Austin in the early 1990s, I saw my job as an opportunity to raise the profile of the state of Texas—nationally and internationally. It was essentially the same responsibility I had for the state of Washington in the gubernatorial administration of Booth Gardner when I lived in Seattle. Integral to that approach was the importance of the University of Texas, both as a source of talent and as a trove of potential new technology relevant to semiconductor manufacturing. The university could be an active partner at every stage of the process. It was during this time that I joined up with Angelos Angelou, who had just left his role as vice president at the Austin chamber to found Angelou Economics (AE), an economic development consultancy. Angelos and I would work together for five years, attracting some of the brightest minds in Texas' economic development community. Amy Holloway, for example, went on to form a highly successful consultancy of her own. It is no exaggeration to say that AE was a talent incubator for economic development. It was also through my work at AE that I came to appreciate the importance of the Austin Area Research Organization (AARO). This nonprofit organization has long functioned as a kind of think tank and "future's forum" for Austin's overall growth. Its past presidents have included Neal Spelce, Neal Kocurek, Ron Kessler, and Elizabeth Christian, all of whom influenced my thinking and were unstintingly supportive. More recently, Sandy Dochen, past board chair, spent countless hours discussing Austin's growth with me.

In our support of the Samsung recruitment—and in Austin's semiconductor initiatives generally—Ben Streetman was a key influencer. Ben was the dean of Engineering at the University of Texas and had founded the Microelectronics Research Center (MRC). I would get to know Ben well a few years later when he, Angelos, and I traveled to Carinthia, Austria, to help them establish their own tech strategy in 1998. (See sidebar, Lessons in Economic Development: Ecosystem and Branding.) As with so many of

Austin's visionary leaders, he was unassuming, easily approachable, and more than willing to share his considerable knowledge.

The second and equally important vision factor that drew Samsung Semiconductor was seeing Austin as a *technopolis* and the fact that the city's leaders—public, private, and academic—had all gotten behind that vision. Austin knew it did not want to be an oil-and-gas town like Houston or a cotton-and-cattle transportation hub like Dallas/Fort Worth. It wanted to carve out its own personality distinct from energy, beef, and banking. Austin's technology presence had already gestated to some degree by the time MCC had arrived and the technopolis was truly beginning to manifest. But the powers that be wanted confirmation. So, soon after MCC settled in and not long after an *Austin American-Statesman* cosponsored conference centered on the city's technological future, the Austin Chamber of Commerce invited the Stanford Research Institute (SRI) to town. The chamber's goal was to discover what the world's leading technology entity thought Austin's future was. Austin was seeking both a road map for continued economic success and validation of a tech strategy. SRI responded—nearly as fortuitously as Dustin Hoffman's neighbor had with "Plastics" in *The Graduate*—with "information technology."

SRI's prognostication nonetheless surprised Pike Powers, who had been instrumental in the MCC deal. "I was sort of shocked," he told me, with "the way we boiled it down to information technology and [how] people were content with that." Not that Powers balked at the notion, I'm sure—until then, Austin, despite a population spike of nearly 40 percent in the 1970s alone, had in fact remained, at least in spirit, a "sleepy" college town; painting it as a nascent technopolis, then, surprised many, even those with their economic developer's ear to the ground. What I'm convinced did not shock Powers, however, were the ineffable charms SRI waxed poetic on in its report: Austin is a "uniquely livable city," it read, and "is also in an excellent position to take advantage of another driving force in the transformation of the United States from an industrial to an information society—the revolution in values and lifestyles. . . . The 'inner-directed values' among scientists, engineers, technicians, intellectual[s], and entrepreneurs . . . place a high value on schools, cultural richness, amenities, clean water, and the like." There it was again, that quality of place factor.

Pike understood that as well as anyone. In numerous conversations that Pike and I had, he laid out not only the steps the community took to secure

MCC and SEMATECH, but also what it meant to embrace a larger vision of Austin as a technology hub. And he was wonderfully direct in his appreciation of George Kozmestky's role in that vision:

> "This guy was something else. He was a ball of fire. I couldn't understand half of what he said to me, but he was a ball of fire. I was telling a group about how he embedded me with all these things. I would be driving down I-35 and say, 'Holy cow! That's what George meant when he said this five years ago.' Little implant bombs into your brain."

Values and lifestyles. Cultural richness. Abundant water. It seems as if the kind of vision attractive to high-tech businesses, or to the individuals who would seek employment with them, went beyond standard economic-development incentives and the practical needs of business growth. It went directly into a relationship between people, place, and innovation that is becoming a driving force for industry everywhere.

Not at all surprisingly, it is these same factors—caring about green space, neighborhood integrity, a culture of openness—that were held dear by those fearful of growth in the early 1980s and afterward. Ironically, the efforts to preserve quality of place aspects in the face of aggressive progress actually served to fuel that growth. In other words, there is a strange congruity between the tech community (and economic developers seeking high-wage tech employers) and the very forces that seek to limit their growth. This tension is both inevitable and unresolvable. It means that the conditions that attract talent are compromised by its success. (A possible solution to this conundrum is the subject of our last chapter.)

Austin began to see "high tech" potential in all companies, not just those associated with the semiconductor industry, and those businesses, in kind, saw potential in Austin. A host of software companies took root or relocated. Concurrent with those corporate transplants and startups, the support structure for technology was also growing—from university-funded programs, including the University of Texas Austin Technology Incubator (founded in 1989 by—you guessed it—Kozmetsky) to venture capital firms to patent attorneys and marketing agencies. The "seat of empire" was now clearly anchored in technology, which took on a momentum that has not slackened. Austin was, as futurist and *Megatrends* author John Naisbitt dubbed it, a "megatrend city"—one defined primarily by high technology, global influence, and long-term thinking.

For those in their twenties and thirties—and even some folks in their forties—the historical developments that paved the way for Austin's current tech dominance are most likely unknown or not seen as relevant. This dismissal or ignorance of the past isn't unusual with generational shifts—it's usually onward and upward. Indeed, the emergence of the internet and ecommerce opened up a new sector of tech growth that spawned a fresh generation of entrepreneurs, ones not wedded to microelectronics or to chip manufacturing. App and software developers, and those at the forefront of the sharing economy—whether Austin-based Pervasive Software, HomeAway, or dozens of others—owed no allegiance to the past. Yes, they may have known they were beneficiaries of past efforts, but they were no more beholden to them than modern-day Boeing is to the Wright Brothers. In short, they were carving out their own path.

Laura Kilcrease, venture capitalist and former director of the IC² Institute, recognized the gap between Austin's tech leaders in the 1980s and '90s and those who were now setting the pace. In a conversation we had in 2018, after she accepted a position in Alberta, Canada, Laura further explored that transition. We wondered whether there was an inevitability about an evolution between traditional, hardware-based tech growth and more entrepreneurial (and software-based) companies. In any case, US anxiety over Japanese chip production that led to SEMATECH in the 1980s was ancient history. MCC had succeeded; the threat was past. Similarly, the role of chip manufacturing was of little direct significance to app developers now. What was more important was that Austin was adapting, moving with the times, and again at the forefront of technology, whatever form it might take.

Lessons in Economic Development: Ecosystem and Branding

In 1998, I visited Carinthia, Austria, along with Ben Streetman, to help its city leaders expand upon their own tech visions. The Austrians wanted very badly to brand their region as the "Silicon Alps." But this was doomed to fail on two levels, at least one of which remains a lesson to this day. The first problem with becoming the "Silicon Alps" was that Carinthia had only a single semiconductor lab, and a single lab does not make you a center of technology. What Carinthia lacked was a technology ecosystem. The concept of a series of interwoven individuals, companies, resources, and supply chains that reinforce technology growth was simply not present. To build it would take years, and more than the recruitment of new companies. Notably absent, and perhaps the most critical element, was a major research center. Technology transfer requires cutting-edge research, and that research was not grounded in Carinthia. Finally, Austria's lack of tech entrepreneurship also meant success was not likely. What Carinthia did have, however, was a brilliant industrial design infrastructure, which continues to propel the economy.

In addition to these fundamental needs for establishing a self-sustaining ecosystem there was another issue. That issue concerned the use of the term "Silicon X." Ever since the emergence of Silicon Valley, regions throughout the world have been trying to bottle the magic—to become a new Silicon X. We have local efforts to brand Austin as the Silicon Hills, Portland as the Silicon Forest, multiple Midwestern communities as the Silicon Prairie—and the list goes on and on. The simplest advice for those intent on this branding? Don't do it. There is only one Silicon Valley. Efforts to cash in on that brand are not a show of strength but an acknowledgement that there are no new ideas to be found in your community.

Challenges to Growth and Competing Visions

Along with Austin's rising prominence as a national tech center, there was increasing anxiety about the effects of the city's growth. Not surprisingly, this anxiety had roots that predated even the more prominent corporate success stories. When *The Wall Street Journal* published an article in December 2020 bemoaning the loss of Austin's unique character, it was just another in a long series of similar stories.

Beginning in the early 1980s, many felt the emerging vision of Austin as a tech hub to be antithetical to the city's reputation as a laid-back retreat for the hippies and cowboys that haunted the Armadillo. In fact, the venue's demolition in 1982 to make way for a high-rise was partially responsible for activating renewed no-growth sentiment. Gibson and Rogers chronicled these and other key events in the city's Reagan-era tech boom in their book, noting that Austin's 1970s counterculture society feared the consequences that growth dragged with it, among them traffic congestion, higher property taxes, and new golf courses instead of new music venues. And the counterculture certainly was not open to any threat of polluting the city's springs and river, those crown jewels prized since Lamar's era.

The no-growth sentiment among Austinites during the 1980s was ubiquitous. "Many Austin residents were not pleased that their city was becoming a center for high-tech growth," Gibson and Rogers wrote. "They remembered the good old . . . days when Austin was a quiet, folksy place; a university town; and not much more. They looked back fondly to when there was no traffic congestion . . . [and when] rising real estate prices [did not force] the closure of live music venues, some of which were demolished for office building construction." Striking about that passage is how, though it is referring to the early 1980s, it would seem current in an *Austin American-Statesman* edition published tomorrow.

Whereas Austin may have been "one of the first Sunbelt towns to question growth," according to Naisbitt, it is difficult to argue that 1980s Austinites were categorically against growth (and change). Many had either lived through or were the beneficiaries of massive efforts to transform the region's landscape. The Highland Lakes, for instance, the seven sparkling bodies of water pooling from dams along the Colorado River, which a first-time visitor can see out of the plane window upon descent into Austin-Bergstrom International Airport, are the result of millions of dollars and millions of man-hours—in large part thanks to giant federal Public Works Administration investments. The creation of these great reservoirs advanced opportunities for Austin in entirely new ways. Historian Anthony Orum described the "coastal climate" vibe they created in *Power, Money & the People: The Making of Modern Austin*. (Incidentally, the Highland Lakes project was a collaboration between government and private interests—such partnerships existed long before Kozmetsky championed them, of course, especially in a state like Texas where good ol' boy networks flourished. Such backroom deals were not the kind of collaborative "sharing of knowledge" Kozmetsky advocated, but there's no denying they yielded results. Lawyer, businessman, and onetime Texas statesman Alvin Wirtz, for instance, a man described by Lyndon B. Johnson biographer Robert Caro as "hugely influential," orchestrated completions of several dams using his role both as a senator and a lawyer representing construction companies, benefitting personally financially while also gifting the region with a beautiful, natural legacy.)

So the antigrowth sentiment that began in the 1970s with the establishment of hundreds of neighborhood and preservation associations, and that continued after the Armadillo was razed, may have been directed more at the agents of growth than at growth itself: Developers and corporations who did not share in the same vision of Austin. "The kinds of people obsessed with a vision for the future expansion," Orum went on to write, "changed markedly." One camp wanted to preserve and nurture Austin's unique geography and laid-back aesthetic, an organic unfolding to enhance the quality of place aspects. The other camp, to put it bluntly, wanted to make money. Not all developers should be painted with such a broad brush, but many architects of the city's growth in the 1980s and '90s were driven predominately by economic rewards and expansion, expansion, expansion. Caught in the middle was the increasing presence and power of technology. Neither camp, I would argue, doubted Austin's emergence as a "technopolis." It was certainly part of the equation. But it wasn't at the heart of it. The tension surrounding the city's growth was less centered on technology companies than on where development occurred—the "not in my backyard" (NIMBY) collective—and the builders and investors driving that development.

Still, tech proliferated, further fueling growth. By the time MCC officially closed its doors in 2004, twenty years after landing in Austin, it had not only captured more than a hundred patents and created models for turning research into products and applications—a critical development in a burgeoning knowledge economy and helping ensure a "win" against Japan—but it had also left in its wake an Austin nearly unrecognizable to longtimers. The "digital revolution," launched in earnest with MCC's arrival, and having survived through a mid-1980s economic decline that persisted until the early 1990s, had "transformed the simple, unpretentious city into Silicon Hills," reported *The New York Times* in a November 2001 article (predictably falling into the Silicon X branding trap).

In fact, the new Austin was, as a separate 1997 *New York Times* piece quipped, "where venture capitalists and software engineers [roamed]." The final five years of the twentieth century alone produced seventeen thousand additional millionaires in the city. By 2017 the Austin Technology Incubator had raised $3.5 billion for startups, and IC² had pumped $3 billion and more than six thousand jobs into the local economy, figures cherry-picked among countless such success stories. In 2020, *Inc.* magazine ranked Austin as the number one best place to start a business and one of the top five cities in which to raise early-stage fundraising. Yet in what seemed like a distinctly non-Austin perspective, a 2018 South by Southwest Interactive panel was titled “Third Coast: Can Austin Be the Next Big Tech City?” As if it weren’t already. “This is a lifestyle city,” one of the panelists cited as a reason that was holding Austin back from becoming such a place, the irony of course being that “lifestyle” was cited in SRI’s decades-old report to the chamber of commerce as a driving factor for high-tech growth, not an obstacle to it. Perhaps some of these panelists just hadn’t been in the city for long, hadn’t truly realized how much it’d changed. A more appropriate question for discussion may have been “How Is Austin a Different Kind of Big Tech City?” Ironically, the answer was already present: Austin’s brand was now synonymous with SXSW.

Competing Visions

Impressive as the growth numbers are, however, especially to economic developers, had MCC’s success compromised the city’s laid-back vibe? Had this big-idea vision usurped an older, more lived-in one? Many would not hesitate to say yes, on many fronts. “Years ago,” *The New York Times* reported as early as 1985, “the wilderness crept up to Austin like a timid deer; now it retreats. Besides traffic snarls, water shortages and soaring costs, Austin’s decadelong boom has increasingly meant a loss of the city’s special touch with nature.” Barton Creek, one Austinite worried, “is not gonna be able to accommodate this growth.”

But there was more to worry about than the loss of a “laid-back vibe,” that slacker mindset, so highly prized by a larger part of Austin’s young inhabitants. In particular there was concern about the environmental risks that development brought in its wake. And there was also the question of social equity. In 2012 a group of UT scholars edited an anthology, based on a ten-year study, that criticized a Smilor, Gibson, and Kozmetsky article, “Creating the Technopolis,” published in *The Journal of Business Venturing* in 1989, for having “no mention of income equality or increased breadth of jobs.” The essays argued at length that the technopolis accelerated a “digital divide” that disproportionately left minority and low-income Austinites behind. These groups were, in large part, the victim of Jim Crow-era policies—segregated and poorly resourced schools, and housing discrimination such as redlining—which had been baked into Austin’s 1928 master plan. In fact, the anthology notes that an early critic of the technopolis had already predicted in 1991 that "many nonhigh-tech employees will have a difficult time finding their place on the technopolis wheel." As the anthology's editors noted, the average Austin tech worker's annual wage by 2000 was $100,000; for everyone else, $33,000. And what about music, what about the Armadillo's cultural fate? In 1984, newswire United Press International explored whether Austin's high-tech boom was "strangling" the city's "legendary music scene" and quoted a music manager who said, "We're fouling our nest," and "What's been unique about [Austin] isn't quite there anymore."

Would a vision for tech growth—the kind of vision necessary for Austin to compete economically—irrevocably damage disadvantaged neighborhoods, the vibrant Black and Hispanic communities in East Austin? Did it matter that proponents of the technopolis were "optimistic, assuming a positive transformation for all" even as concerns over gentrification steadily grew?

George Kozmetsky foresaw these issues. His personal belief system was rooted in social equity and fairness. "Your satisfaction is not money," he said to a group of entrepreneurs in 2000. "Your satisfaction is to see others make it." Kozmetsky biographer, Monty Jones, wrote that the idea behind "constructive capitalism" and "creative capitalism," terms Kozmetsky often used, was "an economic system that would not merely earn a profit for shareholders but also help to solve society's problems." (I do a deep dive into capital, capitalism, and their effect on Austin's growth in chapter 3.) It was an "enlightened" system, anchored in meeting "people's needs in a nonexploitative manner."

This perspective was not incidental to Kozmetsky. He believed it passionately. What is most notable—and perhaps most controversial—about his argument is the role he assigns to technology. For him, technology is the means by which social equity can be realized. While tech growth may (initially) widen the gap between the wealthy and the poor, it is also the only means to close the gap. He famously asserted—in speeches and to me and those he conversed regularly with—that "the only solution to the problems of technology is better technology." Technology, he felt, would empower those whose access to information (and therefore to wage growth) had previously been severely restricted. This was, after all, one of the promises of the internet.

In this regard, Kozmetsky differed from other visionaries who came of age in the 1970s. While Kozmetsky makes no mention of E. F. Schumacher and his landmark book, *Small is Beautiful: A Study of Economics as if People Mattered*, the influence is clear enough. Schumacher's book challenges the notion that growth is a worthy goal in and of itself. He posited that the prevailing "bigger is better" approach leads to dangerous unchecked consumption. On the flip side, small, focused, and contained choices preserve the things that serve humans and communities. In other words, growth must not come at the expense of social equity, and it must not exploit the physical resources (especially oil, gas, and coal) that upset the environmental balance of the planet or communities. Therefore, the notion that technology serves the people, and not the other way around, was explicit in Schumacher.

The difference between the two visionaries may be profound, but so is the overlap between them. Kozmetsky believed deeply that technological growth was inevitable and that it could be harnessed for the good. He saw that as a necessary element of the technopolis. Schumacher was more deeply skeptical—doubting whether we could remain technology's master. It is no leap at all to see the echoes of this dilemma play out in our own time. The debates over Facebook's privacy, over Google's de facto monopoly, or over Amazon's labor practices have their roots in concern over who controls the technology and what impact that control exerts on people across the globe.

While this debate raged, however, public officials and economic developers remained largely oblivious to its importance. Their default answer to any criticism was always the same: Our business is to create jobs; without jobs everything else is inconsequential. This is not, on the face of it, a foolish position to take. Indeed, as we will explore further on, it remains the default posture of virtually all elected officials from the president of the United States down to council members of the smallest towns. As technology changed the economic structure of the country, however, it became increasingly clear that "having a job" was no assurance of being able to support a family, create further opportunity for oneself, or afford leisure time for creativity. In short, the "digital divide" was baked into the equation.

Critics would eventually argue that Kozmetsky's view of capitalism was unrealistic—that capitalism would never be collaborative, that it would always be at odds with the environment and with workers. And yes, Austin's tech ascendancy did pose threats to the environment, to social equity, and to art, music, and culture. And to "weirdness." But the communities within Austin who embraced those values did not disappear. They remain vocal. And their voices were not necessarily separate from those of the very people who worked in the tech companies.

The city may have been one of the first in the Sunbelt to question its growth, as Naisbitt put it in *Megatrends*, but that's only half the story. That very question of growth, he continued, "may help ensure Austin's quality of life in the future."

Naisbitt guessed right. In 1986, the city adopted the Comprehensive Watersheds Ordinance designed to help preserve the city's "special touch with nature" that *The New York Times* reported a year earlier was endangered. And in 1990, the Save Our Springs Alliance (SOS) began in earnest when it prevented development near Barton Creek. SOS continued to fight for the creek, and for Austin's environment more generally, well through the 1990s, drawing into the fray notable personalities such as Robin Rather, a longtime Austin environmental activist who served on the board for many years. The battle continues today.

The image that emerged—and that was quickly gaining international prominence—was of a new center of technology that somehow coexisted with a thriving arts and cultural hub (now expanded beyond music) and an increasing commitment to environmental responsibility. The vision of an empire had been realized.

CHAPTER TWO

Something in the Water

To some Austinites, the city's meteoric growth has been a sign of progress worth celebrating. Austin has prided itself on topping lists of fastest-growing and most-desirable places to live. But to others, this same growth is a source of anxiety. The dangers of the downtown skyline resembling that of somebody else's city, of a small-town familiarity disappearing, and of further displacement for vulnerable communities are on the minds of many. For many others, Austin's explosive growth triggers a feeling of ambivalence, an "I'm not antigrowth but . . ." sentiment, as my friend, advertising legend Tim McClure puts it. No matter where one lands on the spectrum, one thing is certain: Austin's magnetism is undeniable and shows no signs of slowing.

Tim had seen the city's transformation in the most direct way—because he helped create that transformation. As the primary inspiration behind the "Don't Mess with Texas" campaign launched at the 1986 Cotton Bowl, Tim's influence was felt not just by the corporations he helped market (Southwest Airlines being among the more prominent) but also by residents throughout the state as well as those nationally and internationally who found inspiration in his slogan.

Tim came from Corsicana, Texas—the "Fruitcake Capital of the World," he likes to remind people. "Austin felt like a bigger version of Corsicana," he told me when I asked him how the city had changed since the 1960s, when he moved to Austin for college. "It had a hometown attitude to it." Tim had arrived, however, just as the city was surpassing a quarter-million residents, as that hometown feel was starting to shift, and as concerns began mounting about the tradeoffs further growth might entail. "It's so different today," Tim continued. "Now you drive down Lamar Boulevard and you get out to the Broken Spoke and you can't find it because it's stuck between two big, shiny residential buildings. I'm not antigrowth, but it is a different city than the one I moved to." Indeed, the Broken Spoke, the squat, red-sided honky-tonk established in 1964 that still hosts several live-music acts a week, offers as stark a visual metaphor as any for Austin's past abutting its present.

In 2017, I asked IC^2 researcher David Gibson what he thought accounted for the city's eternal boom. I had my own thoughts, but I figured as the coauthor of *R&D Collaboration on Trial*, perhaps the most authoritative work on Austin's transformation into a technology hub, he would know better than I. His list of reasons was exhaustive and included many of the ones I explore in this book: creative collaboration, economic incentives, the agglomeration of high-tech companies, visionary leadership, the university's role, state-level support, and so on. Yet similar circumstances exist elsewhere, so I wanted to pin him down on something more essential, a singularity of sorts. What made the difference in Central Texas? Why the innovation and creativity *here*? Why the success in gathering and harnessing capital? Why did the progressive ideals of tolerance and environmentalism that spread so widely during the 1960s take root sooner in Austin than elsewhere in Texas? Why did music matter so much? Why did Austin become a ground zero for the fight between growth's proponents and its detractors? Why was "weirdness" something to aspire to? After all my whys, Gibson, exhausted by my persistence, gave up and said simply: "It must be something in the water."

Gibson was quick to laugh off his exasperated comment. Afterward, however, I became intrigued by the idea that something in the water—or something relating to water—may indeed have been at play. From the beginning, cities have been built along bodies of water, of course; Austin, along Texas' Colorado River, was no exception. In his history of the city, *Power, Money, and the People*, sociologist Anthony Orum captured the dreams of many nineteenth-century Americans—in Austin and beyond—who foresaw great cities springing up across the new nation, particularly along its rivers, cities that would rival golden-age Athens and Rome. Yet the Colorado River was not seriously imagined as—never capable of becoming—an artery for commerce, certainly never the likes of a Missouri River, Mississippi River, or Saint Lawrence River. The steamboat *Kate Ward*, capable of carrying six hundred bales of cotton, docked in the city in

1846 and soon returned downstream to Matagorda Bay on the Texas coast, never to return. Rivergoers paddling today would indeed be shocked to see a shipping vessel pass them.

If Austin's identity—its explosive growth, its growing international recognition—is indeed linked to water, it is not as a result of traditional river commerce.

What of the water, then? What is that "something," and how does it extend beyond commercial opportunity? And if there is something about the water that isn't captured by its economic benefits, is it more than just an amenity, something more than an escape from summer heat? To ask the question in that way is to see in the water something more than commerce, more than recreation. It is to look into the deep ecology of our world, of *this* world, *this* place. Like Gibson, my first reflex is not to leap into a mystical explanation for something just because I can't readily account for it. But there is something about the water in Austin—the river, the creeks, the springs—that isn't captured through any traditional explanation. Gibson's statement rang true, for I could immediately identify the moment I became an Austin convert, and it had much to do with the water, a baptism of sorts. That baptism, it so happened, took place at one of Austin's remarkable destinations, one of many that define what makes Austin special. I didn't realize it at the time, but I was wading into, quite literally, an element at the heart of Austin's antigrowth/pro-growth debate, a complicated and decades-long question about how a city can evolve without compromising what made it desirable in the first place. In short, a debate about Austin's future.

I was at Berkeley in 1973, and at summer's end, when my friend John Aielli invited me to visit him in Austin, I did not hesitate. Despite the recurring malaria, which was only one of the legacies of serving fourteen months in Vietnam, I wanted nothing more than to set myself adrift, free of the inner turmoil of having been an infantryman. The Americal Division I had been assigned to was more than a bad aftertaste to a national tragedy, it was at the very heart of everything that had gone wrong in Southeast Asia. It was a unit of the Americal that was responsible for the massacre at My Lai, an event so horrific that it is still a stain on America itself, in much the way that Abu Ghraib became a symbol of everything wrong about our "liberation" of Iraq. Finishing up my master's degree at the University of Hawaii had been the first stop on my road to recovery (thank you, GI Bill), the two months I had spent on an Oregon commune my second. Hitchhiking to Austin seemed the perfect third. Graduate studies at the University of Hawaii offered no clear answer to the questions I and so many others were grappling with: What kind of world were we destined to live in? The dilemma of growth versus sustainability was encapsulated in the *Whole Earth Catalog* and other countercultural writings—writings that deeply influenced not only environmentalists, but also tech entrepreneurs like Steve Jobs and Steve Wozniak.

My own views of growth were beginning to take shape under these influences, reinforced during my time in the forests of the Pacific Northwest. I was absorbing the ideas of author-economist and growth critic E. F. Schumacher. His issues—about the consequences of growth based on the damaging effect of extracting resources necessary to support that growth—are still very much with us. While he did not explicitly anticipate global warming, the implications are there: Unbridled economic growth has environmental effects whose costs outweigh the benefits.

So when John's invitation came along, I stuck out my thumb on a San Francisco freeway ramp, slept in a tent by the roadside between rides, and with a confidence now regarded as reckless, hopped between cars—those as conventional as VWs and Datsun pickups and as exotic as a Porsche 356 and a 6×6 Gamma Goat—until I made it to the Lone Star capital. None of the people on the rides I shared to Austin—from long-haul truckers to vodka-sipping VA patients, traveling salesmen, and bearded road warriors—asked me about my time in Southeast Asia. This even though I must have looked like a Vietnam vet from central casting with my jungle boots, olive-drab boonie hat, Nomex flight jacket, and camo poncho liner—the "baby blanket" beloved by infantrymen. I was not surprised that my chauffeurs avoided talking about Vietnam—I was not the only one who wanted to forget the war. Instead, most of our conversations centered on the Nixon presidency and the direction the country was taking—polarization was as deep then as it is now. And with everyone my own age, in their early twenties, the conversation veered off into discussions of the *Whole Earth Catalog* and the burgeoning environmental movement.

It was not my first trip to Texas. In fact, I'd lived there before. I had spent most my life in Germany, the child of a German mother and raised by German grandparents. Eventually, however, we followed my father to Killeen, Texas, specifically to Fort Hood, the city's largest employer then and now. I graduated from Killeen High School (along with John) shortly after my seventeenth birthday. I knew little of Austin, however, as near to Killeen as it was (about seventy miles). I had heard growing up that the city differed from the rest of the state—that in some ways it was akin to Berkeley, but more intimate, friendlier. Its alternative vibe was reinforced by its flagship university. Perhaps that was why traveling from the Bay Area to visit John was an easy choice.

Once I reached Austin, John suggested I meet him at his home in Hyde Park, just north of the University of Texas. It had been years since I had seen him. We had met years earlier as classmates in Killeen, where we became close friends. We both liked books and the arts, and neither of us quite fit into the social scene. John, a talented pianist, moved to Austin, as so many musicians had, and not just because of the university. By the time I'd visited, he'd already launched his radio show, *Eklektikos*, which he'd host for fifty-four years. It was easy to live in Austin then. Housing was readily available, and cost was never an issue. Today the talk is about whether musicians can even afford to live in Austin anymore. A "musician's living wage" discussion heated up after a report submitted to the city's economic development department showed that a third of Austin's musicians couldn't pay the rent in the urban core. In 1973, however, the music conversation was mostly about the lineup at Armadillo World Headquarters.

The Armadillo was not, however, the first stop on the tour John had curated for me, nor was any music venue. First, we'd go for a swim. It was summer in Texas, after all. I thought he would take me to Barton Springs Pool, the natural swimming hole I had heard so much about. Instead, we ended up due west of the city, where the land started rolling, vistas turned greener, and the horizon opened up. As we neared Lake Travis, glimmers of its surface occasionally shone through the live oaks, cedars, and ashes that ringed the shoreline. When we arrived at the lake's limestone edge, I was not prepared for what I found. As young adults in the 1960s and '70s, it was not uncommon to see nudity where our parents would not have expected to, but it nonetheless surprised me to see it there, in abundance, on a lakeshore in the middle of Texas. Given his knowing look, John had expected such a reaction from me. Of course, having lived in Austin for years by then, he had long since recovered from the shock of witnessing such a scene, if he had ever been shocked at all. Hippie Hollow, named after the hippies who frequented it, is the state's only officially sanctioned clothing-optional park. When we visited the cove, it was already emblematic of a city far more tolerant than others in Texas. Bathers had been fined in 1971 for swimming sans clothes, which had warranted the park's first mention in the *Statesman*, but very quickly afterward, despite the occasional objection of nearby homeowners, law enforcement began turning a blind eye, and nudity soon thereafter became legal.

Most surprising to me that day, however, was not the bathers. Rather it was the feeling that overcame me as I submerged myself into Lake Travis for the first time. What drew me then was what drew me to the creeks and lakes of the Northwest and to the warm waters of Hanauma Bay outside Honolulu. That water could mean so much in a place where I least expected it had a powerful effect. I knew, simply, that I felt at home. Though within a week I would return to the Pacific Northwest (and spend the next twenty years there), Austin had left its mark on me. I understood immediately why someone would come to Austin and never leave, why many of those who did leave would be drawn back, years later, as would be the case with me. I was beginning to understand, too, why Austin and Central Texas were places environmentalists fiercely protected. That idea of "something in the water"—something about the water, something *of* the water—took hold not as an intellectual exercise, but as a feeling, a sensation, a sense of place, a "quality of place," intimately connected with flow and depth and profound meaning. It was, in a way that Emerson and Thoreau would have immediately understood, transcendental.

We don't have to understand the essence of things to know them when we see them. But once established, this connection between the quality of a place and its economic development has become the calling card of successful business attraction for every city in the country.

Dam Smart

Shortly after my conversation with Gibson, I came upon Anthony Orum's 1987 book on the urban history of Austin. Amazingly researched and still relevant, it reaffirmed the importance of the city's water, and more specifically, its dams. In an interview given after his book was published, Orum explained, "Without the dams,"—referring to six structures created along the Colorado River in the early twentieth century—"Austin wouldn't be the place it is now."

The dams. As prosaic and civic engineering 101 as that may sound, Orum was not referring to their purely practical value. Yes, nearly one hundred thousand dams dot the United States, providing hydroelectric power and drinking-water reservoirs for tens of millions, but those dams did not create a thousand Austins. And whereas the lakes created from Austin's dams—including Lake Travis—serve as vital water resources for more than a million Central Texans, and whereas the dams themselves generate enough hydroelectric energy to power as many as 220,000 homes, most newcomers take the lakes for granted. Each year nearly one hundred thousand people visit one of Lake Travis's many shoreline parks, 2.5 million treks are made on the trails that circle Lady Bird Lake, and a million people swim in Barton Springs Pool, which is fed by waters that emerge from the Edwards Aquifer (the huge, natural filtration system and reservoir that serves millions of Central Texans and a portion of agriculture land) and flow to the Colorado River via Barton Creek.

Michael Erard, an *Austin Chronicle* writer who interviewed Orum in 2003, paraphrased Orum's take in a way that got as close to capturing that "something of the water" singularity as I could find. "The new lakes enabled a relaxed coastal culture," Erard wrote. "And dams made it worthwhile for urban entrepreneurs to shape their vision of the city, and for market entrepreneurs to get rich," Erard went on, alluding to a distinction Orum made between those visionaries driven primarily by a "devotion to the idea of place" and those driven instead by amassing "private fortunes." All those whys I had asked Gibson, about music and weirdness and tolerance, about innovation, technology, and creativity, were summed up neatly in *The Austin Chronicle*. And they all seemed to have something to do with the water. Water, it turned out, was central to the very concept of Austin.

The engineering of the lakes began with Alexander Penn Wooldridge, who served as Austin's mayor from 1909 to 1919 and was one of those "urban entrepreneurs" Orum described. That is, by Orum's distinction, Wooldridge was just as "animated by dreams of expansion" as market entrepreneurs were—only his motivations differed. In many ways, Wooldridge was a visionary and an optimist, a man convinced of humanity's ability to harness the forces of nature. In the late nineteenth century, before his mayoral tenure, Wooldridge argued for the construction of Austin's first dam. Not only would the city spare itself from the Colorado's frequent floodwaters, the thinking went, but the value of the land along the riverbanks would rise, opportunities to harness the hydroelectric power would manifest, and jobs and prosperity would ensue.

In 1890, the Austin Dam was approved for construction, and it was completed three years later, just upriver from downtown. The dam's promise to deliver economic development, however, did not soon materialize, and it failed disastrously at the turn of the century, when it cracked apart during a downpour, causing a torrent that killed eight people. The city rebuilt it more than a decade later, and it failed yet again, but by then city leaders thought a single dam not nearly ambitious enough. In *Power, Money & the People*, Orum pointed to a 1914 chamber of commerce meeting as a crucial turning point in the further development of the Colorado River. It was argued that the city was not developing as fast as it should, that it was too content to rest on its natural advantages, and that the remedy for economic stagnation was industrial development—still more evidence that geography, in and of itself, is of limited consequence to a city's growth. A remedy for economic stagnation was then proposed: industrial development, with "the heartiest support of the University of Texas." William H. Stacy, formerly of the Texas National Guard and later instrumental in the development of south Austin neighborhood Travis Heights, seemed to concur. "The duty of all good loyal citizens of Austin," he said, is "to get behind any proposition that meant the upbuilding of the city." Part of that "upbuilding," they determined, was to expand the number of dams planned for construction.

Walter E. Long, who in 1915 became the chamber of commerce secretary and is today remembered, like first Mayor Edwin Waller, as a father of Austin city planning, helped to oversee much of this development. In 1951, two years after his retirement—and after the city had spent decades harnessing federal capital, with the help of future President Lyndon B. Johnson—not only had the dam that Wooldridge envisioned half a century earlier been permanently repaired, but five additional dams had been completed as well. The Highland Lakes, as they had become known, were complete, as was the first major step in creating that "coastal culture."

The next major step in the creation of Austin's new coastal image was taken by Roberta Crenshaw, a University of Texas alum who had begun her tenure on the Austin parks board around the time the last of the Highland Lakes dams were created. In 1960, an additional dam, the Longhorn Dam, was completed downstream from the city in order to create a reservoir for a power plant. The dam's construction created an urban lake in downtown Austin. Once Town Lake—decades later named Lady Bird Lake (LBJ's wife was an environmental protectionist)—was complete, Crenshaw had a vision for this new urban asset. In Texas, anything below a river's high-water mark was by law public land, she discovered, and she advocated for the creation of a lakeside walking trail. In an effort that signaled the antigrowth efforts to come, she rallied enough support to ensure that the grounds were indeed designated as public parkland. This successfully stymied plans for an expressway and an amusement park. Soon a vibrant space—an arboreal, waterfront respite in the very heart of Austin—was available for everyone to enjoy. Today, Austin without the ten-mile Ann and Roy Butler Hike-and-Bike Trail—named for a former Austin mayor and his wife—which winds around Lady Bird Lake, is as unimaginable as New York City without Central Park. Somewhat miraculously, what began as an economic development growth initiative laid the foundation for an environmentally sensitive gem. And among the related benefits, Zilker Park has become our Central Park.

The effort to create the trails had begun implanting a mirror question to the one posed decades earlier—not whether we were growing fast enough, but whether we were growing too much, and much too fast. Not whether we were resting on our natural advantages, but whether we were now compromising them. Advocacy around the environment and around Austin's sense of place—that coastal culture the city had spent almost the entirety of the twentieth century until then establishing—had begun in earnest, and it seemed on a collision course with growth.

Preservation v. Industrial Growth

In the 1970s, around the time I first visited Austin, commercial and residential development began to threaten the water purity of Barton Springs, one of the city's crown jewels and considered sacred by the Tonkawa long before Europeans arrived. In 1918, the springs had been deeded to the city, which then dammed the creek around them, transforming the spot into a natural swimming pool near the heart of downtown that soon became a gathering place for everyone—children and seniors alike, the working class and the elite. Regulars, such as author and naturalist Roy Bedichek, journalist J. Frank Dobie (who successfully lobbied for the preservation of the Texas longhorn cattle), and historian Walter Prescott Webb would settle under the shade to tell stories with friends. (Today a sculpture of Dobie, whose home near UT now serves as a space for creative writers, rests near the pool's entrance.) Anyone who visits Austin during warm (or hellishly warm) weather is likely to be encouraged by a bartender, hotel concierge, or host to visit the aqua-green pool, where the chilly sixty-eight degree water is a salve during triple-digit days.

The Barton Creek watershed occupies Austin's southwest quarter and is part of the Edwards Aquifer, which is highly sensitive to pollution. (An aquifer, for the non-geologists, is a body of permeable rock under the soil's surface that holds groundwater and naturally filters out some contaminants, slowly channeling the water into the springs. Aquifers also serve as reservoirs for drinking water and agricultural use. The Edwards Aquifer is one of the most productive in the US.) Contaminating any of the city's largest six creeks in the recharge zone—the area where the aquifer is replenished by rainfall—will endanger Barton Springs as well. Development in the recharge zone puts the springs at risk, from septic leaks and runoff from impervious cover, to pesticides, insecticides, bacteria, and other pollutants. The only way to keep the springs clean, to ensure their safety for recreation, and to preserve their wildlife—the Barton Springs salamander, for example, exists nowhere else in the world—is to ensure that the creeks are kept clean.

It was in the same summer of 1973 that another Austin visionary began thinking in earnest about Austin's relationship to water and how to preserve the city's pristine natural resource. Sinclair Black, architect and professor emeritus at the University of Texas, crafted a "creeks plan" with relevance to the future of the city that remains undimmed. His goal: to protect the creeks at all cost. He saw them as part of the identity of the city and instrumental to the health of the larger system of waterways. His vision was only partially implemented—development continues to endanger some of the creeks (and flooding is a growing concern). But Austin's waterways and the open spaces abutting them wouldn't be nearly as accessible and protected if it weren't for his efforts. I wasn't to meet Black for another twenty-five years, during which time he achieved near-iconic status in the city. And like George Kozmetsky, he gave back generously. In the spring of 2019, he donated $5 million dollars to the UT School of Architecture.

Black's influence remains strong. In many ways, his vision for the future of the city—including rethinking the interstate and how to overcome the division it creates between East and West Austin—is a blueprint that has universal relevance. The water in all its forms—lakes, creeks, springs, and the river—are central to what Austin is to become.

Even with preservationists such as Black sounding the alarm in the 1970s about the dangers development posed to the waterways, growth remained a constant challenge to visions of sustainability—and vice versa. In 1982, soon after ground was broken on Circle C—a large, master-planned community in Southwest Austin—developer Gary Bradley told *The New York Times*, "We've got a town with a conscience," and derisively referred to Austin's environmentalists as "the granola army . . . who can beat you without money." Then, as in the previous decade, the "granola army" did not comprise hippies and tree huggers alone. It was stacked with ordinary citizens fearful of their neighborhoods being overrun with traffic. Orum recounts the 1970s saga over the development of Mopac Boulevard, for instance, the north-south freeway west of downtown. At one point, the city council, reacting to vocal concerns about traffic endangering children and ruining landscapes, shut down three of the ramps onto the thoroughfare. After drawn-out objections from developers, the business community, and the Texas Department of Transportation, the council reversed the decision. The war between developers and their discontents was in full swing, but not until the 1988 announcement of a proposed four thousand-acre Barton Creek Planned Unit Development (PUD)—consisting of apartments, shopping and office space, and a golf course—did Austin's most prominent and most vocal environmental-protection organization arise—the Save Our Springs (SOS) Alliance.

Any pollution resulting from the proposed Barton Creek PUD would have contaminated the springs. But that didn't stop its lead proponent, the ambitious developer Jim Bob Moffett, chairman of Freeport-McMoRan, from pushing it. Hard. Moffett quickly became an archvillain to those devoted to the springs' preservation, and not only because he'd set his designs on Barton Creek. Moffett and Freeport-McMoRan were notorious for having run the world's largest gold mine in Irian Jaya, Indonesia, an operation that had been implicated in cases of not only large-scale environmental damage but also secondhand involvement in human-rights abuses. During a June 7, 1990, city council meeting, nearly a thousand Austinites signed up to voice their objections to the development. The meeting lasted throughout the night, and the following day the council unanimously rejected the PUD. Soon afterward, emboldened by the victory, environmental activists galvanized and formed the SOS Alliance to strengthen earlier watershed-protection ordinances so that future "Moffetts" would be thwarted. Their crowning achievement: The city council voted in 1991 to enforce "zero degradation" of the Barton Creek watershed.

Despite the absolutist language, however, the measure was not so sweeping. The council waffled, ultimately approving a compromise with softer restrictions. In response, SOS gathered more than thirty thousand signatures to put the SOS ordinance on the ballot, which a year later Austinites overwhelmingly approved, despite major opposition from developers. The business-friendly state legislature moved to weaken the ordinance almost immediately by authoring Senate Bill 1029, which would grandfather in developments permitted before the new regulations. Governor Ann Richards, who supported SOS, vetoed the bill, but when the matter landed on Governor George W. Bush's desk in 1995, he approved the grandfathering, weakening the SOS victory and giving the go-ahead to development on thousands of acres in the watershed.

These issues were explained to me with a great deal of passion by one of the leading advocates of the SOS alliance, Robin Rather, former chair of the organization and daughter of newscaster Dan Rather. During my work on Envision Central Texas—a proposed plan for land use and transportation for the 1.2 million people who would be moving to the region in the next forty years—she was a consistent protectionist voice at the long public input sessions that were part of that process. And, in the end, she was a strong proponent of the strategies that emerged. The question of where growth could—and should—occur was a constant theme. Unsurprisingly, much of this debate centered on the question of the environment and land values—how a land's use does or doesn't contribute to a city's tax base (parks are nontaxable, whereas residences and business are, for example).

William Scott Swearingen Jr., author of *Environmental City*, which chronicles Austin's environmental movement, described the fight as one between two opposing concepts of the land's value. Many Austinites wanted to preserve the land to be enjoyed for recreational value or simply for its natural beauty. Developers wanted the land for its exchange value, its profitability. "The movement to preserve the environment in the midst of massive unplanned growth," Swearingen wrote, "was part of the deeper movement to preserve an idea of a place, an idea of an 'Austin' that was based on its quality of life rather than the riches people made from its growth." Indeed, the SOS Alliance mission expanded to encompass the preservation of the very character of the city—a character centered around keeping its citizens in touch with the water and green space. "Protecting Barton Springs has always, in part, been about more than just the springs," SOS Alliance cofounder Bill Bunch said in 2012, on the twenty-year anniversary of the ordinance's passing. "It's also about saving our city from the temptation of the fast buck at the expense of the future."

The Myopia of Environmental Activism

After I'd experienced Austin's thoughtfully engineered coastal culture for the first time in 1973, I'd returned to the West Coast, to the Pacific Northwest, with environmentalism more on my mind than ever. Having left academia, I found myself grappling with the question of growth and preservation on a very different level. It wasn't just me. Big questions were being asked nationwide about how to preserve the natural world, and to me—and to many others—the imperative to be good stewards of the earth was often in direct conflict with rapidly growing cities.

My own trajectory had, however, taken a different turn. In 1986, I was recruited to become vice president of a newly formed venture fund in Portland, Oregon. The Oregon Resource and Technology Development Corporation (ORTDC) was initially funded with state lottery money, but the board was decidedly private sector, and the due diligence process was rigorous. Among the investments I led was the Hood River Brewing Company, along with several tech spin-offs from Intel.

I continued to work with startups after leaving ORTDC, including one of my own. I began the Fat Tire Farm, Portland's first exclusive mountain bike retailer in 1988. All in all, I was content to continue in the venture world and to indulge my love of cycling. When the State of Washington came calling, however, I couldn't resist the allure of Olympia and Seattle.

I took a role as the head of a large state-level economic development division. Admittedly, this was no easy fit with the environmental movement I had long admired. But having a front-row seat to the battles waged between environmentalists and developers helped me understand that extreme positions—being either staunchly antigrowth or rabidly pro-development—can sometimes do more harm than good.

As the Barton Springs saga played out in the early 1990s, demonstrating the good that environmental activism could do, I was witnessing an entirely different face of the movement. As a de facto representative of the Washington governor's office, I was asked to be the point person as the Mitsubishi Corporation was looking to develop a four-star resort on the Olympic Peninsula. The company had acquired land for its project but soon discovered it had tread upon a sensitive habitat, a nesting area for bald eagles. A company delegation came to the governor's office with a proposition: They would cede a large portion of their recently purchased land in exchange for a smaller portion of adjoining state-owned parkland that they could build upon instead. It was a win all around for the corporation, the state, and the wildlife. Instead of proceeding, however, the project collapsed under vocal opposition from environmentalists. The state should not relinquish public land for corporate interests, the detractors contended. If the deal had gone through, the total land set aside for environmental protection would have actually increased, and the development itself would have been required to adhere to stringent state standards, but the oppositional uproar drowned out good-faith debate. That the public hearing to contest this Japanese company's proposal transpired on December 7—the anniversary of the day Pearl Harbor was attacked—seemed to me a troubling indication of xenophobia. Ironically—or perhaps not—the measure's opponents lost interest not long after the deal fell through, even once a subdivision, which trespassed into the wildlife habitat to an extent greater than the resort ever would have, was built upon Mitsubishi's land. The experience was another lesson about the complexity of growth and development and the sometimes blind opposition to it. It seemed to me that vocal antidevelopment advocates sometimes cared less about the environment than they did their own ability to win, relying entirely on antigrowth principles and not on actual outcomes.

The lessons I learned from that experience deeply affected my posture toward environmentalism and sustainability. In this case, "defeating the evil forces of development" actually did greater damage to the land than a compromise would have—a Pyrrhic victory in every sense. And while this realization did not change my attitude toward the benefits of protecting sensitive habitats, it did change my sense of the politics around environmentalism. As is often the case, politically heated battles tend to allow no room for a middle ground, no room for compromise.

Once I returned to Austin for good in 1994, I was no longer a vagabond bouncing between communes and universities, more intent on asking questions than offering solutions. I'd had the benefit of seeing both sides of the environmentalism-versus-development issue. Twenty years earlier, I'd experienced Austin's thoughtfully engineered coastal culture for the first time, and I'd returned to the West Coast with environmentalism more on my mind than ever. Having left academia, I found myself grappling with the question of growth and preservation on a very different level. My anti-development/pro-environment views had been tempered by many of the battles I had seen on the job, including this latest with Mitsubishi. I recognized that the nuanced center is often where the best solution lies, for everyone, and that issues should be approached on a case-by-case basis, not categorically.

Austin had changed by the mid-nineties. It too had become a product of forces that had both spurred its growth and resisted it. The vision of technopolis had materialized, yet the vigilance of environmental advocates—and of SOS Alliance in particular—had helped preserve some of the city's most precious spaces. That "I'm not antigrowth, but" ambiguity was everywhere, and it remains so today. Not long ago, for instance, members of my own team at TIP Strategies, who are pro-growth by trade, were wary about the idea of Amazon building a second headquarters here, fearful—just as the opponents of Mopac Boulevard were so many years earlier—of a traffic nightmare.

The opposite had proven true, too: Some of the activists who had been so invested in the city's environmental preservation in the 1980s had, years on, begun to bristle at that effort's unintended consequences. Rather, who in her role as chair of SOS Alliance in 1999 had helped ink a deal that saved thousands of acres from further development in the Barton Creek watershed, publicly apologized in 2017 for the deal's effects on East Austin. Protecting land and water in certain neighborhoods, often high-income areas near green spaces, meant that developers would head to areas that didn't have those protections, namely the east side. That east side neighborhood had long been populated by lower-income families, many of them Black and Latino. "It sounds naïve now," Rather said, "but we created something called 'the desired development zone' that would go east, and we would buy up and protect lands that were west to conserve and protect the aquifer.... I blame myself and all environmentalists at the time. We didn't understand they were talking about gentrifying neighborhoods and displacing people." (Chapter 6 discusses how Austin's east side is dealing with the repercussions of these and other development decisions.)

The issue of gentrification—including drivers such as environmental preservation and its consequences—has remained a recurrent theme both in the planning world and, increasingly, in economic development. While the debate has been raging since at least the publication of Jane Jacobs's 1961 book, *The Death and Life of Great American Cities* (which argued that traditional urban renewal efforts did not really respect city dwellers), it has taken on a different inflection, one that centers primarily on communities of color, i.e., disadvantaged Black and Hispanic neighborhoods. That rising land values are both good for the tax base of a city *and* a burden on low-income residents is a given entirely unremarkable. Nevertheless, this observation continues to come as a surprise—as it did not just for Rather, but also for Richard Florida, a sociologist and author of *Rise of the Creative Class*. Florida has, in fact, turned several books into an extended critique of his original approach to this issue.

Antigrowth/pro-preservation sentiment has had similar displacement effects elsewhere, such as Carmel, California; Sun Valley, Idaho; and Boulder, Colorado. Boulder, through exclusionary zoning (excluding land uses—lot size, multifamily homes—in ways that negatively affect certain communities such as low-income households), height restrictions (no tall buildings means you can't grow up), and tight controls over annexation, was essentially willing to shut down future growth for several reasons, one of which was land preservation. They have asked the question many have asked about Austin—do we really want or need to grow more?—and have answered in the same way Schumacher, author of *Small is Beautiful*, might have: no. Yet as housing supply limits itself in the face of ever-increasing demand, prices skyrocket. And as the city becomes an extraordinarily desirable place to live, the cost of buying, renting, and accessing amenities rises. Just as growth can lead to undesirable consequences so, too, can the battles waged against it.

Even great visionaries can miss the mark, whether they are advocating for growth, preservation or equity. I doubt someone even as visionary as

George Kozmetsky, who was expressly motivated by social-equity issues, could have foreseen just how much a technopolis would price out non-tech workers from Austin's core. As we have seen, Richard Florida had to acknowledge as much and—to his credit—has written what many see as a near-refutation of his original thesis about the desirability of attracting the "creative class."

Shutting off growth and development will not solve the problems Austin faces; in fact, doing so will only exacerbate them, as it has with Boulder. The question of growth, then, becomes not one of *whether* but one of *how.* "Do we grow up, do we grow out, or do we do both?" is indeed the question that animates much of the discussion in the city today. For an expanding contingent of Austin urbanists, growing out—sprawl—is at its core antienvironmental: Less green space means more parking lots, highways, building foundations, and so on, which restrict water from entering the Edwards Aquifer (impermeable surfaces such as cement mean less water is absorbed into the soil) and increase the risk of polluting it. Greater commuter time means more traffic and more congestion and (at least until electric vehicles are more than a novelty) more air pollution. And the less dense the housing stock is in the core, the more expensive it becomes, which means fewer can afford to live near where they work. For the most vocal among the urbanists' opposition, however—many from the same neighborhood associations that fought decades earlier against Circle C, Mopac, and the Barton Creek PUD—density in the core means permanently altering historic, central neighborhoods as more people crowd onto a smaller footprint. Growth and density are fine in theory, in other words, but not in their backyards. A third contingent—those increasingly displaced from the east side after 1999's "desired development zone," for instance—are caught somewhere in the middle. Density may mean greater inner-city affordability in the long run, they might agree, but by then will they have already been fully pushed outward?

The Unforeseen, a 2007 documentary about the fight to preserve Barton Springs—produced by Robert Redford and Terrence Malick and directed by Laura Dunn—captures the many pro-growth and antigrowth forces at work in Austin, the competing visions for what the city should become, and what sacrifices can and should be made in the name of development. The film not only reinforces for me that, yes, there truly is something in the water here in Austin, but it also captures a distinction that should drive discussions of growth. "Growth itself is not the enemy," said documentary interviewee William Greider, an author and journalist. "It is the nature of that growth, the quality within it."

This "quality" Greider speaks of is essential to the question of whether or not growth is "smart." Then again, what is smart is itself debatable. Efforts by Rather and the SOS Alliance in the late 1990s to fashion a "desired development zone," for instance, "gave rise to the city's 'smart growth' strategy that steered development eastward," reported the *Austin American-Statesman* in 2017. That is, the strategy was very smart for the Barton Creek watershed and those who live near it, perhaps, and mostly smart for Austinites at large, all of whom benefit from our waters—recreationally and practically—but not as smart for many in East Austin bracing for displacement, which continues to this day. The question about what is *smart* then becomes not just whether we grow up, out, or both, but how we do any of those things while maintaining that "something of the water"—that sense of place, that coastal culture, that weirdness and tolerance and openness that are meant to belong to all of us, that so many of us were introduced to in ways similar to how I was in 1973, there at Lake Travis.

The protections Austin has put in place, while they exacerbate inequality, have remained a major factor in our attractiveness. We have protected the Colorado River and the creeks and other natural resources while still having incredible growth. Did we get it 100 percent right? No. No one has, and no one can—there are too many variables. But one must always *try* to get it right.

Another factor to the growth equation is at play as well—arguably the most important factor, one that's long been divisive but is increasingly so in today's political climate. It is the very thing that, once mindfully harnessed, gave Austin—via the dams—its "something of the water" and "coastal culture" sense of place to begin with. Many understand its critical value, but, for public-relations purposes, choose to call it something else. Some are fine with it as long as it is wielded by, as Orum called them, "urban entrepreneurs" (the Wooldridges, the Staceys, and the LBJs) and not the "market entrepreneurs" (the Kozmetskys and other technopolis advocates). Still others balk at it—and the system built around it—as instinctively and unquestioningly as those who opposed the Mitsubishi initiative near Seattle so many years ago.

That thing is capital.

CHAPTER THREE

Why Capital Matters

Any effort to explain Austin's success that ignores capital will be woefully incomplete. On the face of it, this may seem like an obvious statement. But we're talking about Austin, where an anti-capitalist, countercultural sentiment has been firmly rooted since the 1970s. Austin's brand *is* counterculture, yet it coexists with capitalism. More than just coexists, the two actually reinforce each other. This ironic juxtaposition is a defining element of Austin's success, and exploring this relationship reveals important lessons about how the city arrived where it is today—and where it's going.

The importance of capital is a given to every economist. It was as basic to Karl Marx as it was to Milton Friedman. The *meaning* of capital, however, opens an entirely different discussion. Is it at the heart of a system whose primary role is the exploitation of workers? Or is it the fuel that powers creativity and innovation? Millennials and Gen Z struggle with this question. A broad disapproval of capitalism in favor of socialism seems to suggest that young people are disillusioned with the importance of capital and the role it plays in our economy. "Occupy Wall Street," the 2011 protest targeting economic inequity, was a slogan that has had staying power. Corporations, it seemed, played by one set of rules, while workers were expendable and had no recourse when capital was put into play. The typical millennial's negative reaction to "capital" centers on the way in which wealth is concentrated in the hands of large corporations and a small number of individuals. Capital is shorthand for unfairly concentrated power.

Today's startup-savvy generation, however paradoxically, tends to mistrust traditional discussions of capital, due in large measure with the direct link to *capitalism*. The protests that galvanized around Occupy Wall Street in 2011 still resonate. In this view, corporations are the inevitable outcome of unregulated capital. Their ability to manipulate markets and to disregard workers continues to be seen as one of society's greatest evils.

Of course, much hinges on the definition we give to "capital." In purely economic terms, it represents the assets of a corporation, including equipment, buildings, raw materials, and even technology. In financial terms, it's available cash and resources that can be readily liquidated. In personal terms, it's just money.

It is no exaggeration to say that calling someone a *capitalist*—someone who favors capitalism—is an effective insult these days, particularly among younger Americans. A 2018 Gallup poll found that just half of those ages eighteen to twenty-nine said they viewed *capitalism* positively, down precipitously since 2010—over twenty points. (Of course, to add an *ism* to any word is to garner a charged response.) Instead, respondents tended toward the share-the-wealth, communal appeal of socialism.

Ironically, however, these same young people extol the virtues of entrepreneurship and innovation: The same Gallup poll found that people of all age groups viewed the terms *small business*, *entrepreneurs*, and *free enterprise* favorably. I say "ironically" because entrepreneurial success is largely dependent on access to capital and because startup businesses do not fit comfortably into socialist economies. Whether millennials are uncomfortable with capital or not, whether they view capitalism favorably or not, having access to capital is a necessary ingredient for the kind of growth they desire.

This push-pull is at the heart of Austin's appeal—and its success in attracting talented and ambitious people. Access to capital for startups—or at least the perception of available resources (which is sometimes as important as the actuality)—is less onerous than in many other communities. Although Austin is not awash in venture capitalists and angel investors in the same way that, say, Silicon Valley is, there is a high enough concentration of wealthy individuals and firms that are willing and able to put up risk capital to fund entrepreneurial ventures when traditional bank loans (which require collateral) aren't a viable route for a startup. This is great news for entrepreneurs of all ages, of course. For millennials, especially—many of whom are distrustful of corporations, or at least what they represent—there is also the sense that Austin continues to resist corporate overreach. While this can easily be argued against (Austin continues to attract major corporations), the vibe is there. Downtown zoning has long favored locally owned enterprises (Austin's iconic independent bookstore BookPeople, for example, has never had to compete with a Barnes and Noble setting up shop around the corner). There is also powerful protection for the waterfront and green spaces, areas that might otherwise be filled with office buildings. In Austin, it seems, you can have your cake and eat it too—you can be anti-corporate and still be profitable.

The reality, however, is undeniable: No matter how "weird" Austin regards itself, no matter how anti-corporate some of its city policies may seem, entrepreneurial creativity is dependent on *capital* investment. It is access to capital—the very essence of capitalism—that makes these ventures possible. In fact, one often becomes a part of the other. Michael Dell was a true "upstart" entrepreneur; now Dell Technologies is a Wall Street darling. The same is true of John Mackey, the Austin-based founder of Whole Foods, who started his deli-sized store on borrowed funds and supersized the organic grocery chain to the tune of $800 billion in national revenue (and then sold it to corporate giant Amazon).

While self-explanatory to any banker making loans for home improvement, the importance of capital has been consistently underrecognized and underappreciated by planners and even by urbanists who place an emphasis on the creative class, i.e., the pool of talented and innovative individuals who help comprise the foundation of a city's growth. Economic developers and civic leaders have more recently been rightly focused on retaining and growing the talent base, but in their assessment of what makes a community appealing, they typically overlook the pivotal role that capital plays. Not recognizing that the accessibility of capital is largely what draws talent is to misunderstand cause and effect. In Austin's case, harnessing capital is as much part of the city's growth as is the talent base stoked by the University of Texas, or the land, rivers, and creeks, or the Keep Austin Weird vibe. And capital cannot be harnessed without a deep commitment to *capitalism*. In an era when sentiment against corporations and against the "billionaire class" is more pronounced than ever, we can't afford to ignore thinking anew about capital.

The conditions that enabled the dual-purpose growth in Austin would not have been nearly as fertile if it weren't for the vision and action of George Kozmetsky, founder of UT's IC^2 Institute, for whom capital was on a par with creativity and innovation. Indeed, he stated that capital is what fuels growth. Anthony Orum, remarking on the role of money and power in Austin's growth, wrote, "All the dreaming and all the hard work are fine, but there must be resources to make everything go."

Debates over the word *capitalism* in Austin economic development have deep roots in the city. At the same time economist E. F. Schumacher was calling capitalism and growth into question in the 1970s, Kozmetsky was developing his technopolis model for the city of the future—and putting capital at the forefront. The fact that Austin is at the center of that debate, dating back nearly fifty years, offers insights more relevant now than at any time in the city's history.

The Kozmetsky Effect

I cannot recall exactly how often during the mid-1990s I woke early to meet with Kozmetsky for coffee, but I do remember how eclectic the conversations were. For someone as widely read, traveled, and experienced as he, that was no surprise. My encounters with him were not unique in this regard. "People at all levels," wrote Monty Jones, Kozmetsky's biographer, "were regularly impressed, if not awestruck by the quickness of his mind and the range of topics on which he was well informed." This was the man who had helped launch a hundred tech companies, was honored by President Clinton with the National Medal of Technology and Innovation in 1993, and was a prolific speaker on a global scale. Anyone who knew anything about Austin's tech ascendancy—how it went from a city once dubbed by *The New York Times* as having a "Birkenstock ethos" to a dominant technology hub—knew of Kozmetsky's primary role in it all.

While Kozmetsky had been born in Seattle, his family's experience under Soviet communism had shaped his positive views on capitalism. As the child of Jewish immigrants, he had a deep appreciation for the United States and did not take for granted the relative ease of access to capital and economic opportunity. In the USSR, capital was inextricably bound up with Karl Marx's *Das Kapital*—the idea that capitalism existed as a means to exploit workers and enrich the owners. Individuals had little or no control over their own intellectual property, nor were they intended to have. In addition, religion and ethnicity could permanently mark you as an insider or outsider, depending on your heritage and affiliation.

Many years later, while leading a seminar on entrepreneurship in Saint Petersburg, Russia, I was asked about Austin's emergence as a tech capital. I mentioned the central role played by Kozmetsky and the importance not only of capital but of intellectual property and the right to own it. After the class, one of the Russian instructors associated with the institute at which I was lecturing engaged me in conversation. I pointed out to him that Kozmetsky was in fact a kind of fellow countryman to him, his family having emigrated from the Soviet Union (now Belarus). "Hmm, Kozmetsky," he mused, dwelling on the name. "No, not a countryman," he said, "a Jew."

It took me a moment to absorb what I had just heard. Apparently, because Kozmetsky's family was Jewish, he could lay no claim to being Russian. Here, in a nutshell, was the origin of Kozmetsky's embrace of the United States and the value of an open society, including free-market capitalism. In America, he was not regarded as the "other" but accepted as a citizen, someone who could not only explore ideas, for his own betterment and for society, but could also be a part of the growth associated with those ideas. This latter part of the equation was crucial to his thinking. The underlying values inherent to Marxist ideology—egalitarianism, humanism (ideas still seductive to many US millennials)—and its economic system could, he believed, be better realized through an economic *and social* system like that of the United States. In short, capitalism was not an evil to be combatted, it was the very means by which entrepreneurial creativity could be unleashed. And without creativity, Kozmetsy believed, a society was moribund.

What I most clearly remember discussing with Kozmetsky during those early-morning coffee meetings were the initiatives he and his team were pursuing at IC², the institute he founded at UT in 1977 and that I described in chapter 1. What I did not learn until many years later, after Kozmetsky had passed away in 2003, was the story behind that institute's squared little initialism, a story that has a lot to do with that much-maligned word *capitalism*.

At the organization's inception in the mid-1970s, "IC²" stood for the Institute of Constructive Capitalism. Its stated mission was signature Kozmetsky: The institute would "subject capitalism to the objective scrutiny of academic research and provide ideas about ways in which the private sector may respond more effectively to help solve society's social equity problems in a time of rapid socioeconomic and cultural change."

Implicit in this wording is Kozmetsky's belief that capital was indeed the fuel of growth, that capital would propel a dynamic and talent-attracting city. But Kozmetsky also understood that while capital had the potential to solve social problems, it could not be relied upon to do so in itself. The purpose of capital—if we can speak in that way—is to expand. That's all. After all, if capitalism were already working just fine to "solve society's problems"—of which racial equity and environmental protections are two of the more prominent—he'd have seen no need to found the institute to begin with.

A question once posed to him by one of his University of Texas students helps illuminate Kozmetsky's singular moment of revelation. When asked when American capitalism had begun to "decay" (a question largely unique to a liberal academic institution), Kozmetsky said that the deadly Watts riots of 1965, sparked by an altercation in the Watts neighborhood of Los Angeles between white police officers and an African American motorist, had driven home the breakdown for him:

> Can I personalize it? Yes, the morning I woke up in my bedroom in Los Angeles and I looked out through our coral tree to the Pacific Ocean and listened to the radio telling me Watts was burning. That is when it struck me. That is when I decided to give up being an executive. The time had come to go back to the university.

Kozmetsky saw that the violent unrest in a Black neighborhood was on a continuum with social equity and that the economics of capitalism, regardless of how beneficial to society generally, could not resolve the equity dilemma on its own.

It was there, in the university's classrooms, and later at IC^2, where he could help to encourage the shifts he wanted to see in the world, to begin bridging the gap between ocean views enjoyed by some and the chaos and struggle endured by others. Capitalism was flawed, yes, and capital formation wasn't a panacea for all societal problems. But he wouldn't abandon it. Kozmetsky's profound understanding of the limitations of communism and an authoritarian government, which concentrates wealth in the hands of the few, kept him firmly rooted in the soil of capitalism and democracy.

Furthermore, Kozmetsky understood perfectly well that wealth alone would not guarantee broader access to capital. We see this in modern-day Russia and in other countries that have built their economy almost entirely on natural resources. Saudi Arabia is a clear and extreme example. It is flush with monetary capital—all related to oil and gas—yet plagued by social inequity and bald-faced, unapologetic oppression of women and minorities. This capital, however, is highly stratified. It rests in the hands of a very small number of people. It is something of a hallmark of economies built entirely on natural resources: They pay little attention to creativity or innovation. The simple explanation for this is that they do not have to do so. As long as the demand (for oil or other natural resources) is there, the money will continue to flow. And it is no big step to see why there is a vested interest in further concentrating that wealth.

I came to the same realization while in Saint Petersburg. While talking about intellectual property as key to building an entrepreneurial ecosystem, I was quickly reminded that IP protection is virtually nonexistent in Russia. The most skilled coders and tech entrepreneurs operate in a kind of gray zone of the economy, a close parallel to the government-supported hackers we now know so much about.

This was precisely Kozmetsky's point. Capitalism harnessed "constructively" was an engine not only of economic growth, but also of social advancement and social justice. Constructive capitalism, then, aims to benefit human lives and not only result in economic growth. He saw technology as leveling the economic playing field, of putting the tools for growth and creativity into the hands of everyone. The link between capital(ism) and social equity both required and furthered the idea of the open society. His goal for IC^2 was to demonstrate how a human-centered capitalism could be accomplished anywhere in the world.

Prefixed with *constructive* or otherwise, capitalism was—and remains—a fraught issue to many academics, particularly those outside business schools. Kozmetsky was sensitive to many of his colleagues' distaste for capitalism, both for its perceived overreach and the increasing stratification of wealth that seemed to follow in its wake. It seemed not to matter to many critics how wealth was generated (natural resources versus innovation and creativity). What did matter was only what furthered social justice.

Referring to the institute by its initials (IC^2) obscured the c-word and was employed by Kozmetsky and others as commonly as the spelled-out name—if not more so. It worked to keep further criticism at bay. Nearly a decade after the institute's founding, however, he officially changed its name to "IC^2" so that the initialism stood instead for "Innovation, Creativity, Capital," the three-ingredient economic-development formula I remember him advancing in the same mid-1990s speech at UT that so captivated me. Public reasons for the name change included Kozmetsky's emphasis on the word "creativity" and his sense that "constructive capitalism" was too often misunderstood. Monty Jones further uncovered Kozmetsky's personal reasons for making the name change: The *ism* in *capitalism* had continued to be three little letters of outsize power. Even among those who subscribed to the institute's mission, and those who may have otherwise been willing to fund and endorse it, advancing *capitalism* was no longer a tenable position for a university to take.

While some would argue that Kozmetsky's vision for IC^2 hasn't fully been borne out on the social justice front (and they wouldn't be wrong), its mere establishment helped ferment Austin's venture capital-rich landscape and helped offer capital access to those who may not otherwise receive it. Not only did it draw additional funding and talent to the university (that all-important talent factor!), it also signaled to companies considering a move here that tech transfer between academic institutions and private companies, the kind that put Stanford/Silicone Valley on the map, was possible and supported. The founding of the Austin Technology Incubator (ATI) in 1989, another Kozmetsky brainchild, further opened the flow of capital from interested investors—private and public—into startup projects in sectors such as agriculture, energy, health care, transit, and more. Over ten initial public offerings (IPOs) owe their success to the ATI, and as of this writing, over five hundred companies have participated in projects that have yielded \$3 billion in economic impact. (Chapter 5 delves into Austin's entrepreneurial ecosystem and all the factors—including capital—that have made Austin an entrepreneurial supercity.)

How Do You Say Capitalism Without Saying Capitalism

My experience in talking with millennial colleagues corroborates the Gallup poll findings and echoes Kozmetsky's own difficulties. Beginning with the Occupy Wall Street movement at the end of the Great Recession, the backlash toward unbridled capitalism has become widespread. In fact, calling it "unbridled" seems redundant to the critics. It was my daughter,

Teresa, who introduced me to the concept of *institutional betrayal*. When I asked Kathleen Baireuther—a millennial who's a former team member at TIP and a former vice president at Our Next Energy—she was quick to explain. Institutional betrayal was evidenced by student loan rates that often exceeded 8 percent while getting a car loan was typically half that amount. I was taken aback. How could that be? But yes, the government showed no interest in writing down loan rates—a simpler solution than forgiving student loans while continuing to generate income. Millennials felt betrayed first for being coerced into believing that higher education would pay for itself and second for a government that then did nothing to ease their burden.

While anticapitalism sentiment is a common theme among millennials, it is certainly not restricted to them. In the 2020s, presidential candidate Bernie Sanders, a self-described democratic socialist who is among the most prominent of capitalism's critics, had a following that includes people of all ages.

In the economic development world over the last twenty years, we see the same trend. Frameworks that refrain from elevating capital have proven enormously influential to urbanists, civic leaders, and economic developers. The most prominent and lasting example of such a framework is that of Richard Florida. His "3Ts of economic development"—talent, tolerance, and technology—first popularized in his 2002 book, *The Rise of the Creative Class*, became something of a gospel. These three elements, the thinking goes, are what drive a city's growth and development, via the in-migration of creative, knowledgeable individuals and the firms who seek to employ them. "What ultimately makes a location attractive to industries are the clusters of talent that it has on hand," Florida reiterated in a 2014 academic article, "and what attracts smart talented people to a place are its natural, cultural, and built amenities, everything from its architecture to its prestigious knowledge institutions—and most of all, the presence of other talented people." But there is no mention of capital in this framework, no recognition that access to capital may be determinative to the growth of creativity. As strong an argument as Florida makes for his 3T approach—and he's not wrong on many counts—using it in an economic development context without accounting for that fundamental ingredient of capital is like celebrating the Fourth of July without acknowledging the

American Revolution. If you don't understand why access to capital makes economic growth happen, the formula will not serve you well. None of it matters without capital.

It is true that Florida has not been silent on the role of capital elsewhere, and his 3Ts encapsulate much of what makes Austin unique and successful. Included in his work are trenchant observations that capture how separate visions—technopolis, weird city, and so on—overlap, and how Austin's eccentric allure attracts talented individuals. Florida wrote of a 2001 visit when he expected to find, as elsewhere, self-serious suits in "lavish" surroundings but instead discovered tieless collars and shirtsleeves; a comparatively friendly venue, the Austin Music Hall; a live band comprising, to his astonishment, venture capitalists; and Michael Dell—all willing to engage with outsiders and newcomers. Florida wrote, too, of a conversation he had with a college graduate who'd recently been recruited by an Austin firm. Asked why he'd leave his northeastern city—a fine, attractive, amenable place in its own right—for his new job, the young man responded self-evidently, "It's in Austin!" Once Florida pressed him to elaborate, he cited a "tremendous amount to do, a thriving music scene, ethnic and cultural diversity, fabulous outdoor recreation, and great nightlife."

The motivation for people to move to a new city was always in the back of Florida's mind. *The Rise of the Creative Class,* he hoped, "would help enlarge the focus of the field of economic development, from one that was almost exclusively fixated on firms and industries to one that also paid due attention to people and places." In this he sounds to economic development as Jane Jacobs did to urban planning: "People make [cities], and it is to them, not buildings, that we must fit our plans." Florida wrote in a 2014 academic journal that "the vast majority of economic development theory and practice, as well as much of urban and economic geography and urban and regional economics, had been focused on the behavior of firms, whether in selecting locations or in organizing themselves into clusters."

He was not wrong. The focus on talent came very late to economic development. And Florida made a strong case that if you do not attract a young—and skilled—workforce, your community will not be competitive. This trend brings us directly back to the magnetic pull of Austin. While we (sardonically) once boasted about having the most educated waiters in the country, we were suddenly of interest to a whole new wave of companies—big and small—who were seeking out Austin because of its talent pool.

In 1988, more than a decade before Florida was talking about what attracted *individuals* to a city, he was citing Kozmetsky and exploring how high-tech cities like Austin were "net attractors of *capital*." In *The Rise of the Creative Class*, Florida highlighted MCC and SEMATECH as illustrations of Austin's embrace of one of his "Ts," technology. The role of capital, however, was not seen as a major contributing factor to the city's success. In calling Kozmetsky a "fabled entrepreneur" under whose leadership Austin "built a thriving entrepreneurial climate," Florida would also need to highlight the outsize role of capital not only as it relates to the University of Texas, but also how it underpins entrepreneurial activity. My criticism of Florida was that he treated trailing indicators as if they were predictive. Had he included access to capital in his analysis, the picture he was painting would have looked different. His occupational classification that comprised the "creative class" served only to underscore what earlier writers (such as Peter Drucker) would have characterized as white-collar workers. As a result, communities scored high simply because they had an abundance of "office workers"—hardly the definition of "creative." Nevertheless, no one should regard capital or access to capital as a guarantee that a community will experience growth. No, capital is not the only determinant of broader economic well-being (as we can readily see in looking at natural resource-rich countries that have not diversified their economic base and therefore have not achieved equitable prosperity), but it always plays a part. More importantly, ensuring access to capital should be the prime consideration not only in attracting talent, but also in ensuring that creative enterprises can flourish.

The question of capital takes center stage in yet another way. Whatever the source of capital, and however easily it can be accessed, the effect is profound once it is reinvested in the community. The history of Austin is a history of constant investment and reinvestment. From the dams that created the lakes to the generous donations from locally grown companies, the connection is direct and immediately visible. This is precisely what Kozmetsky envisioned when he championed the partnership model for growth—corporate, academic, and public.

I understand the conflicted feelings about capital*ism*. That "ism" now confers on capital a philosophy that suggests greed and indifference to the needs of the community as a whole. (The solutions to runaway capitalism are in the boring details of tax policy and regulation, the stuff that few politicians and city leaders want to bother themselves with—and which can fill an entirely separate book.) It is true, narrowly speaking, that capitalism lays no claim to social or moral issues one way or the other. It is not a path toward social equity in the way that Marxism or socialism purport to be. The February 16, 2019, issue of *The Economist* featured a smiling young woman proclaiming, "The Rise of Millennial Socialism." This captures the mood of the time perfectly. Capitalism bears the brunt of reaction against the widening wealth gap, the concomitant loss of the traditional middle class, and both racial and gender inequity. But as *The Economist* points out, the remedy for these very legitimate grievances is not achieved through a rejection of capitalism. An economic system that accepts the benefits of capital formation, access to capital, and the right to own one's own ideas is not at odds with the need for social justice. This is precisely Kozmetsky's point.

Discussions of capital, capitalism, and social justice are never easy. I debated them on a commune in a forest clearing in Oregon, in classrooms at universities in Oregon and Washington, and with Richard Florida at a forum we gave jointly in Wisconsin. I remain mindful of economist E. F. Schumacher's criticisms of unchecked growth and of capitalism's willful indifference to the effects of a growing wealth gap.

Not long ago I purposefully rattled a conference room full of business-friendly fellow economic developers by suggesting that our entire profession was an exercise in socialism. If we really believed in the free market, in the benefits of capitalism, why did we feel the need to intercede through incentives and inducements? Why not just let the market do what the market does? Let corporations locate where it is to their greatest direct advantage. Why appropriate taxpayers' money to influence their decision and effectively skew the market?

The fact that my audience was shocked suggests that they were out of step with the criticisms leveled against the profession, both by "millennial socialists" and by Tea Party libertarians. On the one hand, you had accusations of "corporate welfare" and on the other "taxpayer fraud." In both cases, it means that economic developers have not thought through a rationale for their profession, one immune to criticism from both sides of the political spectrum.

What we need to do is to see capital (which, of course, includes financial incentives, which I discuss in chapter 4) within the context of talent, innovation, and creativity. The point is that these interrelate, and in its interrelation lies the key to Austin's growth. Former New York City Mayor Michael Bloomberg weighed in with a 2012 op-ed. "Talent attracts capital," he wrote, "far more effectively and consistently than capital attracts talent." And Richard Florida eventually cited Bloomberg's op-ed as a validation of his ideas and prescriptions among policymakers. But it's one thing for a major metropolitan mayor to make this claim and another entirely to understand how connected these factors are. Venture capital remains highly concentrated in the San Jose-San Francisco region, with the NYC-DC-Boston triangle accounting for most of the rest of the nation's venture wealth. The simple reality is that capital and talent, inspired by ideas (creativity and innovation) *attract each other.* Capital alone, if I'm to be generous to Bloomberg's argument, is not enough in itself to attract talent, let alone "effectively" or "consistently."

Capital made *accessible,* however, changes the equation. When coupled with the intent to attract enterprise to a city or region, it often succeeds in doing so. North Carolina's Research Triangle Park (RTP), established in 1959, comes to mind. "Rather than coming about organically," wrote one scholar presenting his 2010 research to an economic-development symposium, "[it] was entirely planned by state and local officials . . . focused on attracting the research divisions of major corporations." Today, RTP is home to nearly two hundred organizations and more than forty thousand workers. Yet would RTP have the same starstruck effect that Austin had on Florida's young interviewee, even if his salary prospects were comparatively the same? Doubtful, unless that young man had a peculiar affinity for office parks. And what attracts individuals to Austin is at the heart of Florida's entire claim, and why in 2010 the Research Triangle Foundation commissioned a firm to review the region's old master plan in an effort to "make it more competitive at a time when companies are flocking to urban areas that offer employees more amenities." In time we will be able to determine whether RTP's endeavor is successful, but to put as fine a point on it as I can: The capital, in any case, came first. Widely sought-after amenities that enhance the quality, the vibe, the fun, and the human scale of places are indeed crucial, especially during an era when employment isn't tied exclusively to geography. By themselves, however, they are not enough to turn metros into the new cosmopolitan powerhouses that will define an increasingly urban future.

We need such an understanding and appreciation now more than ever. Today's national conversations about capitalism and its consequences are front page news. Kozmetsky and others at IC^2 feared as much when they warned of an impending global confrontation "between the haves and have-nots." In the journal article "Creating the Technopolis," he and his colleagues wrote, "The very success of the development of a technopolis can lead to greed and many dissatisfactions" and "can be a shattering of the consensus that originally made the technopolis possible." Florida, belatedly, came to the same conclusion and has spent the past few years expressing regret that he did not anticipate the deep divisions that resulted in our national polarization. Clearly, there were warning signs, and not just from George Kozmetsky, Dave Gibson, and others.

Bill Bishop, another former Austin resident, predicted the political ramifications of this emphasis on the "creative class" with astonishing prescience in his landmark book, *The Big Sort: Why the Clustering of Like-Minded America is Tearing Us Apart*, which details how we've "sorted ourselves," to our own detriment, into cultural, economic, and political polarization. In a conversation I had with Bill, he related a call from Richard Florida that began—without preamble—with Richard blurting out, "We are so fucked!" Bill wasn't sure exactly what Florida was saying, but he guessed that it was a blunt admission that the consequences of the "sorting out" of talent and creativity within and among very few metro areas—including gentrification—had unexpected social consequences and political ramifications.

Is there a way to embrace the power of capital (especially as expressed through tech innovation and entrepreneurship) as well as the aspirations of a younger generation seeking great social equity? The answer is a highly qualified "yes." A "yes" dependent, in other words, on a willingness to reshape the *social compact*. It is not a fool's errand. An attempt to reverse the trend of capitalism-as-repugnant—by acknowledging its necessity—is a worthwhile endeavor, one I would argue is at the heart of our industry and nation's potential for successful and equitable growth. Austin is at the forefront of what can be seen as a movement, a movement born out of the idea of the technopolis, a movement to redefine the relationship between economic growth and social equity. We are still grappling with it, still trying to find ways to leverage capital to fuel social justice—a challenge Trayce

McDaniel discusses in chapter 6. But are we poised to turn Kozmetsky's vision into a reality?

Regardless, without a deeper appreciation for the role of capital, talent attraction will not confer the competitive advantage that cities are hoping to find. It's that simple. This takes nothing away from the placemaking that communities are engaged in. It simply reaffirms that the growth of corporations *and* the entrepreneurial initiative of individuals rest on access to capital.

The task that cities (and economic development organizations) must tackle is to identify and mobilize capital sources. Nothing accomplishes this better than harnessing both local dollars and seeking new infusions of capital from outside sources. This infusion of capital, along with creativity and innovation, are the engines of entrepreneurship and why Austin is setting the pace for national job growth, an influx of tech companies, and record numbers of millennial transplants.

CHAPTER FOUR

An Open Society

“e have the best quality of life of any city in America!” Economic development consultants and site selectors hear variations of this claim virtually everywhere. And here’s the irony: For those in privileged positions, it’s true. It’s true because for the chambers of commerce, for civic boosters, and for many residents, it is their reality. This is their home, and for them it is an affirmation of where they live, where they invest, and what their future is tied to. In short, “quality of life” is a proud statement of what their city means to them. But what if we were to change the terms of the equation? What if we ask about the perception of the community held by those who are not residents? The perception of those from elsewhere? And perhaps not just “outsiders” in the literal sense, but those who live in the community and are regarded as outsiders? What are their feelings about this “quality of life”?

Having visited and worked in scores of communities across the country—from Wasilla, Alaska, to Charlotte Amalie in the US Virgin Islands—I felt we needed to nuance the notion of quality of life from the perspective of the outsider. We needed to ask how someone who is not from the community experiences the city. We needed to give this perspective a name. My company, TIP, appropriated the term “quality of place,” which in economic development terms is traditionally defined as the interplay between the built and natural environment, along with residents’ health and happiness. It is the connective tissue between the social aspects of a community and the larger cultural context. The contrast with “quality of life” is the insistence that the outsider’s perspective be taken into account. I had personally experienced an air of suspicion toward outsiders in more than one community—the wariness below the superficial welcome. To then put myself into the shoes of someone who might look much less conventional than I, or who was not Anglo, who might be pierced or tattooed or wearing dreadlocks, or flamboyantly dressed—then how might I be perceived by residents? What would be the "quality of life" for me, a nonresident? An emphasis on *quality of place* would account for the way in which the stranger, the outsider, would be received by the community. And by this standard, very few communities ask: Are we welcoming?

Quantifying and measuring "quality of life" is not especially difficult, even when statistics don't quite measure up to the community's image of itself. Crime statistics, school performance, and cost of living are among the obvious metrics, and those can be spun any number of ways. Quality of place is more difficult. Economist and futurist Rebecca Ryan worked on this question and delivered provocative presentations to underscore her findings. Richard Florida tried to capture it in his discussion of *tolerance*. What is at stake is more than whether a community is friendly or welcoming (though these are consequential in their own right). The question is whether a community is reflective of an *open society*. This phrasing takes the quality of place perspective into another realm. Place speaks not only to the physical layout of a city, its geography and its built environment, but also to the sense of place that its inhabitants have. The effort to capture that human essence has roots in political philosophy, in the writings of philosopher of science Karl Popper, whom I alluded to in chapter 1. Popper believed that a community's ability to embrace new people and ideas was as important as any other measure of community and that it significantly influenced whether it would flourish or stagnate. The practical ways this plays out in the world of economic development is worthy of closer examination.

Can a case be made that an "open society" directly results in greater economic vitality? The answer is yes, but in order to make that argument we need to define what constitutes openness and how it ties to job growth, higher wages, and a more resilient tax base. That connection can best be understood with a contrast to a closed society—one where there are both institutional and legal barriers to accessing capital. Openness, however, can also be seen as reflecting additional principles that any community can work toward.

The first of these principles speaks to the accessibility of capital across a broad spectrum of individuals and institutions. In a closed society—such as we see in oil-rich Middle Eastern nations and in oligarchies generally—capital does not flow freely and is not accessible in a way that talented and creative people can use it to create both new products and new companies. It speaks to the availability of risk capital, the willingness to invest in ideas and individuals, and to anchor both ideas and individuals in the community. An open society is in direct opposition to one dominated by oligarchs, to a disproportionate concentration of wealth. When George Kozmetsky or architect/urban planner Sinclair Black donates money back to the University of Texas, when Michael Dell endows a children's hospital or a children's museum, when Isaac Barchas, CEO of Research Bridge Partners, volunteers his time to mentor young entrepreneurs, who in turn reinvest profits into the community—these are examples of how an open society and capital flows reinforce each other. They link directly to the economic vitality of the community, and their intent is to create open pathways to additional capital investment.

A second aspect of an open society is one in which collaboration is built into the economic fabric of the community. Collaboration (a favorite theme of Kozmetsky's) says that wealth-generating ideas should flow laterally as well as vertically. What this means is that innovative ideas are deliberately and consistently shared across public and private platforms. Individuals and institutions who are not necessarily the originators of new ideas are actively pulled into a collaborative framework. Silicon Valley, dependent as it traditionally was on Stanford University, represents that kind of model in the link between venture firms and university technology transfer. That "transfer" of ideas is not wholly, or even predominantly, dependent on formal mechanisms, such as university offices of tech transfer. Instead, it is the recognition that talent is anchored in the community, along with financial players who understand the acceleration of capital. To reference Isaac Barchas again (he also headed up the Austin Technology Incubator for nearly a decade), *network density* is everything. That phrase is shorthand for the importance of closely interconnected individuals, institutions, and technology to access and deploy capital.

The third component of openness speaks directly to the acceptance of diversity and inclusion. After the murder of George Floyd in 2020, diversity, equity, and inclusion (DEI) became a national focus. For many, this was a belated awakening to systemic injustices. But efforts to drive diversity and inclusion as Kozmetsky and others understood them have been going on for decades and predates the Black Lives Matter movement (birthed in 2013) by a generation. The Watts Uprising of 1965 predated the assassination of Martin Luther King Jr. and the riots that ensued after the police assaulted Rodney King (also in Los Angeles) in 1991. Kozmetsky reacted to the Watts Uprising on a visceral level. He saw it linked to the way Jews were persecuted and excluded from the social fabric of the former Soviet Union. This "exclusion"—as I detailed in chapter 3—persists to this day not only in Russia but in numerous countries, including the United States.

Purely from an economic perspective—imagining for a moment that we put aside the ethics of the situation, that we have no moral compass—the willful exclusion of individuals based on race, ethnicity, or religion is a squandering of resources and talent. That exclusionary impulse also motivated the historical marginalization of women, denying them not only the right to vote, but also the right to own property or to have agency over their own bodies. It is no coincidence that the most successful global economies create economic opportunity for women instead of excluding them from the workforce. (For example, the top five economies in Europe are also in the top ten for gender equity, according to the 2024 World Economic Forum's "Global Gender Gap Report.") The same is true for marginalized communities: Projected estimated GDP of the US goes *up* when racial inequities are eliminated. Without the inclusion of everyone (which goes to the very heart of an *open society*), we not only squander talent, we also increase the economic burden on everyone through higher taxes and through spending on everything from health care to housing to crime.

What links these factors is that they create a fertile ground for economic growth. But to make a case for growth—and to link that growth to capital, collaboration, and the acceptance of those not from the community (to include immigrants)—also involves two critical components. The first is the willingness to defend the benefits of growth from those who would oppose it, in essence to fight xenophobia. And the second is to ensure that growth does not occur at the expense of the environment or at the expense of disadvantaged populations, which is addressed in chapters 6 and 8.

Xenophobia?

Naturally for Austin, xenophobia is drenched in a signature irony. It is a kind of irony afforded to knowing that the city will continue to grow at a prodigious rate. This is a city that attracts nearly 150 new residents a day and ranks consistently among the most rapidly growing metros in the nation. Nearly every major event and every institution, from Austin City Limits Festival to the University of Texas itself, has transformed itself from a part-time occurrence (whether for four days or for some portion of four years) into a magnet that that can turn visitors into permanent residents. In fact, SXSW is a sort of showcase in that regard. Each March there is a growing cadre of real estate agents with bright-yellow signs reading, "Thinking of moving to Austin? Talk to me."

At the same time, and directly related to this growing influx of visitors, is a "visit but don't stay" mentality. "Do Not Come Here" sentiments are not against newcomers on principle. How could they be? Most of Austin's residents are transplants themselves. The transplanted and locally born alike live in a city that for nearly two centuries has almost never *not* grown, has never *not* been one of newcomers; a city, capital of the "friendly state," that is absent the social "chill" I have felt in other cities; a city where longtimers ask newcomers how they can help; and a city that has long cherished the same values of openness, plurality, and tolerance expounded upon in 1945 by Popper in *The Open Society and Its Enemies.*

"Do Not Come Here" may be symptomatic of a deeper anxiety. And it is an anxiety deeply ingrained in the city. In 1884, the *Austin Daily Statesman* wrote of the ramshackle buildings scheduled for destruction to make room for the Driskill Hotel. "A few years hence," it wrote, "the citizen of thirty years ago will be a comparative stranger in the home of his youth with no familiar objects to greet his eye save the eternal hills on which the capitol city sits enthroned as a queen in her royal beauty and the sparkling Colorado at her feet."

This concern continues unabated, whether it is the shuttering of the Armadillo World Headquarters or the loss of Las Manitas, a downtown Mexican restaurant where I once sat with Quentin Tarantino as he held court over breakfast tacos. Or even in the relocation of Mellow Johnny's—the bike shop established by Lance Armstrong—to a slick new space now indistinguishable from any high-end retail store. What is different today is how many of those old fears—about decreasing affordability, overburdened infrastructure, and economic stratification—have since been realized not only in Austin but in the nation at large. It is perhaps not surprising that other rapidly growing cities—especially ones with identities that feel threatened by waves of new residents—struggle with this issue.

In Bend, Oregon, a popular bumper sticker reads: "BEND SUCKS. DON'T MOVE HERE," superimposed on an outline of the state. When *Forbes* magazine nominated Bend as the "#1 Coolest Place to Travel to" on an Instagram post, the reaction was swift: Please don't make it so that more people want to live here! This sentiment is, in many ways, a continuation of a sense of Oregon's "exclusiveness" that harkens all the way back to Governor Tom McCall. Himself a visionary, he promoted a series of "ungreeting cards." The most popular of those cards read: "Welcome to Oregon. Enjoy your stay . . . *then go home!*" And of course, the state map was helpfully outlined as well.

This attitude, paradoxically, had the opposite effect from the intended one. Young people especially loved the quirkiness of the message and wanted to become part of what felt like an exclusive club—one whose members had a special identity. In that regard, Bend today is not so different from Oregon (and Portland) in 1973—a favored destination for many creative individuals. From an economic development perspective, the advantages of a growing population are obvious. But there is a huge difference between a droll "visit but don't stay" message and a deep suspicion of those who are not rooted in the community or whose values seem different from those of longtime residents.

"Do Not Come Here" is not a refutation of Karl Popper's idea of an open society but rather a recognition of the threats to it: economic anxiety, displacement, and a sense that increasing congestion—beginning with traffic—places increasing strain on our sense of well-being. Pluralism and inclusivity risk becoming victims of an increasing flow of people, where the challenge is not just to accommodate them but to ensure that the ethos, the culture of Austin, is not compromised.

I am optimistic that the vision Austin has embraced since its founding will prevail. Harnessing of capital, not just for its own sake but to ensure a shared quality of place, is inextricably bound to its embrace of an open society. Yes, the Colorado River may indeed overflow its banks, just as the population seems to be dangerously overflowing its limits now. But this is a risk we must accept. We are not a community that defines itself by walls and barriers. Rather, it is the embrace of change and growth that defines us.

Many other cities and regions, from Seattle to Nashville, have some of these open-society ingredients and are working to add others. Because of that mindfulness on their parts, their long-term futures in an increasingly competitive environment—one in which talented individuals drive economic growth—are all but assured. The same is true of smaller, less ambitious, towns. While they may not dream of becoming "seats of empire" or leading economic and cultural engines of the future, they are learning to capitalize on their assets. Hood River, Oregon, once known for its unrelenting winds rather than as a talent magnet, has reinvented itself as a global windsurfing mecca and a year-round circle of artists and outdoor enthusiasts. In addition, the Hood River Brewing Company, on whose board I served, continues to draw a national following.

By contrast, those cities and regions that refuse to capitalize on their historical or geographical advantages and who, by contrast, want to limit access only to insiders, are suffering a sad but predictable economic decline. I have known such places.

Years ago I was asked to advise leaders in Vermont who, like some of their counterparts in neighboring New England states, were wondering why they were having such difficulty either attracting people, youth in particular, or keeping them from fleeing the region. "Look," one state official pleaded with me, "saving even a handful would be a success." A "handful" was a polite understatement but revealing of a sort of desperation. Burlington had more or less the same number of residents it had had forty years earlier, and while its wider metropolitan area served as home to tens of thousands more, its total population, too, had stagnated—a sobering reality for a city that said it was eager to grow, or at least to not shrink.

The University of Vermont (UVM), whose students and staff comprise more than a quarter of the population within the Burlington city limits, seemed to me as good a place as any to begin searching for answers. Universities are, after all, powerful engines for developing the skilled, knowledgeable, and talented individuals so many employers seek. Academic institutions had for that reason, along with access to intellectual property, been key to the technopolis framework. If UVM could not retain its alumni, something must have been off. My own team and I knew, for instance, that many University of Texas students stayed in Austin after earning their degrees. These alumni continually replenished a deep local talent pool that helped both to quench the thirst of employers already here and to attract employers looking to come. Today the Austin area retains nearly 40 percent of graduates from its four-year institutions of higher learning.

What then, I wondered, did Burlington's alumni retention look like? Accurate figures were hard to come by and still are. Austin's numbers came from a study later contested by several cities urging other variables be considered. That study's alumni-retention results did not include Burlington, but if we were to take at face value its results for New England neighbors Providence, Rhode Island (32 percent), and Hartford, Connecticut (26 percent), we would probably be close to the mark. Though I did not have hard data, it soon became plain that University of Vermont students were not staying in the state, their diplomas still warm from the printers.

From the start I had my suspicions as to why, but for further insight, I met with some of those who had not yet fled at a young professionals' group from IBM. The company's Burlington-metro facility employed 8,500 at its peak, though many thousands fewer by the time I visited. On our team was Rebecca Ryan, an early pioneer on the subject of talent migration and on the preferences of young workers when it came to choosing a place to live. "Where would you move to," she asked this roomful of nearly one hundred skilled IBM professionals, "if you were given the option to leave Burlington?" A risky question, given the embarrassment it might cause for our clients with the State of Vermont's economic development office. To our surprise, the audience overwhelmingly chose Austin. I suspected some of the young workers might have chosen Austin, but this was a tidal wave. It was an awkward moment. Yes, IBM had a home in Central Texas, too, one decades older than Burlington's. Yes, an intracompany transfer to Austin would have been simpler than a move and a job search from scratch. Then again, "Big Blue," as IBM is nicknamed, had branches far and wide, and whereas its Burlington facilities still specialized in microchip manufacture, its Austin offices—which until 1986 had built many if not most of the company's 13 million Selectric typewriters—had by the late 1990s pivoted primarily, as scores of Austin technology companies had, to activities further upstream: research, innovation, and design. So why Austin, then?

The city's burgeoning reputation as a hip place—a reputation borne in large part by SXSW's "maximum symbolic impact," as one *Guardian* writer who authored a book about music festival cities put it—surely helped fuel the current appeal. The reasoning the young IBM employees ultimately voiced, however, was more pragmatic and broadly applicable to other technology hubs. In Austin, they said, plenty of firms besides IBM would welcome their skills.

The possibility of finding other employment if things were not to work out with IBM had profound implications that go beyond the IBM experience. It gives another dimension to the importance of industry clusters. Michael Porter has written extensively on this subject, and I had the pleasure of working with him on the Texas Strategic Economic Development Plan a few years earlier. His *The Competitive Advantage of Nations*, published in 1990, remains the seminal text on economic development and how nations (and cities) grow. While the theory behind cluster growth was predominantly linked to supply chains (the "verticals"), and customers and technology (the "horizontals"), he could not have foreseen the pressure that would be created in the search for a skilled talent base. In other words, the clustering of competitive businesses would become increasingly linked to the presence of a skilled workforce.

While the argument for clustering was growing weaker as supply chains were becoming less place-based, the need for talent clusters was growing. Yes, emerging Asian markets allowed for cheaper labor, and shipping costs were coming down due to containerized cargo, but technological advances were already beginning to replace inefficient labor, regardless of how low the cost. In an unexpected way, the COVID-19 pandemic and the disruption of foreign supply chains has only accelerated this trend.

Of course, IBM management understood the changing dynamics of the market, but for government officials this was still too much to absorb. The young semiconductor employees were not wrong. IBM-Austin's focus may have changed from IBM-Burlington's, but these talented IBM employees could have nonetheless found a new home in its offices, or, if not, then in the familiar furnishings of Austin's high-technology fabrication environment. This environment was strengthened in 1987 by Kozmetsky, who, just a few years after MCC's arrival, had been instrumental in attracting to town SEMATECH, a manufacturing consortium. These freshman IBMers, then—many of them UVM graduates themselves—had options. Austin had impressed upon them the attractors that growth-minded civic leaders and economic developers nationwide strive to cultivate, maintain, and broadcast. These attractors are no less relevant today—opportunity for related work made possible by industry clusters increasingly tied to crosscutting innovation. Add to that an entrepreneurial ecosystem with relative ease of access to capital, and the choices of desirable communities quickly narrows. And, finally, mix in the quirkiness and relative affordability of a city like Austin, and the choice seems obvious.

Burlington—and the state as a whole—was in a tight spot. It could have redoubled its efforts to enhance and highlight its quality of place, but would that have been enough to staunch the flow of people searching for opportunity elsewhere? It could have strategized how it might have harnessed its financial and intellectual capital to become the next Austin or Research Triangle Park or Silicon Valley—that is, to concentrate innovative industry within Burlington—but time was their enemy. Most importantly, how many cutting-edge firms would want to arrive only to discover that the skilled people they could have employed were not committed to the community? It could have instead focused its efforts on propping up its small-business community. It could have experimented with programs to partially reimburse homegrown firms for new-hire wages, as San Francisco has; to encourage local-business loyalty by subsidizing customer discounts, as Cleveland has; or to extend lines of credit or provide loans for companies who'd had little luck with banks, as St. Louis has. Yet those businesses need foot traffic, of course—what to do, then, when the state was hemorrhaging its young?

These were all questions Burlington and Vermont had asked of themselves in some form or another; all outcomes, pessimistic or not, they had considered; experiments they entertained. They did not have the luxury of conducting a chicken-or-egg debate about what came first—capital, talent, vision, or quality of place. Sans a golden goose, they needed all the chickens and all the eggs, the whole farm, and they needed it straight away.

Crisis demands triage, however, so, considering the UVM alumni exodus from the city and state and the viewpoints expressed in the IBM town hall, I suggested to my clients what their first step might be. The University of Vermont was Burlington's—and the state's—prized jewel. Founded in 1791, it, like the University of Texas, had for decades been considered a "public ivy," a valuable institution that few cities have and many states envy. Even though its enrollment was dropping and had been for years, it remained the state's most reliable and most readymade people magnet, both locally and nationwide. Today the vast majority of students come from outside the state, as those from inside it are increasingly lured by universities elsewhere. Might then Vermont's leaders focus their next efforts on designing programs aimed chiefly at keeping more of these geographically diverse UVM alumni? No university wants 100 percent of their alumni to stick around, of course—graduates working inside far-flung organizations act as ambassadors, spreading worldwide the message and substance of an institution's influence, research, and innovation—and no doubt regions larger than Burlington already have a leg up. "Graduates from top tier universities [in smaller cities] often move to larger cities after they graduate to pursue high skill jobs available there," as a 2017 *Cornell Policy Review* article put it. But given the dire circumstances, even a modest spike in UVM's alumni-retention rate might help stem the tide.

For four years, give or take, you have a captive audience of talented, ambitious young people, I told my clients, and you can help persuade them to remain in the state after graduation—and critically, by extension, have them continue contributing to its economy. "Go there and speak to them," I advised. "Make them feel at home, not just on campus, but in the city and the state, too." The actual selling points would have to be ironed out, of course. Making the message of hospitality itself clear, however, would have been relatively quick, inexpensive, and elementary. I anticipated my suggestion to be a welcome one—an inoffensive one.

I was wrong. In the next instant, I was reminded of the "freeze" I'd long ago felt elsewhere, reminded that not all cities or states habitually ask their newcomers how they can help, that not all "Do Not Come Here" messages are ironic, that not all societies are open ones. One of the officials, aggrieved, answered me by saying of the UVM students, "We don't really think of them as part of who we are as a community." Case closed.

On my return flight to Austin, I concluded that it did not matter how eager state officials may have been to attract business, or how appealing the beauty of the state, if there was no commitment to change the culture of exclusivity. If behind closed doors leaders were prepared to exclude entire classes of people, then success was a pipe dream.

Vermont continues to struggle: "The economic hub of the city and state . . . continued its long-run population stagnation," reported the *Burlington*

Free Press in 2018, though it also noted that select municipalities in its greater metropolitan area had seen some net-positive population growth during the same period, reasoning—tellingly, in my estimation—that said growth might be tied to diminishing home prices. Population growth anywhere in Vermont remains particularly newsworthy in light of its continuing statewide decline: Between 2010 and 2018, it remained among the four slowest-growing states. As of 2023, Vermont was one of the five slowest-growing states between 2022 and 2023 with a mere 0.05 percent uptick in population, according to a Pew analysis of US census data. I cannot argue an undeniable causation between Vermont's posture then and its circumstances now. I cannot with certainty make a case, either, that embracing the warmhearted idea of a more inclusive state would have sufficiently prevented further economic deterioration. I cannot avoid conceding that other cities with social "chills" or "freezes" have thrived. What I remain convinced of, however, is that—in today's economy and in that of the future—the adoption of an open society has a major role to play. A role so vital, in fact, that its effects can be transformative.

Long after I'd visited Burlington, I stumbled upon a satirical headline in *The Winooski*, Vermont's own *Onion*: "Vermonters Overwhelmingly Oppose US Border Wall, Support Vermont Border Wall," it read. Funny, I thought, but perhaps funnier if it were of another brand of irony, not one reflective of a truly dire economic conundrum. I had also become familiar with what a "flatlander" was, a pejorative ascribed to outsiders, according to one Vermont-based website. A flatlander, the site explained, "implies a person who visits the state or lives here that brings negative qualities from their home to our state, . . . a person who is unfamiliar with traditional Vermont ways." Dismally, it goes on, "Even if they assimilate to Vermont culture and reside here for 50 years, they can never rid themselves of this label." Perhaps the attitude I had heard Vermont leaders express years earlier was not so behind-closed-doors, after all; perhaps it was in fact the waters that Vermonters swam in, an object of longstanding cultural pride.

More recently, Vermont has sought to address its continuing talent outmigration by awarding $10,000 to out-of-staters relocating there. This is an economic-development experiment also attempted elsewhere in the country. "It's just for pulling people in," a state lawmaker was quoted as saying of the program. As an added aim—one that sounds very familiar—that same lawmaker was paraphrased by the *Burlington Free Press* as saying that he "hopes the incentive will help [out-of-state] college students to remain in Vermont after graduation." An open society is not merely a nice-to-have, it would seem, but a must-have, even if communities come to that conclusion in their own time.

In 2014, the IBM facility I'd visited near Burlington years earlier nearly shut down. It was saved in the final hour when another company purchased it. Public officials there were elated. They displayed a "collective sigh of relief," it was reported, at this "shot in the arm."

A few short years later, Austin was displaying much different gestures, those more akin to shoulder shrugs and dismissive hand waves, when Amazon, after a monthslong and highly publicized search for its second headquarters location, announced that Central Texas would not become its new home. Austin was already a technology hub, which accounts for much of the nonchalance, but the news tapped into that familiar "Do Not Move Here" anxiety. Only this time, it did so in a way that added to a broader discussion about big business; a discussion that prompted one *New York Times* columnist to argue, not long after Amazon initially picked Queens as one of its second headquarters, that the tech industry in fact did not "mesh" with the "slow, open-society, regulatory-heavy, greater-good mission that defines city living"; a discussion that cuts to the very heart of economic development itself and to one of its most longstanding, and increasingly controversial, tools: corporate tax incentives. These incentives, as we will see in the following chapters, may not be at odds with the entrepreneurial spirit Austin hoped to build on, but they certainly change the dynamics of how cities grow and of who gets to be a part of that tech growth.

CHAPTER FIVE

ELSIE L. ECHEVERRI-CARROLL
AND EVAN JOHNSTON[1]

Austin's Tech Entrepreneurial Ecosystem

"The most intensive areas for entrepreneurial potential are in well-known entrepreneurial ecosystems like Silicon Valley, Boston, and Austin."
—Jorge Guzman and Scott Stern, in "The State of American Entrepreneurship: New Estimates of the Quality and Quantity of Entrepreneurship for 32 US States, 1988–2014."[2]

ustin's love affair with tech entrepreneurship is a match made in Hill Country heaven. The city attracted global attention in 2015 and 2016 when it ranked first in the Kauffman Foundation's annual index of metropolitan areas' startup activity in the United States. More recent data on business registrations from the Texas Secretary of State (TSOS) show that the average number of new businesses in the Austin Metropolitan Area has risen to more than twenty-nine thousand in the last ten years. That exceeded the rate of growth in the previous twenty years, when the average number of new firms was only about six thousand, by 357 percent.

Austin's fertile startup landscape is tightly tethered to Austin's technology economy. That economy has thrived for decades thanks to the location and local expansion of major employers, including IBM, 3M, AMD, Oracle, Google, Apple, and Tesla. But it isn't only these imported tech giants that have fueled Austin's tech growth. Homegrown tech startups that became large corporations, such as Dell, Tivoli, Silicon Labs,[3] Indeed, Trilogy, and National Instruments, were also instrumental in Austin's rise to tech dominance. Since the 1980s, groups of engineers and other professionals have exited these companies to create new generations of Austin-based tech startups. Factoring in hopeful entrepreneurs, who come to the city to fulfill their startup dreams, it's no wonder that today, local entrepreneurs create an average of one new tech startup per day, according to TSOS data.

The question of how Austin became a magnet for *large* high-technology firms (many from California), which in turn fuel tech startups, is one I have investigated for years. Early in my career, I wondered what factors were unique to the top five metropolitan areas in Texas, including Austin, in attracting these large high-tech firms. In 1996, I set out to answer this question systematically by interviewing CEOs and mailing a survey to 1,772 high-technology firms in Austin, Houston, Dallas, Fort Worth, and San Antonio. I found that "quality of life" was the attribute with the highest score for all firms, but that three additional attributes were unique to the fastest innovators:[4]

- the presence of other tech firms that help attract skilled workers
- the local number of college-educated people (a source of local skilled workers)
- the availability of direct flights (to stay connected to other high-tech regions)

Austin scored well on these factors, which boosted its tech growth beyond that of other similar cities. But nearly two decades later—during which time Austin has become not only a locus of large tech firms but also of entrepreneurial activity—a new question emerged: What has driven the emergence and rapid growth of Austin's tech-based entrepreneurial ecosystem? To answer this towering question, my coauthor Evan Johnston and I began to study the genesis and evolution of Austin's tech entrepreneurial ecosystem in 2016, with support from a grant from the Kauffman Foundation. We interviewed more than one hundred local tech entrepreneurs and economic development stakeholders, including those from large firms, serial entrepreneurs, venture capitalists, economic development officials, and professors from the University of Texas at Austin (UT) in computer science, electrical engineering, and the business school. We also reviewed more than five hundred archival documents.[5] After years of analysis, we finally had an answer. Or rather, answers, as it became clear that several key ingredients came together over time for Austin to arrive at its superstar status.

Some findings were as predicted, such as the important role of UT, which Jon Roberts discussed in previous chapters. As an institution, UT increased research activity and the pipeline of graduates in fields related to computers, semiconductors, and software, aligning with the city's increasing specialization in these three high-technology clusters. Not surprisingly, collaborations between UT, the state government, and the private sector were also important. A few special elements, however, stood out.

While UT played a significant role, our research indicates that Austin's tech entrepreneurial success is best explained by two key factors: the attraction of growth-oriented, tech-driven companies (incubating firms), and the development of a critical mass of experienced entrepreneurs who reinvest (recycle) their knowledge and resources into the local ecosystem. Crucially, our analysis of Austin's trajectory emphasizes the dynamic interplay between these two processes and how they have evolved over time.

We analyzed the average number of tech startups and identified three inflection points where notable increases occurred, revealing three distinct phases: nascent, growth, and self-sustaining. In the following sections, we explore how the rising presence and expansion of incubating firms, along with entrepreneurial recycling processes led by experienced entrepreneurs, contributed to the tech entrepreneurial ecosystem's advancement through each of these phases. Briefly, these phases are:

Phase 1: Nascent: Laying the Groundwork with Incubating Firms (Before 1990)

A distinction is important here. The term incubating firm is different from the well-known "business incubator," which is created to *intentionally* provide nascent entrepreneurs with low-cost services (e.g., space) and networking opportunities. In contrast, we define incubating firms as research-oriented (innovative) firms where tech entrepreneurs worked before founding their first startups. These incubating firms provide employees with significant autonomy and, often *unintentionally*, serve as incubators by providing resources, new technologies, and networks that catalyze their decision to enter into entrepreneurship.[6] The efforts of the Austin community to build long-term friendly relationships (external networks) with large corporations, entrepreneurs, and economic development organizations in California (mainly in Silicon Valley) brought many large corporations to

Austin. These firms not only created direct and indirect quality jobs in the city at an unprecedented rate,[7] but more importantly, they nurtured many entrepreneurs who—after convincing their peers to leave their secure jobs at an incumbent corporation—turn their dream of creating a technology startup into reality. The successful relationship with California is particularly striking given the well-documented rivalry between Silicon Valley and the Route 128 tech corridor in Boston.[8] (Austin's beneficial friendly attitude toward Silicon Valley supports Jon's careful explanation in chapter 4 of how open societies tend to be more innovative.)

Phase 2: Growth: Building Entrepreneurial Network Density (1990–2009)

Entrepreneurs in Austin have strategically cultivated local networks serving as mentors, advisors, serial entrepreneurs, angel investors, venture capitalists, and partners in accelerators or incubators. This *entrepreneurial recycling*—the reinvestment of experience, knowledge, and resources through local networks—has been a critical factor in the sustained success of Austin's entrepreneurial landscape. And, it's not only about their wins: The experience gained and the resources released in *failed* ventures are also recycled through the ecosystem, similarly contributing to its growth. A prime example is David Altounian, founder of Motion Computing and partner at Capital Factory. He recounted that in 1992, Motorola invested in General Magic—a company once described by *The New York Times* as Silicon Valley's most closely watched startup. Although General Magic ultimately became a spectacular failure, Altounian emphasized the significant lessons it offered. The company's collapse led to the emergence of several successful ventures, including Nest, which Google acquired in 2014 for $3.2 billion.

Phase 3: Self-Sustaining: Achieving Critical Mass of Experienced Tech Entrepreneurs (2010–Now)

Both mature and young firms need to foster an employee-led startup process to help the ecosystem achieve a *critical mass* of well-connected, experienced entrepreneurs capable of sustaining entrepreneurial activity. Success requires the "system" to be both open and closed. What this means, somewhat paradoxically, is that entrepreneurs must be committed to the growth of the Austin community while actively cultivating outside relationships.

Clearly, none of this happens overnight. It takes decades to move through the process and develop a self-sustaining entrepreneurial ecosystem, and, frankly, some serendipity as well. There is no step-by-step game plan for prosperity. Austin's success story does, however, hold valuable lessons for economic developers and public officials seeking to support their tech sector and encourage entrepreneurship, no matter where they are in the process.

Practical Lessons from Academics on Building an Entrepreneurial Ecosystem

Before telling the story of Austin's evolution, it's important to understand that there is a divide in the research on entrepreneurial ecosystems. When Evan and I first set out to understand Austin's entrepreneurial explosion, we learned that there is no fixed definition of what a tech entrepreneurial ecosystem actually consists of—surprising considering that these systems have existed for decades. We discovered that academic scholars and practitioners studying the drivers of entrepreneurial ecosystems essentially fall into two distinct camps: incubating firms and entrepreneurial recycling.

The Incubating Firms' Camp:[9] Many studies from business scholars consistently find that the most powerful predictor of future entrepreneurship for a city is the presence of established, or incumbent, firms. Since most entrepreneurs emerge from established firms, this holds up.[10] Edward Glaeser and William Kerr,[11] of Harvard Business School, find that a 10 percent higher base of incumbent firms is associated with a 6 percent higher number of local startups. Jasper Sørensen and Magali Fassiotto,[12] of Stanford Business School, estimate that nine out of ten entrepreneurs have worked in established firms before founding their first startups. This research camp notes that though largely unintentional, incumbent firms "incubate" entrepreneurs by providing their employees access to intellectual property, knowledge, and resources that facilitate their transition to entrepreneurship.[13] This is particularly true for tech entrepreneurs, as many of them start their entrepreneurial firms by commercializing a new product or process developed at the parent firm.[14]

Three findings from this camp help us understand the role of incubating firms as one driver of Austin's entrepreneurial ecosystem growth. First, new entrepreneurs tend to stay in their incubating firm's region—they need the local social networks of former associates and employees to grow their startups,[15] and it's easier to find high-productivity employees among their familiar talent pools.[16] Second, entrepreneurs who employ workers from their parent firms tend to have startups that survive longer, due in large measure to the reduced initial recruiting costs.[17] Third, small, young incumbent firms are better incubators of startups than older, large incumbent ones because they not only provide prospective entrepreneurs with new ideas and resources but also educate them in the entrepreneurial process.[18] As author and professor Ed Malecki,[19] a leading voice in urban geography, stated, "Regions with high levels of entrepreneurship will tend to spawn further entrepreneurs."

It is natural to think that creative individuals would switch from being employees to entrepreneurs at times of rapid economic growth, fueled by expectations of significantly greater opportunity and driven by a vision for better products or processes and personal gain. However, research shows that individuals can also commit to entrepreneurship during periods of slow economic growth when layoffs are high.[20]

Simply put, this research camp shows that while tech entrepreneurial expertise certainly arises from formal training, previous experience in high-growth firms—particularly young ones—is crucial.[21] Over time, this cumulative incubating process seeds multiple generations of spin-offs. This, in turn, leads to a self-sustaining ecosystem endowed with a large network of experienced entrepreneurs (network density) who reinvest their resources and knowledge in new businesses, perpetuating the cycle.

The Entrepreneurial Recycling Camp: The question of what drives entrepreneurial ecosystem growth has also been of particular interest to scholars in geography and regional development.[22] Their most recent contributions offer a *process-view perspective*. In this perspective, ecosystems grow in stages. These stages are based on the capacity of experienced entrepreneurs to reinvest their resources in newer generations of entrepreneurs.[23] They also recognize that the experience gained by entrepreneurs, including those who failed, is recycled through the ecosystem, contributing to its growth.

These scholars propose that ecosystems mature through an *entrepreneurial recycling process* in which multiple generations of experienced entrepreneurs—successful and unsuccessful—reinvest their wealth and knowledge into the ecosystem as mentors, advisors, top managers, serial entrepreneurs, business angels, venture capitalists, or incubator/accelerator partners.[24] Ben Spiegel and Richard Harrison, in an article in *Strategic Entrepreneurship Journal*,[25] indicated that the volume of recycled entrepreneurial resources and networks increases as an entrepreneurial ecosystem evolves in three phases over time. Simply put, these scholars focus on the networks of experienced *entrepreneurs* through which resources and knowledge flow within the ecosystem (not their incubating firms) as the core forces that drive an entrepreneurial ecosystem's growth with new innovative startups.

A New Integrated Analytical Framework: Once we studied and considered the research from both of these camps, it was natural to apply all the findings to our understanding of the local entrepreneurial process in Austin. What emerged was what could be considered a new camp, or as we call it, a new *integrated analytical framework*, in which both experienced entrepreneurs' networks and their incubating firms drive the transformation of the ecosystem over time. As we cover Austin's history over several decades, we'll see that the actions of incubating firms *and* entrepreneurs are fundamentally entwined and therefore must be addressed jointly. This integrated analysis follows the theory of Daniel Isenberg, who popularized the entrepreneurial ecosystem concept with his publications in the *Harvard Business Review.* He is a big believer in the symbiotic necessity of large companies and entrepreneurial ventures living side by side: "You simply cannot have a flourishing entrepreneurial ecosystem without large companies to cultivate it, intentionally or otherwise."[26]

The following section explains how the location of high-tech firms from advanced regions, mainly Silicon Valley, nurtured Austin's new entrepreneurs and how these entrepreneurs transformed the local ecosystem across three distinct phases: nascent period (before 1960), growth (1990–2009), and self-sustaining (2010–now).

The Evolution of Austin's Tech Entrepreneurial Ecosystem (1960–Now)

Figure 1 depicts Austin's general (not necessarily high-tech) entrepreneurial trends measured by for-profit corporation registrations with the TSOS.[27] It reveals three inflection points when the average number of new startups (not just tech) jumped from virtually nothing to 347, then to 6,711, and to 30,681, which represents three growth phases of Austin's entrepreneurial ecosystem, 1960–1989 (nascent), 1990–2009 (growth), and 2010–2021 (self-sustaining).[28]

Phase 1: The Nascent Period of Austin Tech Entrepreneurial Ecosystem (Before 1990)—the Contribution of Academic Spin-Offs

Between 1960 and 1989, when a few large tech manufacturers were located in Austin (IBM, Motorola, National Instruments, AMD, and Texas Instruments), the average number of new tech firms was eight per year, according to data from TSOS. The University of Texas was the most important source of new startups. UT populated the nascent local ecosystem with a few high-growth academic spin-offs (startups founded by professors to commercialize technology developed at UT that benefited from military funding), and some were later acquired or became large corporations. More importantly, these first-generation academic spin-offs seeded further generations of other private-sector startups.[29]

Austin and other successful high-tech communities in the United States were initially shaped and subsidized by federal military funding to universities during the Cold War.[30] Although most defense spending was funneled to a select pool of elite institutions (e.g., MIT and Stanford), UT also benefited through its Defense Research Laboratory (DRL), founded in 1945.[31] This federal support for applied military research contributed to the creation of thirty-four UT spin-offs between 1939 and 1968.[32] However, UT played a key albeit passive role in the formation and development of these spin-offs.[33] While it fostered the talent and ideas that could lead to commercialization, it provided little institutional support to academic entrepreneurs in critical areas such as securing capital, expanding markets, patenting innovations, or effectively managing and scaling startups.

The most consequential UT spin-off for the birth of the Austin entrepreneurial ecosystem was Tracor, an academic startup spun off from UT's

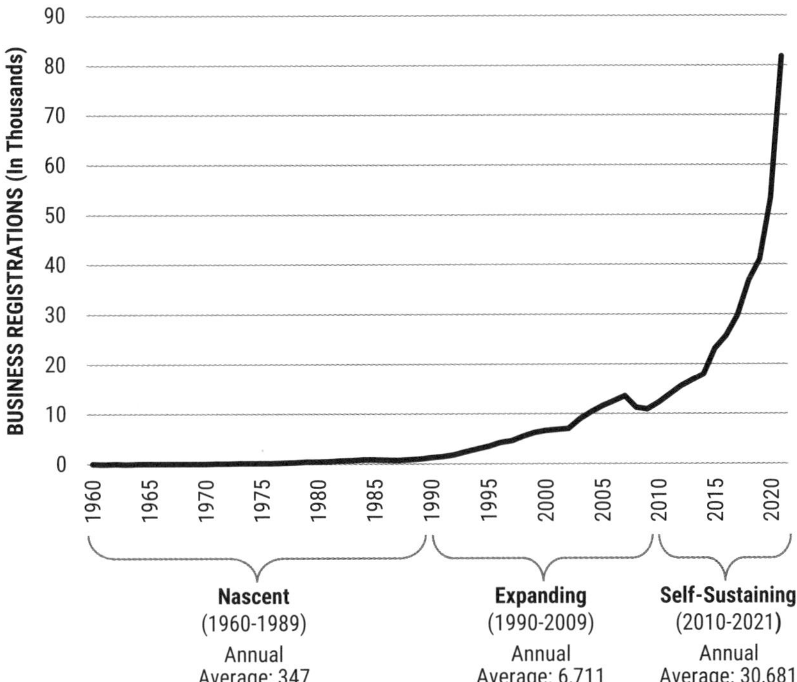

Figure 1. Figure created by Evan Johnston and Elsie L. Echeverri-Carroll; edited by Meredith Eberle.

DRL in 1962, and its spin-offs (and their spin-offs). Tracor (Texas Research Associates) manufactured electrical instruments and components mainly for the US Department of Defense and the US Navy, and it became the first Austin-based company listed on the stock exchange, as well as the first Austin-based Fortune 500 company. True to its role as an incubator, the company spun off more than twenty local companies (many working in nondefense-related products)[34] before its acquisition by General Electric Company in 1998. One of its spin-offs was Radian Corporation, founded in 1969, which in turn spun off four new companies by 1989.[35] Radian eventually merged with Dow Chemical in 1995. National Instruments, another DRL software spin-off founded in 1976, became a major corporation with approximately 2,700 employees in Austin in 2023. MRI Systems

Corporation, a database software developer founded in 1965 and acquired by Intel in 1979, is widely regarded as the first significant software spin-off from the University of Texas' computer science department.[36]

Although Austin's high-tech manufacturing roots date back to the mid-1950s, the city was still in the early stages of developing a high-tech research-based economy in the 1980s, when only a handful of large tech firms were conducting major research activities.[37] These included IBM, Motorola, 3M, and Texas Instruments. Most large high-tech firms were manufacturing operations; as a result, the private sector was contributing with just a few innovative tech spin-offs. Bottom line: Despite the birth of dozens of UT startups during the 1950s and '60s (and their spin-offs), the number of tech entrepreneurs before 1990 was simply too small to catalyze the growth of the local tech entrepreneurial ecosystem.

Phase 2: The Growth of the Austin Tech Entrepreneurial Ecosystem (1990–2009)—Spin-offs and Importing Incubating Firms

"George [Kozmetsky] knew that as we began to build a base of technology employers—that ultimately, we'd reach this critical mass where we'd start to see a surge of entrepreneurship. That we'd see people spinning out of those technology companies and starting their endeavors."—Glenn West, president of the Austin Chamber of Commerce from 1987–2000

After winning two national research consortia, MCC and SEMATECH, at the end of the 1980s, large research-based high-tech firms (many from California) began locating in Austin at an unprecedented rate.[38] As Glenn West noted, "We went through a period in the 1990s in which we were probably attracting twenty-five to forty California [tech] companies a year." The dynamic location of tech firms in Austin and the swift growth of homegrown Dell Corporation (founded in 1984), National Instruments (1976), and Silicon Labs (1996), made the Austin region a true leader in computers and semiconductor clusters during the 1990s. Between 1990 and 1996, Austin created more new jobs in the semiconductor cluster than Silicon Valley, though Austin was only half its size.[39] Austin also created more jobs in the computers and peripheral cluster—that is, equipment for computers, such as keyboards, mice, and printers—than in any other region in the United States during this period.[40]

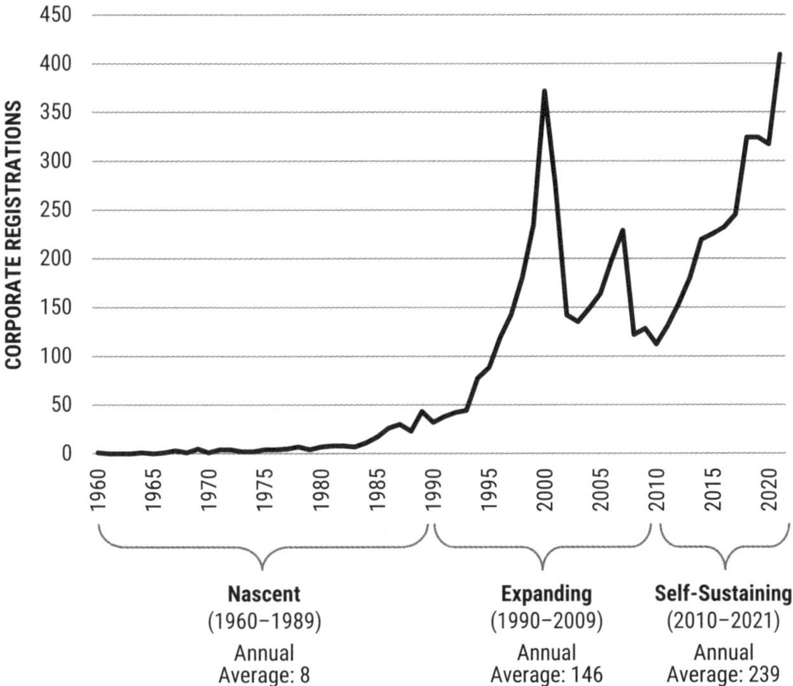

Figure 2. Figure created by Evan Johnston and Elsie L. Echeverri-Carroll; edited by Meredith Eberle.

Given the empirical evidence that most tech entrepreneurs had previously worked in an established firm before starting their first company, it is natural to expect that the rapid location of large research-based high-tech firms in Austin after 1990 would parallel a similar trend in innovation-driven startups, many created by ex-employees of these firms. We use the number of for-profit corporation registrations in Delaware with an address in the Austin metro area to estimate the growth of innovation-driven startups.[41] (Many high-tech startups are incorporated in Delaware because the state has a well-respected and established corporate court system and business-friendly tax, legal, and regulation policies.) Figure 2 shows that the annual average number of tech startups jumped from eight during the entrepreneurial ecosystem nascent period (1960–1989), to 146 during its growth phase (1990–2009), and to 239 when it became self-sustaining (2010–2021)—growing at an impressive rate of 265 percent since 2010 despite the 2020 pandemic.

Of course, the rapid growth of large firms in Austin is not the only source of tech startups during this growth phase. In general, as noted earlier, the spin-off rate in young innovative firms exceeds that of large tech firms over time. These spin-offs also tend to perform better, partly because young firms offer prospective entrepreneurs the experience of learning how to create and scale up companies by participating in the entrepreneurial process alongside more experienced entrepreneurs.[42] Additionally, they are exposed to suppliers and customers accustomed to dealing with startup companies.[43] Roy Kaham, the cofounder of Indeed, recalled that his previous experience as a successful entrepreneur "taught us how to shape and grow a business."

Despite the impressive growth of tech startups in Austin during the 1990s, Austin's entrepreneurial stakeholders identified two startups, Tivoli (an IBM spin-off) and Trilogy (a startup imported from California), as the key drivers in establishing Austin as a world center of tech entrepreneurial activity and in moving the city solidly into a growth phase. Tivoli founders *recycled* their talent and a huge volume of resources in the local ecosystem when they sold their company. Although Trilogy was never sold, it brought a large volume of talent from the most prestigious universities in the United States to attend its unique program called Trilogy University—a three-month boot camp in Austin where new employees were given significant responsibility to lead projects, build new products, and even start a company under the Trilogy umbrella,[44] populating the local ecosystem with a large network of entrepreneurs.

Tivoli, founded in 1989 by three former IBM employees, completed an initial public offering in 1995—just one year before IBM acquired it for $743 million (equivalent to $1.4 billion in 2023). The former IBM employees saw an opportunity to commercialize an idea that IBM was not ready for. As Bill Wood, Austin Ventures' partner and founder, noted, "They [employees] see customers paying a lot of money for problems that large corporations are not addressing." Through its acquisition, Tivoli powered the local ecosystem with multiple generations of spin-offs whose founders continue to recycle their wealth and experience within the Austin ecosystem as serial entrepreneurs, advisors, managers of other startups, partners of business incubators, and venture capital/angel investors.

Using data from LinkedIn, we built Tivoli's family tree of spin-offs or startups that were created or managed by the founders and ex-employees of Tivoli (those who worked at Tivoli between 1989 and 1996 when it was an independent startup). Figure 3 shows that Tivoli founders and ex-employees launched at least thirty startups in Austin and became top managers of at least another nineteen local startups between 1990 and 2013. Even more interesting is the fact that only three of the thirty new firms had not been acquired or had not received outside funding by 2016. The extraordinary growth of Austin's entrepreneurial ecosystem since 1990 suggests that other large and young high-growth firms also nurtured successive generations of tech startups.

Trilogy was Tivoli's twin sister. Together they sparked the entrepreneurial big bang in Austin. Originally founded in Silicon Valley by Joe Liemandt, who left his undergraduate studies at Stanford to start the company in 1990 along with four of his university friends,[45] Trilogy relocated to Austin in 1992. "Trilogy never had that big sale moment like Tivoli had when IBM purchased it for $743 million," noted Trilogy Chief Scientist David Franke in our interview. But as Bruce Porter, then chair of UT's Computer Science Department, explained in 2016, "What is special about Trilogy is that it brought to town the brain trust, that then *scattered around like pollen* [emphasis added], and created a whole bunch of great things in town."

Trilogy aggressively pursued a large pool of college students from the most prestigious universities, spending millions and earning industry attention for its ability to beat out Microsoft Corporation for the brightest graduates from Harvard, MIT, Princeton, Stanford, and Carnegie Mellon.[46]

While Trilogy's valuation fell during the 2000 dot-com crash, the quality of talent that Trilogy hired through the 1990s stayed on. They became known as the "Trilogy mafia" and populated the top management ranks of Austin-based companies formed in the 2000s. These included Indeed (2004), HomeAway (2005), Bazaarvoice (2005), Vast.com (2005), Capital Factory (2009, a leader in Austin's self-sustaining phase), and WP Engine (2010).

Austin's ecosystem benefited from the entrepreneurial talent coming to the city from Silicon Valley but also from other advanced high-tech regions. Austin Ventures was founded by Joe Aragona, Ken DeAngelis, and Bill Wood, who met in graduate school at Harvard before moving to Austin to join Rust Capital in the early 1980s—the precursor to Austin Ventures, formed in 1984.[47] Austin Ventures would end up becoming the city's oldest and largest venture fund and would fuel Austin's most successful startups,

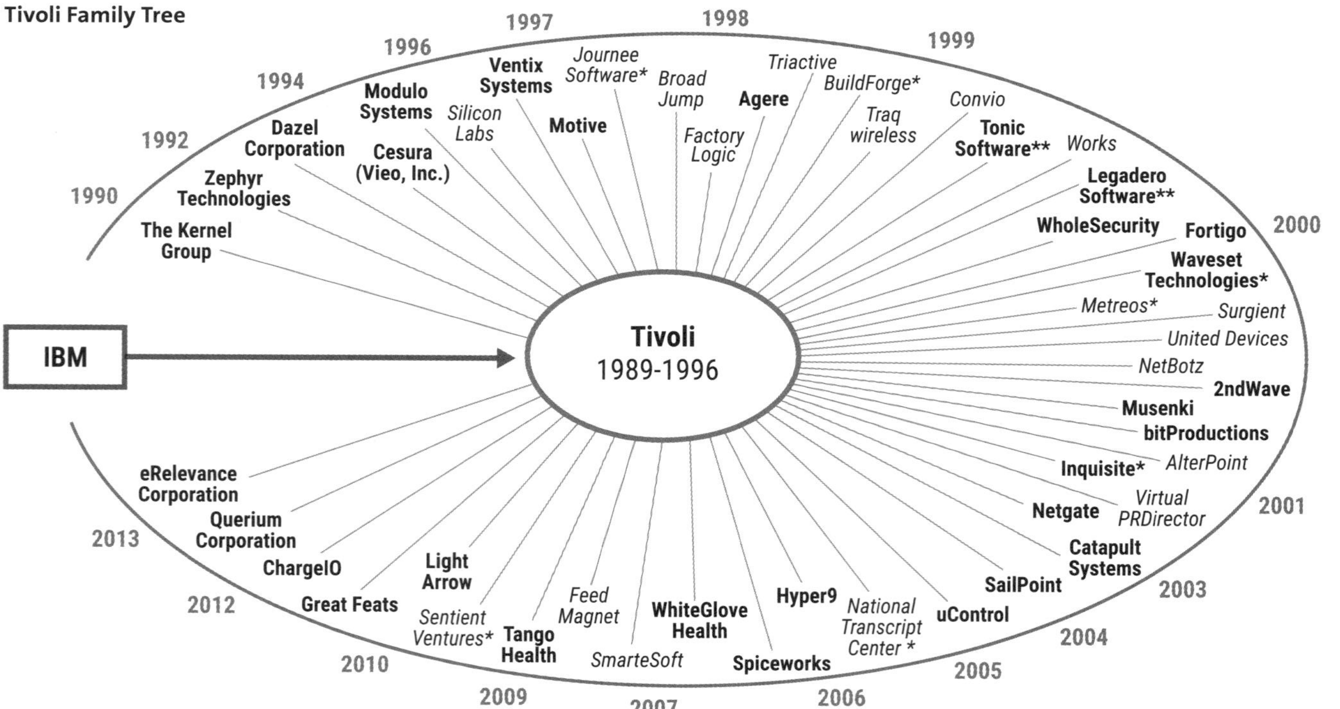

*Indicates founding year sourced from the National Establishment Time Series.

Indicates founding year sourced from other independent inquiry. Thirty of these firms, indicated by **bold text, were founded by former Tivoli employees. Nineteen of these firms, indicated by *italicized* text, included former Tivoli employees as managers.

Figure 3. Figure created by Evan Johnston and Elsie L. Echeverri-Carroll; edited by Meredith Eberle.

including Tivoli, Silicon Laboratories, and HomeAway. Austin Ventures financed twenty-six new startups in 1996 and 166 by 1999.[48] In an example of entrepreneurial resource recycling, Tivoli founder Bob Fabbio became Austin Venture's general partner in 1997. Austin Ventures brought operating experience, technical skills, and networks of industry contacts, as well as cash, to their funded ventures.

Austin Ventures not only advised and funded many generations of entrepreneurs but was also the anchor for the attraction of startup-oriented business service providers from other highly developed tech regions. Two venture banks from California, Silicon Valley Bank and Imperial Bank, established Austin-based loan production offices in 1996. They provided funds only to startups that had already secured angel or venture capital from Austin Ventures or other venture capital firms.[49] Despite the significant contribution of Tivoli, Trilogy, and Austin Ventures to the local entrepreneurial environment, the reality was that Austin's entrepreneurial ecosystem in the 1990s still had not reached critical mass. Chris Hyams, Indeed's CEO, noted, "In 1999, there was not a startup community. Companies did not interact with each other." Similarly, Bob Fabbio described Austin's ecosystem and the lack of an entrepreneurial community in the 1990s, when he was building Tivoli, in the following way:

> I felt like I was every day in a dark room where there were no lights, and most days I was just crashing into walls or just trying to stay away from crashing into walls because I had never run a company before, and I wasn't in a world like Massachusetts or Silicon Valley, where there were people I could talk to that were like me doing it. I was a young thirty-three-year-old guy that had a burning desire to go conquer the world with this really great idea, but I had nobody around me to help me or advise me, so it was pure instinct.

Phase 3: Self-Sustaining Entrepreneurial Ecosystem (2010–Now)—Contributions of the Local Entrepreneurial Community

"If Tivoli started two years ago [2014] and Capital Factory's resources were available to me, it would have been hugely impactful. . . . At Capital Factory, if we see entrepreneurs banging on the walls like I was, we tell them to stop and turn on the lights. We provide direction to new entrepreneurs and keep them from having all the bumps and bruises that I had."—Bob Fabbio, Tivoli cofounder and Capital Factory partner

After 2000, Austin continued to attract large innovative firms from other high-tech regions and helped companies such as Apple and Oracle build large campuses after 2010. In contrast, its tech entrepreneurial activity experienced a bumpy road during the three recessions. Figure 2 shows that registrations fell sharply after 2000, declined again after 2008, and fell little at the onset of the COVID-19 recession in 2020. This bumpy trend was followed by a consistent rise in registrations after 2010, reaching an all-time high in 2021. The outcome of the strong growth of tech entrepreneurial activity after 2010 is the emergence of a *critical mass* of experienced entrepreneurs whose large network density now drives and sustains the local entrepreneurial ecosystem.

Austin's tech entrepreneurial ecosystem was hit hard by the 2008 Great Recession. High-tech startup activity dramatically dropped from a peak of 229 in 2007 to 122 in 2008. However, the trend recovered after 2010, reaching a new high of 409 new registrations in 2021 (despite the 2020 pandemic). The growth of Austin's entrepreneurial ecosystem since 2010 has been extraordinary if one takes into consideration that the average number of tech startups was just eight during a period of thirty years at the nascent period of the ecosystem (1960–1989) and 146 during twenty years of the growth phase but then jumped to 239 in the most recent decade (2010–2021).

Today, it's clear that Austin's entrepreneurial ecosystem has entered a self-sustaining stage. Comparing Austin's present situation to that of the 1990s, Marc Yagjian, Tivoli's partner, said, "We didn't have that startup community that is now just living and breathing throughout our city." This sentiment is echoed by Bill Harrison, founder and CEO of Frontera Software, who said, "There is such an infrastructure and system around entrepreneurism [in Austin today]. . . . You're not swimming against the stream to be an entrepreneur now." Chris Hyams, Indeed CEO, said, "There was no real structured way for people to get access to mentorship. . . . Capital Factory, at its base, is this sort of network. It's a collection of investors; it's a formalized mentorship network and office space."

Austin now has a *critical mass* of well-connected experienced entrepreneurs who have built a local *startup support infrastructure* that is accelerating the creation and sharing of entrepreneurial resources and knowledge. A particularly important component of this infrastructure is the large number of active investors in the city today. There are currently over four hundred investors headquartered in Austin with at least one recorded investment round in the last ten years,[50] including the Central Texas Angel Network, which is considered the most active single-chapter angel group in the United States by the Angel Resources Institute. This trend contrasts with the paucity of venture capital firms in the past. Laura Kilcrease, who founded Triton Ventures in 1999, noted that "there was only one venture capitalist in Austin in 1985: Austin Ventures." Her view was complemented by Bob Fabbio who noted, "It [Austin Ventures] was really the only source of money in town," and Marc Davis (a Trilogy ex-employee) who highlighted, "If they [Austin Ventures] didn't like a pitch, there was nowhere else to turn for finances. One could try to find outside VC, but many outside VCs were no longer looking to invest in Austin after the dot-com bust." Carmelo Gordian, an Austin-based lawyer who started advising local tech startups in the 1980s, added, "It wouldn't surprise me if over 80 percent of the startups in Austin, that we think of today, were supported in part by Austin Ventures."

Local entrepreneurs are also building new incubators, accelerators, and coworking spaces. We surveyed the thirty-nine of them existing in Austin in 2016 and found that only seven (18 percent) started between 1980 and 2009, while thirty-two (82 percent) started between 2010 and 2016. Some, however, are adopting a *new* business incubator model—the *networked incubator.* The networked incubators rely heavily on experienced individuals with ties both to traditional corporate growth models and entrepreneurial energy. We researched Capital Factory's talent stock in 2016, using LinkedIn, and found that its 129 partners had a collective 857 years of startup experience and 826 years of experience in large corporations. As Laura Kilcrease noted, "Capital Factory has done a very excellent job, and part of this comes down to the types of people running it: Entrepreneurs."

Similar to traditional business incubators, the new networked incubators are making the Austin entrepreneurial ecosystem more efficient by helping novice entrepreneurs resolve uncertainty around their companies' quality. Identifying issues early allows them to make funding and exit decisions accordingly.[51] But these networked incubators have a dual mission: They scale up companies and serve as an effective platform where the entrepreneurial community can interact and develop a common social identity in the emergence of new ventures—creating the environment that Bob Fabbio explained was lacking in the 1990s. In this regard, interviewees note that Capital Factory has become a physical and virtual space where experienced and novice entrepreneurs can network, facilitating the flow of entrepreneurial resources within the ecosystem.

In emerging ecosystems, entrepreneurial networks happen mainly at *informal* socializing venues (e.g., cafes, bars, and restaurants).[52] In self-sustaining ecosystems, the role of scattered, informal venues is enhanced by *the thousands* of *institutionalized socializing events.* These are organized at networked incubators in which the large entrepreneurial community interacts and develops a common social identity. In these institutionalized encounters, entrepreneurs informally network with peers with similar or more advanced entrepreneurial skills. Jason Ford, founder of FeedMagnet, a provider of social media content, explained, "Capital Factory was the environment where I networked and met Marc [Ygjian], and I'm certain that I would not have been as successful without Marc; I don't know if I would have sold my company without him." Similarly, he noted, "Capital Factory serves as a town square and a meeting place."

New incubators' central role as networking platforms for entrepreneurs is reflected in the large volume of events they organize. Josh Baer, a Capital Factory cofounder, noted that they had held more than one thousand events that brought over fifty thousand participants together in 2016—creating an "energy that is magnetic" to investors and entrepreneurs alike. Similarly, Gordon Daugherty, another founding partner, noted, "We want every tech and entrepreneurship event to happen here [Capital Factory]. We are the center of gravity of entrepreneurship. We cooperate with other incubators because we want every tech entrepreneurial event to happen here at Capital Factory. Out of all the events run here, I promised only 1 percent are Capital Factory events, and 99 percent are other people running their events here."

By institutionalizing longstanding practices of informal cooperation and exchange, new networked incubators such as Capital Factory are formalizing the process of collective entrepreneurial learning. Scott Francis (a former Trilogy employee) explained this change in the following way: "What Capital Factory did differently was that they didn't approach building a coworking space as this is a place where you rent some space and do your business. They approached it as building a community around a startup. . . . The focus on startups and community led to the office space, not the other way around." Furthermore, he said he regards Capital Factory as "incredible for the community in terms of building critical mass" and noted that Josh Baer and cofounders understood early on that "density and critical mass really matter." In his view, a "big part of the value of creating a coworking space or a startup-hub kind of space, is just the *incidental opportunity to meet* [emphasis added]."

In sum, after 2010, two main forces explained the explosive growth of technology entrepreneurship in Austin: First, the availability of a critical mass of experienced entrepreneurs who built a robust entrepreneurial infrastructure (e.g., venture capital firms and networked incubators such as Capital Factory). Second, the rapid location and expansion of large high-tech firms continued to provide new entrepreneurs with opportunities for new technologies and resources. In seeking lessons that could inform communities in other regions, two closely related policy questions arise: What strategies enabled Austin to attract the *large* high-technology firms (many from California) that helped fuel its startup scene? And, can direct support for entrepreneurs effectively drive the development of a local entrepreneurial ecosystem?

Local Strategies to Attract High-Tech Firms and Promote Entrepreneurship

The Austin community employed a dual strategy to expand its local entrepreneurial ecosystem. One approach focused on attracting large high-tech firms—primarily from Silicon Valley—while the other concentrated on directly supporting local entrepreneurs through initiatives such as traditional business incubators and seed-stage funding programs. Which one drives the growth of the local entrepreneurial ecosystem?

Austin Community Efforts to Attract Large Technology Firms

The recruitment of large technology firms has been a part of Austin's game plan since the mid-1950s. The initial objective in attracting high-tech firms to Austin was to generate high-paying employment opportunities for University of Texas graduates, who had historically migrated to established technology hubs on the East and West coasts. Austin's sustained success in attracting high-tech firms can be attributed to the local community's longstanding capacity for collaboration, both within the city and with external stakeholders. A critical examination of these efforts over time reveals that collaborative networks and community-driven partnerships have been the primary factors influencing firms' decisions to locate in Austin—rather than the monetary incentives (e.g., loans and grants) provided by the state and city since 2000, a commonly held but misleading belief.

FIRST COLLABORATION (MID-1950S TO 1970S)

During this period, the Austin Chamber of Commerce partnered with other leaders (bankers, realtors, representatives from local government, and some UT professors)[53] to assist a few manufacturing-branch plants of electronic companies. These included IBM, in 1967, and others that chose to locate in Austin following the arrival of IBM, such as Eagle Signal, which made computerized traffic-control systems, in 1975, and both Data General and Advanced Microdevices, in 1978. They used simple recruiting strategies such as organizing tours of UT's Balcones Research Center, mailing promotional brochures and stickers, media advertising, yearly industry appreciation dinners, and Aqua Fest—a festival to publicize Austin's abundance of water. Despite these few successes, as already noted, before 1990 (Austin's entrepreneurial nascent period), most local tech spin-offs were UT's academic startups, not spin-offs from these private companies. Nevertheless, these few tech manufacturing companies did help the community bring MCC to Austin. After all, a "high-tech cluster" was one of the criteria adopted by this consortium's selection committee.[54]

SECOND COLLABORATION (MID-1980S)

The chamber became an important partner in a *regional* collaboration led by the Texas governor's office and UT to win two national large private research consortia, MCC in 1983 and SEMATECH in 1987, which represented the major players in the computer and semiconductor industries, respectively. After a vigorous national competition, MCC chose Austin over fifty-seven cities and SEMATECH chose it over 137 other competing cities. As Pike Powers, legislator and executive assistant to the governor at the time, noted, "Before winning MCC, Austin had achieved some early success as an outpost for manufacturing operations, but winning MCC positioned Austin as a center for advances in research, information, and technology."[55] These two research consortia charted a distinctly new course for the city, giving birth to Austin's research cluster of computer, semiconductor, and information-technology companies—ones that were located in the city for the first time (e.g., Hewlett Packard and Apple) and those that were already in Austin but significantly expanded their research capabilities when they became members of MCC or SEMATECH (e.g., Motorola and IBM).

During its peak in the mid-1980s, MCC employed almost four hundred workers.[56] David Gibson and Everett Rogers noted in *R&D Collaboration on Trial: The Microelectronics and Computer Technology Corporation*, "When MCC came to Austin in 1983, many of the community's public and private leaders expected the city's economic growth to be spurred by spinouts from the R&D consortium, even though MCC officials emphasized that this was *not* what the consortium was about." They explained that there were institutional barriers that limited the contribution of this large influx of science and engineering workers to create their spin-offs. In particular, MCC's shareholders had three-year development rights to the consortium's products, and decisions about spin-offs emanated from the shareholders' widely dispersed corporate headquarters rather than from Austin. Similarly, local leaders expected many spin-offs to emerge from SEMATECH, which employed about eight hundred researchers in Austin.[57] In reality, only a few spin-offs resulted from this consortium, since it was mainly involved in basic research that did not have immediate commercial applications. Therefore, scientists and engineers were hired based on their reputations for research excellence and not their proficiency in technology transfer.

THIRD LOCAL COLLABORATION (1990S)

Despite their limited direct contributions to local spin-offs, MCC and SEMATECH together became a major pull force for over three hundred companies—most of them tech-related—to locate branch plants in Austin in the 1990s.[58] The chamber collaborated with UT professors, representatives of the state's economic development division and the City of Austin, and executives from the few high-tech firms located in Austin during their visits to California. Glenn West talked about how these companies were "intimately involved in the sales pitch for Austin." West explained how "once Austin had both MCC and SEMATECH, the presence of those two made it much easier to get companies to come over from California." These newcomers were able to drive spin-off activity because they did not have the institutional restrictions that slowed down the consortia members' spin-off contributions. This became an inflection point in the evolution of Austin's entrepreneurial ecosystem moving it to its growth phase. Innovative startups (proxied by Delaware-registered corporations in Austin) grew at a rate of 1,000 percent from thirty-two in 1990 to 372 in 2000. Despite the sparse *direct* contribution of the two research consortia to the local entrepreneurial ecosystem, their *indirect* contributions provided a long-term stimulus for the location of additional research-intensive, large high-tech firms, which ended up driving an explosion of innovative entrepreneurial activity and strengthening the local entrepreneurial ecosystem.

A RISKY NEW STRATEGY (THE 2000S)

The dynamic growth of imported tech firms in Austin continued after 2000. Local leaders continued to collaborate in their recruitment efforts, providing more data and insights on the evolution of Austin's economy to prospectus relocations. At the same time, Rick Perry allocated large monetary incentives for (mainly) large high-tech firms to locate in Texas, including Austin, when he became governor of Texas (2000–2015). The splashy incentives seemingly worked wonders, but a closer look reveals they were not nearly as instrumental as one would think. The state's flagship incentive program is the Texas Enterprise Fund (TEF), which launched in 2003 and continues today. It provides cash grants from the state, on top of other state and local incentives, to companies that decide to locate or expand and create jobs in Texas. As of 2020, the TEF was the largest deal-closing program in the nation, allocating over $600 million since its creation.[59] Nathan Jensen, a professor of government at UT, and Calvin Thrall, a professor of political science at Columbia University, published an analysis of the program in 2021. They found that many of the benefited companies failed to meet their job-creation promises, which led to a non-disbursement of their incentives or repayment of their incentives plus interest,[60] and they concluded that the program has had little impact in attracting new high-tech firms or local expansions to Austin. The City of Austin also provides incentives, including Chapter 380 agreements, which offer cash incentives to companies for investing in the municipal region with requirements to create jobs and meet other conditions. Jensen found a similar effect with these incentives: Most companies dropped out of this incentive program (e.g., Dropbox, eBay, Facebook) before the city paid a single dollar because they could not meet the job requirements.[61]

The question then becomes: How many companies that relocated to Austin actually asked for relocation or expansion incentives? To answer that, we compared the relocations of firms in Austin and their use of three incentive programs—TEF, Chapter 380, and the Emerging Technology Fund (ETF)—between 2016 and 2022. Table 1 shows that 94 percent of the

TABLE 1. Business Expansions and Relocations to Austin by Incentive

Incentive	2016	2017	2018	2019	2020	2021	2022
Texas Enterprise Fund Recipients	5	1	3	1	1	2	1
Texas Emerging Technology Fund Recipients	1						
Chapter 380 Agreement Recipients	3		1			1	
Not a recipient of TEF, ETF, or Chapter 380	95	111	132	133	130	191	143
Total Business Expansions and Relocations	**101**	**112**	**135**	**134**	**131**	**193**	**144**

NOTES: Includes companies based in the Austin metro area. Counts of incentive recipients and nonrecipients may not add to total since a company may receive multiple incentives. Incentive recipient companies are manually matched to expansion and relocation announcements reported by the Austin Chamber of Commerce.

companies that relocated to Austin or expanded in the city in 2016 did not use any of these incentives. Even more striking, despite the rapid growth of large firms that relocated to Austin (43 percent between 2016 and 2022), only one used any of these three incentive programs in 2022. Only a few of the firms attracted to Austin asked for monetary incentives offered by the state or the city, and most of them ended up not meeting the employment requirements, which disqualified the funds for use. The bottom line: Data show that these monetary incentives (loans or grants) have not been the force behind these firms' decision to locate or expand in Austin. (Jon Roberts discusses the relationship—or rather the lack of one—between tax incentives and job creation in chapter 9.)

Austin Community Efforts to Directly Support Nascent Entrepreneurs

When George Kozmetsky became dean of the University of Texas School of Business in 1966, he envisioned the growth of the local entrepreneurial ecosystem as being driven by spin-offs from an influx of large high-tech firms. This vision was shaped by his earlier experiences in California, where, in the 1930s, he worked at Litton Industries—one of the pioneering startups that helped lay the foundation for Silicon Valley's emerging electronics industry.[62] Kozmetsky and a coworker left Litton to found the electronics company Teledyne in 1960, a firm whose extraordinary growth led Kozmetsky to make *Forbes* magazine's list of the nation's four hundred richest men in the United States in 1985.[63] Their decision was not unique—many employees were leaving innovative firms in California, particularly in Silicon Valley, to create technology startups. These events influenced the two visionaries' decisions to become entrepreneurs and helped Kozmetsky recognize the importance of spin-offs in building Austin's entrepreneurial ecosystem.[64]

Kozmetsky also saw government-funded business incubators as well positioned for nurturing the next generation of entrepreneurs. A collaboration between the IC^2 Institute, the Austin Chamber of Commerce, the City of Austin, Travis County, and the University of Texas supported the founding of the Austin Technology Incubator (ATI) in 1989. Although located within UT, ATI's focus was not on academic entrepreneurs but rather on assisting new and potentially high-growth local companies. Pike Powers noted that ATI graduated about seventy-five companies between 1989 and 2004, an average of five local firms per year. While important in other respects, ATI did not graduate a large enough number of companies to drive the growth of the local entrepreneurial ecosystem. Moreover, its contribution was relatively smaller after 2010 when the number of local tech incubators and accelerators exploded.

In 2005, Governor Perry developed a new incentive program, the Texas Emerging Technology Fund (ETF), intended for startups seeking seed-stage money. It gave out $400 million before being shuttered in 2016.[65] The program faced criticism for its lack of transparency and investments in high-risk companies. Several grant recipients went bankrupt, and not all kept their promises to create jobs.[66] Overall, local efforts to directly help nascent entrepreneurs benefited a relatively small number of startups (i.e., ATI) or were distributed in a process biased by a lack of transparency and accountability (i.e., ETF); therefore, they do not seem to have had the ability to drive the growth of the local entrepreneurial ecosystem.

Advice for Economic Development Leaders in Other Regions

If we want to understand not only how to create an ecosystem, but also how to keep it dynamic, we need a new analytical framework that considers an ecosystem's entire life cycle—creation, growth, and self-sustainability.

Austin's case illustrates that a milestone in creating a sustainable entrepreneurial ecosystem is the emergence of a *critical mass* of experienced entrepreneurs. When this benchmark is reached, a large number of networked entrepreneurs recycle (reinvest) substantial entrepreneurial resources and thicken the ecosystem with startup support organizations (e.g., venture capital firms, angel investors, and networked incubators), driving the growth of the entrepreneurial ecosystem.

What does it mean to be self-sustaining? It means that outside capital and talent are no longer the main drivers of the ecosystem's growth. This is not to say that outside resources are superfluous in advanced ecosystems. Capital and talent cannot live in a bubble, so a thriving ecosystem is never closed. An entrepreneurial ecosystem has to remain open. The distinction here, however, is whether local entrepreneurial activity relies *primarily* on outside capital and talent, or other outside resources. In Austin, the system became self-sustaining precisely because local entrepreneurs routinely reinvested in the community, supporting several generations of tech entrepreneurs that over time produced a critical mass of experienced entrepreneurs.

What strategies can local leaders adopt to increase the number of experienced entrepreneurs in a city? Local leaders (and academics) often propose measures that intend to make a direct impact on both the local entrepreneurial learning process and the availability of entrepreneurial resources, such as funding entrepreneurship classes at local colleges or universities, supporting traditional business incubators, or providing direct monetary incentives to entrepreneurs (e.g., ETF). However, the Austin case illustrates that these *direct* entrepreneurial efforts, although helpful for some entrepreneurs (e.g., ATI graduates), affect too few startups to drive the growth and evolution of an entrepreneurial ecosystem. Business incubators and universities certainly played a role, but they alone could not ensure success. Furthermore, it also shows that public monetary incentives for innovation-oriented startups could be biased by individual payoffs, like winning political donors, rather than helping local entrepreneurs.

A more effective approach to creating a critical mass of experienced entrepreneurs is to recognize, as professor and entrepreneur Daniel Isenberg does, that economic leaders cannot create a flourishing entrepreneurial ecosystem without large companies cultivating it, intentionally or otherwise. Although Austin community leaders' goal in attracting large firms was primarily to create quality jobs for UT graduates, they also understood that an unintended benefit of rooting these firms in the city would be to spark the local entrepreneurial ecosystem.

When MCC and SEMATECH arrived in Austin, local leaders had high expectations that the incoming one thousand-plus high-level researchers would jump-start the entrepreneurial ecosystem. Unfortunately, MCC and SEMATECH had institutional restrictions that stopped them from directly contributing to the local entrepreneurial ecosystem. However, their indirect contributions to the growth of the local entrepreneurial ecosystem were vast. They sped up the interest of large high-tech companies to locate in Austin and became a learning ground for "best practices" in recruiting future innovative firms (e.g., 3M's Division for Research and Development in 1984 and Samsung in 1996). With all this in mind—and understanding that there is often a bit of kismet involved as well—these are some of the evidence-based practices that could help fuel a self-sustaining entrepreneurial ecosystem in other regions.

Best Practices to Attract Potential Startup Incubating Firms

1. *Attracting large high-tech firms is a cascading process that starts by building long-term relationships with the economic development community in a few advanced high-tech regions.* During the birth and strengthening of the Austin entrepreneurial ecosystem, Austin community leaders visited Silicon Valley and focused on building strong, long-term relationships with the chamber, the *San Jose Mercury News*, and prospective high-tech companies in San Jose. These early efforts would benefit local entrepreneurs during all growth phases of Austin's entrepreneurial ecosystem. The importance of this strategy is evident in the early flow of startup service providers from California (e.g., Silicon Valley Bank and Imperial Bank) to Austin, which complemented the role of Austin Ventures during the rapid growth of the local entrepreneurial ecosystem in the 1990s. As the entrepreneurial ecosystem advanced over time, Austin leaders' linkages cascaded to other high-tech regions. Measuring Austin's linkages with more advanced high-tech regions by the number of direct flights from Austin to five top-tech regions (San Jose, San Francisco, Boston, New York, and Seattle) shows a trend of increased regional diversification. In the 1990s, 96 percent of these direct flights were to two California cities,

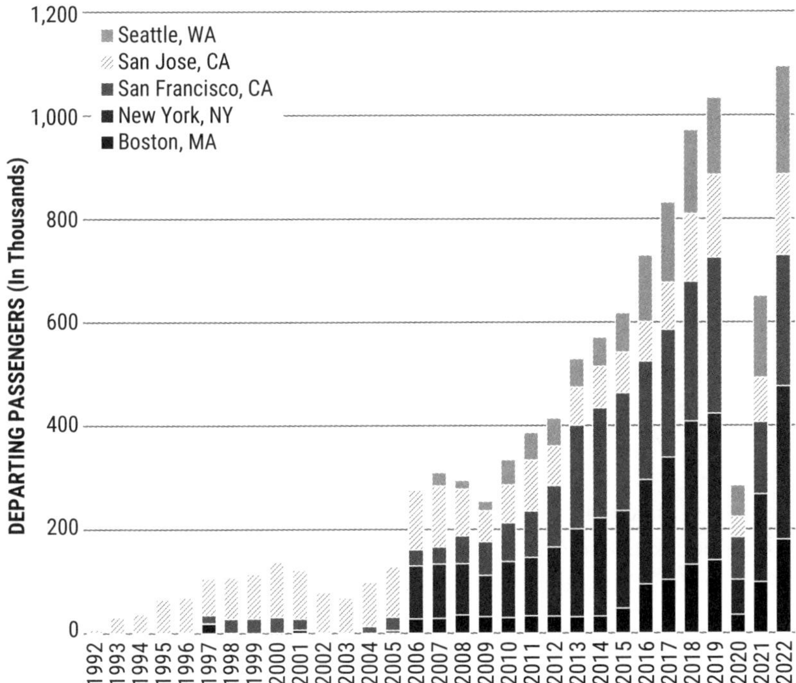

Figure 4. Figure created by Evan Johnston and Elsie L. Echeverri-Carroll; edited by Meredith Eberle.

San Jose and San Francisco, while only 37 percent were to these two cities in 2022. (In 1990s, the direct flight from San Jose to Austin was so packed with tech industry workers and employees that it was nicknamed the "nerd bird.") As figure 4 shows,[67] over time, the city diversified its linkages with other top high-tech centers, coinciding with the beginning of the self-sustaining phase in 2010.

2. *Commit to fulfill future needs of relocated firms.* Recounting Austin leaders' success in winning one of the research consortia, Glenn West noted, "The SEMATECH people felt like we had a team here, that they can count on its help if they have a problem, or that this group who had recruited them will be there for them if they needed some support." In particular, he highlighted how Austin Community College (ACC) played a big role in winning SEMATECH "by promising companies

that ACC would offer the technical training that these companies were looking for." Indeed, since 1995, ACC has partnered with a significant number of local large and small semiconductor companies in a two-year training program. Some of these companies have donated many expensive machines that are critical tools in training students, making ACC's semiconductor program one of the best in the country. Its prominence is evident in the unusually large number of visits by community college representatives from across the US and other countries.[68] ACC has also offered special certifications for other high-tech companies, such as software giants Oracle and Microsoft, since the 1990s. The high-tech cluster's long-term partnership with ACC has been very important for the growth of the high-tech industry in Austin since most of the technicians it employs are local.

3. *Build the local infrastructure high-tech firms need instead of relying on monetary incentives.* Austin did not win MCC simply because monetary incentives came into play. What played a more decisive role was building excellence in microelectronics and computer science research and graduate education at the state's two premier universities—UT Austin and Texas A&M University, according to Gibson and Rogers. These investments promised to help UT establish thirty new endowed professorships in electrical engineering and computer science, increase the number of PhDs in these fields from ten to fifty a year, and dramatically increase graduate student stipends and research facilities (including a new microelectronics research center). The relevance and strong potential of long-term research-oriented investments is clear when you contrast it with monetary incentives (e.g., loans and grants), which the state has offered since 2003 to relocate firms with the promise of employment (e.g., TEF) or with the possibility of commercializing technologies via nascent startups (e.g., ETF), both of which have had limited success.
4. *Community efforts to grow a high-tech economy should be more supported by local governments.* Increasing the number of innovative (high-tech) firms, large and small, is now a major focus of regional economic development policy. The follow-on effects on higher-paying jobs and an increased tax base are easily documented. One might then assume that *all* city governments would like to spark a high-tech cluster of large and young firms, but the Austin case illustrates that

> local governments do not always perceive these benefits. For instance, no Austin government representatives were involved with the collaborative efforts to attract MCC. Gibson and Rogers, in citing Adm. Bobby R. Inman's interview, explained, "The timing was such that the rally causes against growth were preoccupied with getting candidates elected. So, they [the city of Austin] were not involved in the MCC decision. Then they were bypassed entirely in 3M's decision to move to Austin." Perhaps the most important lesson from these events is that collaboration of the local community with state government and leaders from other states and cities can overcome the "short-term" resistance of a city government to collaborate in building a high-tech cluster.

In sum, our framework and advice offer a practical guide to community leaders—especially in those cities struggling to create an entrepreneurial culture. In particular, a focus on attracting large innovative firms through "best practices" can yield dividends. Developing long-term relationships with a small set of advanced regions and technology firms, and building the local infrastructure these firms need (e.g., the number of direct flights to other tech regions and university research capabilities), is a sound approach.

And what advice do we give communities with established ecosystems? The rapid growth of tech startups in Austin after 2010 and entrepreneurial support organizations are tied to the continuous relocation and expansion of high-tech firms from other regions that started more than twenty years prior. What incentivized large high-tech firms to continue to expand and relocate in Austin throughout this period and up to the present day? Economists have a term for the benefits that a large geographic cluster of technology firms gain from spatial proximity: agglomeration economies. This refers to the specialized services, specialized workers, and knowledge externalities (access to free knowledge that spatial proximity brings to firms in large spatial clusters). The dearth of agglomeration benefits in Austin's sparse ecosystem in the early 1990s explains the eagerness of high-tech firms to collaborate with other community leaders in recruiting more high-tech firms. Glenn West noted that the support of incumbent major industrial employers, like Motorola and IBM, had a huge impact on California CEOs. He recalled how these incumbent firms were on the schedule for prospects to visit, how they talked to potential new companies about what it was like doing business in Austin, and how they even sent people to California to market Austin and its community. In contrast, when agglomeration economies are large, firms already in the city would have less incentive to collaborate in industrial recruitment or to take advantage of the benefits offered by the state or the city.

The Austin case signals that, at this advanced stage, community leaders should direct their collaborative efforts to expand the infrastructure that facilitates the flow of entrepreneurial resources and ideas within the city (e.g., transportation mobility)[69] and with other high-tech regions (e.g., airport expansion and connectedness), and to maintain the quality of life that attracted these firms and their employees in the first place and that are also important for attracting entrepreneurial talent and relocating startups. The availability of skilled workers drives this argument to an increasing degree. Without focusing on what attracts and retains tech workers, for both large and young firms, the entrepreneurial culture will wither. Essential to this approach is the willingness to address sometimes controversial issues. Kozmetsky recognized that the wealth gap between Black, Hispanic, and white communities was a broader equity issue and should not be divorced from economic vitality. While tech companies and entrepreneurs do not speak with one voice on this subject, the importance of recognizing who benefits from tech growth is more urgent than ever.

CHAPTER SIX

TRACYE MCDANIEL[1]

Ambition, Exclusion, and the Erasure of Black Culture

"Whatever you do, don't go to East Austin," my father cautioned me as I loaded up my car for the drive from Waco to Austin to enroll at the University of Texas (UT). It was 1978, and my protective father was understandably nervous about my safety as I launched into the world beyond my hometown. He had attended Huston-Tillotson University in the 1960s, an HBCU on the city's east side—the area just east of Interstate 35 and downtown—and while he had a good experience as a student, he worried that it might be unsafe for his beloved daughter on her own.

So, what was the first thing I did? I headed straight for East Austin. There was a bit of a rebellious daughter in me, but mostly, I was searching for a Black community. I hadn't been able to find my community at UT (the percentage of Black students enrolled in 1980 was under 3 percent), and I didn't have family in Austin. I craved a sense of belonging in a community where I could experience a warm embrace of acceptance and the kind of tight-knit camaraderie I'd grown up with as a fourth-generation Texan. After connecting with the Black culinary staff at my dormitory cafeteria and asking where they went to church, what restaurant had the best BBQ, and, most importantly, which beauty salon did the best hair, I realized that East Austin—Central East Austin, to be specific—was where I wanted to be.

I didn't know then that this neighborhood, Austin's mecca of Black culture, which had held fast to its identity for nearly a century, would soon be

East Austin and the Eastern Crescent

The Eastern Crescent is shown by contiguous census tracts identified as undergoing gentrification or susceptible to gentrification.

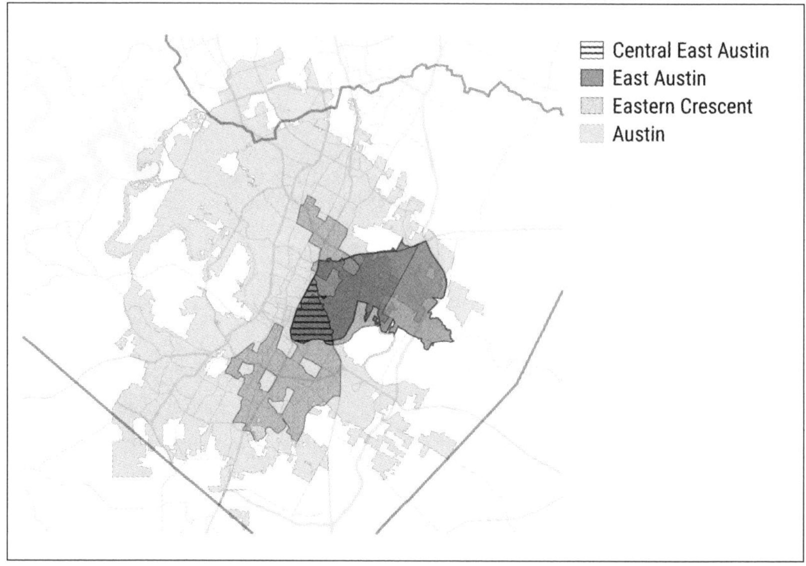

Figure 5. Figure created by Evan Johnston; edited by Reece Neathery and Meredith Eberle.

dramatically changed by the city's economic growth. As tech companies proliferated over the next few decades, and as more people moved to Austin, many Black residents in East and Central East Austin would leave or be forced out, and the disparity between white and Black prosperity in the city would widen. Nowhere would the gap be more pronounced than in Central East Austin, where most of the city's Black residents lived.

In the early 1900s, roughly one quarter of Austin's residents were Black. Today, Austin's Black population stands at a mere 8 percent, or seventy-nine thousand—the number of people who can comfortably assemble in the football stadium of the University of Texas at Austin, my alma mater. Over fifty years—from 1970 to 2020—when the national Black population rose from 11 percent to 13 percent, Austin's Black population shrunk significantly, from about 12 percent to 8 percent. Equally striking, between 2000 and 2010, *Austin was the only major city in the US that had experienced substantial growth while also experiencing a net loss of Black residents.*

For those Black residents who did remain in East and Central East Austin, the ability to create wealth through traditional avenues—being well employed, business ownership, and owning a home—stalled and lagged. From 2012 to 2022, Black home ownership in East Austin dropped from 32 percent to 27 percent, even while home ownership among *all* East Austin residents rose (from 47 percent to 50 percent). The percentage of STEM (science, technology, engineering, and mathematics) jobs in Austin held by Black workers during this time was lower than the national average—7.6 percent compared to 9 percent. The bottom line is that the wealth-building opportunities available in East Austin were not shared equally across all racial groups. All of this came when Austin's tech sector was exploding. The city's pursuit to become a technopolis was, arguably, blind ambition, undertaken without consideration for the downsides of unchecked growth.

There are exceptions hidden in these numbers, however, experiences of prosperity that detour from the main plotline of exclusion. The story of Black Austin and technology and growth is not a monolith, and there are several bright spots to note. A 2023 SmartAsset survey of the country's thirty-nine largest metro areas found that the Austin metro area, which includes the suburbs of Georgetown and Round Rock, ranked number one for Black entrepreneurs (data points included employment rate, new business success, and job security). A Lending Tree analysis of 2021 census data looking at prosperity for Black households placed Austin second out of the one hundred largest US metro areas, thanks to low unemployment rates and a stellar ranking for education: 33 percent of Black adults have a bachelor's degree or higher (although a breakdown of those degrees finds that less than 3 percent of Black residents twenty-five and older studied in a STEM field). One other small but significant positive development: Over ten years, from 2012 to 2022, the median Black household income in the Austin metro area rose from $51,400 to $68,600, a gain of 33 percent. So while Black households still earned less than white households (whose median income rose from $87,000 to $104,000 over the same period, a 20 percent increase), the accelerated gain among Black households represents a 6 percent *reduction* in the gap between Black and white household median income.[2]

But from the thirty thousand-foot view, the picture is this: Austin's tech growth and economic prosperity have left much of the Black population behind, particularly long-standing residents. While most other high-growth tech hubs across the country have attracted enough Black talent and residents to outpace the out-migration of Black people, Austin has not. The percentage of tech workers who were Black or Hispanic dropped about 5 percent from 2000 to 2016.[3] When looking at the broader category of STEM jobs, a proxy for technology jobs, Black participation has not kept pace with the Austin metro region. *What is behind Austin's outlier status? How does a city with such an open and progressive reputation, where entrepreneurial opportunities seem to abound, find itself as a stark example of Black economic exclusion?*

Hispanic Austin and Technology Growth

While the Hispanic population's experience with the city's tech explosion somewhat mirrors that of Black residents, there is a unique and larger story to tell about Hispanic participation in Austin's technology boom, a history which could fill its own book. In brief, while much of East Austin is Hispanic (43 percent), Hispanics' community and culture has also been affected by gentrification and displacement. Overall, the Hispanic population in Austin has shrunk over the last decade, dropping from 36 percent in 2010 to 32.5 percent in 2019 (this is in contrast to a statewide increase of 21 percent). It is also important to note that a higher percentage of Hispanic people participate in Austin's technology workforce than Black people. As of 2024, Hispanics or Latinos made up 15 percent of technology employment in Austin; Black people made up 7 percent; Asians made up 24 percent; and white people constituted 54.34 percent.

There are several key reasons to unpack—ones that go beyond gentrification—but to understand the origins, we must travel back to 1928. Nearly a century ago, Austin's city government adopted the 1928 master plan and created a "negro district." This plan's legacy continues to shape Austin's future. Before 1928, the city's Black populace was robust and scattered around the city, living in neighborhoods west of East Avenue (west of today's Interstate 35), such as Clarksville, Kincheonville, the Wood Street Settlement at Shoal Creek, Wheatville, and Bouldin. Central Texas was less racially oppressed than East Texas, and many freedmen communities, nestled in the rolling green hills close to the winding Colorado River, were able to flourish.

The 1928 master plan, however, disrupted these organic communities. The plan's goals were twofold: to define a citywide land use blueprint, which included moving all of Austin's African Americans to one area to save city resources, and to solve the desire to segregate the races (even though race-based zoning was ruled unconstitutional in 1917).

The plan called for Austin's entire Black population to move to a six-square-mile radius in Central East Austin known as Six Square, roughly between Seventh and Twelfth streets. To make this happen, the city threatened to cut off sewer service and not pave the roads in neighborhoods where Black people were previously living, coercing them to move to the east side with a promise that they would be offered public services, parks, and a public school exclusively for Black children. Whole generations were uprooted from neighborhoods where residents had built churches, schools, and thriving businesses. *This single decision made nearly a century ago, concentrating Austin's Black population in one discrete area, would result in disproportionate displacement and economic segregation throughout the decades, especially when the city's tech success began to accelerate.*

In Six Square, Austin's Black community re-created what they'd lost and then some. They erected restaurants, pharmacies, and grocery stores. They opened the famous Victory Grill, a US Chitlin Circuit club where B. B. King played. The Victory Grill also provided a place for returning World War II vets to gather at a time when they could not attend clubs frequented by white veterans. Six Square retained a majority Black population throughout the 1940s, 1950s, and 1960s, not only because it was a tight-knit community but because redlining and predatory mortgage lending practices had limited out-migration to other parts of the city. In addition, the construction of Interstate 35 in 1962 created a physical barrier between Austin's west and east sides, cementing the divisions (quite literally).

By the late 1970s, the Six Square district was beginning to change partly due to desegregation. New opportunities outside the neighborhood—higher-paying jobs, more affordable homes, better education—created a significant migration movement out of the area. But the neighborhood still offered what I wanted. In 1980, most Central East Austin residents were Black, and although some folks had started moving out and Hispanic families were beginning to settle in, it still felt like a vibrant Black neighborhood that welcomed other ethnicities but preserved the Black cultural identity so important to me.

I graduated from UT with a degree in organizational communications after discovering I could command a better starting salary than with a degree in journalism, my first love. I also recognized that a career in journalism would extract a toll I wasn't willing to bear. My internship with a local news station—where I'd covered a violent, hate-filled KKK rally at the state capitol and the murder of a young Hispanic man, whom I later learned was the son of a kind woman I'd met (she'd returned my wallet to me after I'd left it on the bus)—had shown me the dangers and despair I'd face in that profession. I was thrilled to land an internship at the Austin Chamber of Commerce, where I spent six months learning the ropes of public-private partnerships, networking, business development, and advocacy . . . and doing tedious tasks, like replacing the paper in the copier machine (I was an intern after all). While there, I met Austin legends such as Mayor Lee Cooke, Glenn West, Vic Mathias, and Angelos Angelou, who would become lifelong inspirations and mentors.

In 1984, the chamber loaned me to the recently established Capital City African American Chamber of Commerce (incorporated in 1982, the CCAACC is now known as the Greater Austin Black Chamber of Commerce). The CCAACC, or the Black chamber, as everyone referred to it, was founded by community, business, and political leaders primarily to bring awareness to the enormous revenue generated by Black consumer spending across the country through travel and tourism. And because the city's hotel tax was a significant source of the Black chamber's funding, our main objective was business development efforts to attract Black conventions, business travelers, and business development. In 1985, I was invited to be CEO—only the second one in the Black chamber's short history—a role I embraced. I was just twenty-six years old—and as green as they come—but I was energetic and excited to join the organization. I had an inspiring opportunity to meet and work with Black public and private sector leaders, along with community activists in Austin, such as Tommy Wyatt (as founder, owner, and publisher of the African American newspaper *The Villager*, he is credited with being one of the founders of the Black chamber); Rev. Norris Carr (past chair of the Black chamber and owner of a printing business); Eric Mitchell (a city council member, business owner, board member of the Black chamber, and an architect of the Austin Revitalization Authority); Dr. Charles Urdy, PhD (he served five terms on city council and is past chairman of the Austin Revitalization Authority); Dorothy Turner (known as queen of Austin civil rights activists, the unafraid crusader with a heart of gold served as the longtime president of the Black Citizens Task Force—founded by her friend and fellow activist Velma Roberts—among other causes); and so many others who impacted my trajectory of advocating for Black businesses and the Central East Austin community.

The Black chamber was meeting our goals on the travel and tourism front—recruiting and hosting associations such as the National Coalition of Black Meeting Professionals (NCBMP) and the National Bar Association, and meeting planners from business, civil rights, church, and fraternal organizations. However, the role gave me a high perch, revealing that the Black business community was poorly integrated into the city's larger economic development ecosystem. Black entrepreneurs and leaders were underrepresented in strategic discussions about growth, business development, and the city's future. We did not have seats at the table. And I don't mean a proverbial seat, but a literal seat. At the time, no members of the Black chamber were on the board of the Austin Chamber of Commerce. Information and invitations were shared on a need-to-know basis, and if we were lucky, we would receive trickle-down information from the headlines, political leaders, and other resources. To help close the knowledge gap, I floated an idea that was well-received by the Austin chamber's president at the time, Lee Cooke, who had an ear for inclusivity—to create a board member exchange between the Austin chamber and the Black chamber. The mutual exchange created an opportunity to rotate members, and it was a game changer for the Black chamber. This rotation brought fresh perspectives and expanded both chambers' networks for collaborations and fundraising opportunities, and the knowledge sharing greatly benefited our members and strengthened the organization. Early in my career, it impressed me how important it was for marginalized groups to simply be in the room to learn about what was happening and for those in leadership positions to provide a formal network to share that knowledge with all communities. (The first Black member of the Austin Chamber of Commerce was the late Marcellus "Andy" Anderson, who paved the way for future Black businesspeople in many respects. He was the first Black Texan to receive his real estate license, to serve on the Austin Planning Commission, and to be a city bank director, among many "firsts.")

While this change helped strengthen relationships between the Black chamber and the Austin chamber, looking back, there was a significant lack of inclusion of Black business leaders and the Black community in the advancements taking place in the tech sector. At this time, Austin was in the throes of its technology revolution. Behind the scenes, the power players, having committed the city to technology early on—not manufacturing, oil, or agriculture—were seeing their labor bear fruit. A couple years before I started at the Black chamber, the city had scored an enormous feather in its cap: Microelectronics and Computer Technology Corporation (MCC). As detailed in chapter 5, MCC was the nation's first-of-its-kind tech business consortium formed to compete with Japanese microchips. Austin was chosen as its site over fifty-seven other national applicants. In 1984, 3M relocated its research and development division to Austin from St. Paul, Minnesota, to take advantage of Texas' tax-friendly environment.

Among the influential forces behind Austin's tech boom was the rise of Dell Technologies. Founded in 1984 by Michael Dell, a University of Texas student, Dell quickly became a global powerhouse in the personal computer market. The company helped create a ripple effect that attracted many other technology companies, vendors, and suppliers to the area.

In 1987, Austin won the bid for SEMATECH (another consortium that competed with Japan's growing semiconductor industry). In 1989, George Kozmetsky launched the Austin Technology Incubator (ATI) at the University of Texas, a regional economic development catalyst that became a national model for business technology incubation. Even through the recessions of the 1980s—which hit Austin hard in the banking and real estate sectors—the city continued to prosper by staying focused on tech growth. Austin was actively recruiting tech companies with remarkable success. The city's high quality of life, coupled with lower living expenses and construction costs, compared favorably with California's Silicon Valley and the Research Triangle in North Carolina. New and emerging companies continued to flock to Austin, and homegrown tech startups began to proliferate. The payoffs for these "gets" were huge economically and reputationally over the next decade. Austin was becoming a true tech hub, gaining a name for offering an abundance of "gold collar jobs"—positions that not only paid a good salary but were also located in a place filled with open green spaces, water, and music.

Despite the seismic growth in the technology sector, the Black chamber continued to focus on travel and tourism (due to a service agreement with the City of Austin) and supporting Black businesses. It made sense then, but in retrospect, it was too limiting. The connection to the burgeoning Austin tech economy was tenuous at best. In addition to the tech blind spot, the neglect in addressing and improving the economic conditions of established Black and Brown communities would have far-reaching consequences, exacerbating many of the economic disparities that exist today.

While I didn't interact much with Austin's tech gurus, I did have a significant run-in—and I do mean run-in—with the godfather of Austin's tech boom: Pike Powers. It was a rainy day, and I was headed from the Black chamber's offices to the old Robert Mueller Municipal Airport to catch a flight. I was asking a lot of my Ford Fiesta's worn-out tires as I maneuvered down Manor Road, but I was running late and determined not to miss my flight. Suddenly, my car slid into another vehicle, a Jaguar. I was shaken but physically OK. Embarrassed, I exited my car to see how the other occupant was doing. He told me he was fine, too, and we exchanged cards. I told him I would call him when I returned from my trip to settle up, secretly terrified I wouldn't be able to pay for the damage to his car, even with my insurance. I returned to the car and read his card: Pike Powers, Partner in Charge, Fulbright & Jaworksi. I immediately called my dad, in tears. "I can't afford to pay for the damage to a Jaguar. And he is with a powerful law firm." My calm and logical dad told me to contact my insurance, report the accident, and call Mr. Powers as promised. When my plane landed in Austin, I rang Mr. Powers and offered to cover any damage in installments. I also shared that it was my first job out of UT to help explain my inability to pay in total up-front. I'll never forget what he said. "I appreciate this call, and you don't owe me anything," he responded. His kindness touched me. "Let's stay in touch." And I did. As I learned more about him over the years, I was blown away by his vision of innovation for Austin and his role as a dealmaker—he was pivotal in bringing MCC and SEMATECH to Austin in the 1980s and Samsung in the 1990s. Years later, when I sat with him on a panel about best practices for economic development (*I was on a panel with Pike Powers!*), I reminded him of how we met "by accident." He'd forgotten about the young woman in a Ford Fiesta who dented his Jaguar. After that, when we found ourselves together at various functions, he often told the story of how we met.

In 1991, I was recruited for a position at the Texas Department of Commerce's Tourism Division under Governor Ann Richards. I was excited to work for a female governor; the role was a logical and exciting next step.

A few years later, I met Jon Roberts, who was appointed head of the state's business development efforts. His team was directly across the hall from mine, and we chatted every morning. These kinds of fortunate "collisions" marked so much of my life in Austin.

I continued as director of tourism under Governor George W. Bush and joined the economic development and tourism team under Governor Rick Perry. Governor Perry created a business climate swagger that attracted key industries, including tech, to the Lone Star State. I learned the vast value of private-public-academic partnerships. This collaborative trifecta helped convince Texas Instruments to keep their microchip plant (a $3 billion investment) firmly rooted in Richardson, Texas (yes, there was a time when TI was window-shopping in other states). Helping to land Toyota's manufacturing plant in San Antonio, I understood firsthand how important it was for personal relationships between different cultures to be nurtured and respected.

Because my jobs were centered on economic development at the state level, I wasn't too focused on the inner workings of Austin's business ecosystem. However, as a resident of Austin, I began to witness how the city's growth, bursting with energy and prosperity in so many neighborhoods, bypassed Central East Austin. A 2001 report by the Austin Revitalization Authority found that as of 1997, 83 percent of the neighborhood's streets were substandard. Twenty-four percent of land parcels were vacant. There was extensive need to repair storm drainage pipes and a lack of safe open space. It seemed the historic Black neighborhood and longstanding residents were intentionally neglected. And, in part because of the neglect and vacancies, violent crime was five times higher in the area than in the city as a whole.

Beginning in 2000, the displacement of Central East Austin residents accelerated, driven by both voluntary relocation due to the neighborhood's changing character and higher property taxes. New developments accelerated rapidly. One major trigger was a 1998 city zoning initiative that was hailed as a great success but, in retrospect, further splintered Central East Austin's Black community. As tech businesses swarmed the city—the number of high-tech workers living in the region more than doubled between 1990 and 2000 and accounted for more than one in four jobs—some leaders were understandably concerned with how unchecked development would affect the city's delicate aquifer system, the Barton Creek Greenbelt (miles of intracity trails dotted with natural watering holes and bouldering spots), and its unique system of waterways. So, in 1998, under Mayor Kirk Watson, the city council passed the Smart Growth Initiative (SGI), an urban growth boundary plan that satisfied both pro-growth developers and urban environmentalists (not so endearingly referred to by some as NIMBY—aka the "Not In My Backyard" camp). After all, the city's natural beauty was a big part of the allure for tech workers and companies, and the plan got buy-in from both sides. SGI divided the city into three development zones: the drinking-water protection zone (close to the Edwards Aquifer and Barton Springs), the desired development zone, and the desired urban development zone. The first zone—in Southwest, West, and Northwest Austin—was generally protected from development to safeguard the watershed and sources of drinking water (and endangered species who lived there). The latter two, where development was heavily encouraged through incentives and investments, were located in, drumroll please, . . . East Austin and Central East Austin. Real estate and business development ensued, followed by gentrification and displacement. Many longtime Black and Hispanic residents were priced out when housing values and property taxes skyrocketed. In 2000, home appraisals, which were up across Austin and Travis County, had gone up the fastest in East Austin. This pattern of rapidly increasing property values has continued through Austin's more recent housing booms. According to data on typical home values from Zillow, the monthly median typical home value in East Austin between 2017 and 2021 was the same or higher than the rest of the city. Rapid growth and development, driven in this case by the tech industry, are the hallmarks of gentrification.

Gentrification, a term thrown around a lot, is the process of urban revitalization where higher-income households and businesses move into a neighborhood and displace low-income residents and small businesses, thus changing the neighborhood's character. The effect it typically has on longstanding residents includes increased property values, rents, and amenities, as well as a shift in demographic makeup. Gentrification can have positive and negative impacts; it can improve infrastructure and services, but it can also contribute to social inequality and the displacement of longstanding residents. Forcing residents out of their neighborhoods can shake the stable factors essential for promoting well-being and quality of life. For those who stay, gentrification erodes important community anchors such as neighbors, churches, and small businesses—the things that constitute the fabric of an area. This all can culminate in the erasure of community history, culture, and economic opportunities. Some experts have begun using the term "whitetrification" to describe the process of gentrification when it happens (as it most often does) in Black and Hispanic communities, resulting in an influx of non-Black and non-Hispanic residents.

This is exactly what happened in Central East Austin. Between 2000 and 2010, the *Black population in the area decreased by 66 percent, the Hispanic population decreased by 33 percent, and the white population increased by 442 percent.* (That is not a typo.) It was a literal draining of color and culture, a "whitetrification." Eric Tang, PhD, of UT's Institute for Urban Policy Research and Analysis, explored these figures in a 2018 survey, "Those Who Stayed: The Impact of Gentrification on Longtime Residents of East Austin." It is an illuminating and sobering read. For those who had lived in the neighborhood for over a decade, 74 percent described the changes as "negative." Over one-third described the neighborhood as "no longer one of color." Ninety percent perceived property taxes as too high, even though nearly three quarters of those surveyed paid "little to none" on their mortgage (almost 38 percent of those surveyed were on a fixed income). Reading the interviews of survey respondents, what struck me was the passion and persistence of those who remained despite seeing their neighborhood change so drastically. The majority were second-, third-, and fourth-generation householders with deep family histories in the neighborhood. One woman said, "This is ancestral land. Blacks are in Austin; we were raised in East Austin. If we leave Austin, we can't trace our family." This response, what scholars call "the right to stay," signals the embrace of a heavy responsibility: a resolve not to be erased.

In my recent discussions with other longtime residents of East Austin and small business owners, this sentiment of erasure of culture and community is echoed. Homer Hill, co-owner of the iconic The Catfish Station live music venue featuring jazz fusion on Sixth Street (now Mr. Catfish & More) and cofounder of the annual Urban Music Fest (now Urban Cultural Festival), explains, "Growth destroyed the community. I have lived and owned businesses in East Austin my whole life, and none of the growth has impacted me positively. There was a big disconnect and a lot of broken promises. When I hear urban renewal, I think, 'The support should start with the people already there. Help us build our events, help us with housing.' There has been no seat at the table." Frustrated with being over-policed and not finding sponsorships for The Catfish Station, Hill opened a satellite venue in Atlanta with a partner in the early 2000s and experienced the kind of business and city support he rarely found in Austin. "It was the inverse of Austin. Businesses were beating down our doors," he explained in 2020 on the podcast *Pause/Play*. "I love Austin, but it made me sad. Atlanta was a haven for me, a place where there is potential for everyone to benefit."

It's important to note, again, that this experience of exclusion and displacement did not describe every Black experience. According to Gregory Smith, president and CEO of the Austin Revitalization Authority (ARA), a development company committed to the preservation of Black heritage in the Eleventh and Twelfth streets commercial corridor (the beating heart of Central East Austin's Black community), many folks were given a fair shake by the city, which offered subsidies and cost-of-living allowances for several years for them to stay or purchase homes at fair (and rising) market prices. "Not everyone was pushed out," he says, "but there was flight. Some people chose to leave, and others could not afford to stay." No matter the reason, the cultural losses were palpable. Mainstays of Black community life started disappearing. Churches serving the neighborhood for decades began to relocate when congregants became sparse. Several well-established neighborhood stores shuttered because proprietors couldn't afford the increased rent or their customer base was dwindling. Freshly planted, higher-income residents began to patronize new restaurants in the area or hop in their Teslas for a trip to Whole Foods.

I moved to Houston in 2006, becoming chief operating officer (COO) of the Greater Houston Partnership, an organization that "strives to make the Houston region the best place to live, work and build a business." (The partnership serves as the primary advocate for the greater Houston business community.) The role allowed me to stretch my skill set and get outside the Austin bubble, expanding into the corporate landscape. In 2011, I worked in New Jersey as the COO of Choose New Jersey, a startup organization led by business leaders and Governor Chris Christie. Choose New Jersey was a slogan I could get behind, considering I'd *chosen* New Jersey as my new home (I often opened presentations with this quip). My time on the East Coast gave me an excellent point of comparison, opening my eyes to navigating economic development in a new state and culture. My persistence in building on the fantastic attributes of New Jersey and getting business and policymakers aligned earned me the nickname of "Lone Star Moxie" among my colleagues.

I wouldn't return to Austin until 2015, when Governor Greg Abbott was elected. I was offered an opportunity to lead the Texas Economic Development Corporation, a public-private organization responsible for marketing Texas as a premier business location. I was thrilled to be back in Austin and to join the governor's team. It was an incredible moment for me when I was invited to Governor Abbott's announcement of his cabinet members. Having my dad and sisters by my side made it all the more special. Looking back on the day I arrived in Austin over thirty years earlier, I realized how far I'd come and what an influence Austin had on my career.

By this point, Austin was an established tech hub with a reputation that attracted diverse tech companies and startups. The city's tech diversification had gone well beyond semiconductors and included software development, data analytics, cybersecurity, and more. The growth of tech events, like SXSW (South by Southwest) Interactive, bolstered Austin as the epicenter of innovative tech and entrepreneurship. Austin was FIRE!

I always knew I would return to Austin, but when I stepped off the plane at the new Austin-Bergstrom International Airport from Newark, New Jersey, I had to recalibrate my understanding of the city. The stark changes in East and Central East Austin quickly became apparent. For one thing, living in my beloved neighborhood was no longer affordable. At the time of this writing, my former Central East Austin home is valued on Zillow at nearly $750,000, up from under $100,000 when I lived there. It had changed so much that I wasn't sure I would have planted roots there even if the price of entry weren't so high. So I ventured west, about thirty minutes from downtown, and discovered that there, too, changes were afoot—the area, which had felt isolated thirty years ago, was now flourishing with new housing and new amenities.

During the time I'd been away, the demographic trends that had begun in the early 2000s showed no sign of slowing. Black population growth continued to slow compared to other racial demographic groups, and rising property values and living costs in East and Central East Austin led to further displacement for longtime Black residents. They faced widening challenges related to employment opportunities, income inequality, affordable housing, and educational attainment. As often happens when such inequities surge, community activism and advocacy also intensified to address the effects of unchecked economic growth: racial inequality, housing affordability, and social justice.

In 2017, ready to venture into entrepreneurship, I founded McDaniel Strategy Ecosystems, which focused on economic development advisory services and consulting for strategic planning projects. For one of those projects, I joined TIP, the economic development consultancy and advisory firm founded by my friend and former colleague Tom Stellman. Tom and TIP managing partner Jon Roberts invited me to join the organization in 2019 as president, and I have not looked back. Having a team with diverse experiences, insights, and national perspectives has dramatically enriched my career in economic development. The deep bench of talent and experience brings much-needed understanding and innovation as we address opportunities and challenges in communities like Austin, realizing supersonic growth in the tech industry.

Today, East Austin and Central East Austin are considered eclectic and trendy. Due to its unique vibe and culture, the area is often marketed as "authentic" Austin. But the historical authenticity is being eclipsed. I recently picked up a publication at the airport focused on East Austin and flipped to an article highlighting dozens of faces of entrepreneurs on the east side. I did not see diverse faces featured.

Bridging the Gaps

While Austin carries the distinction of being named one of the best places to live in the country, it was also recently designated the most economically segregated in the nation by the Martin Prosperity Institute in a study coauthored by urban studies legend Richard Florida. (The study looked at income and included educational and occupational segregation.) In addition to economic segregation, Austin's Black community has experienced geographical and racial segregation. It's a complex and formidable force that contradicts Austin's branding as "the human capital." While the tagline (adopted by the city in the early 2000s) may have aimed to showcase Austin as a hub for human capital and talent, the outward migration trend of the Black community reveals the city's complex social dynamics and that not all people are necessarily supported. Underlying challenges must be addressed to ensure inclusivity and equity for all residents. This is our current position, but where are we headed?

In 2019, I became the chair of the International Economic Development Council (IEDC), an association with over 4,500 members in economic development. At this point, more than ever, I understood the responsibility of our profession and how *we* may have contributed to the disparities in communities in our country. We focus on job creation and target industry attraction and capital investment for growth and prosperity. But prosperity for whom? We all have heard that "a rising tide lifts all boats," which means economic growth and improvements will benefit all. This premise is flawed.

Despite the evidence of the racial wealth gap—data that is readily available and disseminated by major media outlets and economists—the severity of these inequalities is met with complacency and a lack of urgency. (Wealth is defined as assets—real estate, investments, money, and valuable possessions—minus debt.) The racial wealth gap has become such an integral part of our society and culture that we are desensitized to how it is harming our communities and the collective economy. Closing the racial wealth gap, improving job quality and training for economically disadvantaged communities, and ensuring economic opportunity exists for everyone are vital. We must encourage a culture where the *entire* workforce can fully participate and entrepreneurs of all backgrounds can flourish. Breaking down systemic barriers that prohibit citizens from full participation in the economy should become a vital focus of the profession of economic development. The goal is to build sustainable communities where everyone participates, is engaged, and is *retained*, where the human factor is considered alongside the economic outlook.

The City of Austin has begun to address some of its past injustices to Black residents in gentrifying areas. In 2015, Mayor Steve Adler acknowledged systemic inequities and—after efforts from community advocacy groups—established the city's first Office of Equity. The aim is to help guide city council decisions by considering how policies would economically impact communities of color. In 2016, the council formed a Task Force on Institutional Racism and Systemic Inequities cochaired by Colette Pierce Burnette, then president and CEO of Huston-Tillotson University, along with cochair Paul Cruz, AISD superintendent, and representatives from the business, housing, educational, and criminal justice communities. They offered over two hundred recommendations, including a plan to repopulate gentrified areas with original residents, provide housing development funding, and provide business incentives to tutor low-income students. In 2017, the city created the Anti-Displacment Task Force to help expand affordable housing for longtime residents. The report pointed out that Austin was spending significantly less per capita on housing issues than Portland, Philadelphia, Denver, San Francisco, or Boston. While the city did approve $300 million in funding in 2020, which it has been dispensing over many years, much more needs to be done (only twenty-eight homes were tagged for the first disbursement).

The Black and Hispanic communities have long been focused on bridging economic disparities and stemming the loss of a shared culture. These include nonprofits, educational institutions, health organizations, financial institutions (which help fund nonprofits and entrepreneurs), certain private companies and residents, and economic advocacy groups such as the Diversity and Ethnic Chambers Alliance (DECA), which includes the Asian, Black, Hispanic, and LGBT chambers. The vast inequality between Black and white populations would likely be even broader if it weren't for the consistent support coming from the Black community itself. Organizations such as Austin Revitalization Authority, Six Square (focused on the historical preservation of the original "negro district"), Austin Area Urban League, African American Leadership Institute, the local branch of the NAACP, and Equidad ATX continue to bridge the equity gaps, often with limited resources and capacity to fully realize transformational impacts.

Equidad ATX's novel approach to revitalization is focused on place-based planning and including the voices of people and their visions for the community they live in. (Revitalization is defined as the effort to rejuvenate the vitality and economic health of a low-income community that's been underinvested in.) Its target is the "Eastern Crescent," an area shaped like a backward C (see fig. 5) that's considered an "urban desert" adjacent to Central East Austin and near Tesla's electric vehicle manufacturing plant. (The region includes connecting areas in Central East Austin, Colony Park, Del Valle, Dove Springs, Montopolis, and Rundberg.) Here, communities are fighting to retain their heritage and cultivate an equitable quality of life in an area with limited access to health care, financial and professional services, retail options, and fresh food. At the time of this writing, there is still no major grocery store in the area, even though large chain stores, like Texas grocery giant H-E-B, have located in other low-income neighborhoods while still offering high-quality, fresh food at lower prices. (A sign of progress: In late 2024, H-E-B made a $1 million donation to help fund affordable housing in East Austin and announced plans to open two new stores on the east side.) The Eastern Crescent faces many of the same challenges that Central East Austin experienced as a direct result of the 1928 master plan.

Austin has a long way to go. Nationally, Black people make up only 9 percent of employees in tech jobs, with under 3 percent in C-suite positions. Austin's percentage is lower. Unless major interventions are pursued, that disparity is likely to widen. The downstream effects of lost wages, home ownership, and wealth building are staggering. By 2030, Black households nationwide stand to lose out on more than $350 billion in tech job wages, according to a McKinsey Institute for Black Economic Mobility analysis.

There are, however, reasons to be optimistic. One example of a private industry-university collaboration is a partnership launched in 2020 between Tesla and Huston-Tillotson, Austin's only HBCU and the city's first university. Tesla offers students and graduates learning opportunities (research and faculty collaborations), internships, and apprenticeships. The partnership essentially creates a pipeline of talent from the university to one of the country's most impactful technology companies, helping to populate the local tech culture with talented Black and Hispanic people, raising the chance of keeping these students in Austin and flourishing after graduation. Other private companies are making strides in different ways. Austin-based WP Engine hires many racially diverse employees and offers job opportunities to individuals without requiring a college degree. NXP Semiconductors, a Dutch company committing millions to Austin-area manufacturing investments, has signed on to the City of Austin's living wage requirements and has partnered with the city to reimburse property taxes and contribute to childcare assistance. Google Austin partners with Code2College, which works to place underrepresented high school students in paid internships. Google has also offered free digital coaching to local businesses owned by people of color and has seeded Black-owned Austin startup companies with $100,000 as part of its national Startups for Black Founders fund. The Austin Urban Technology Movement, founded to bridge the tech gap for Black and Hispanic Austinites, partners with companies such as AT&T, Austin Community College, IBM, and Microsoft to provide jobs and resources.

Tech-oriented cities like Austin can also access federal funds to increase STEM education in minority-serving institutions. The CHIPS and Science Act of 2022 has tagged funding for undergraduate scholarships, fellowships, and traineeships in STEM-related areas with an eye toward diversity and closing gaps. There is also money dedicated to outreach to HBCUs and labor organizations.

These interventions formalize a way of doing business that acknowledges *past* injustices, assesses how past decisions have affected *present* circumstances, and plans for greater inclusivity in the *future*. It's a 360-degree view backward and forward in time that should be taken by anyone in a position of influence—from a CEO or public official to a small-business owner, teacher, or loan officer. The goal is, ultimately, to not have to create another task force on inequity or funding tagged for STEM education for underrepresented communities, because there would be no need for it. Ideally, each business's practices and every public policy decision would consider all groups when enacting small and big decisions. We are far from that point, but that is the ideal.

A word about the "D" word: diversity. Jon Roberts and I participated in a 2024 panel discussion at the IEDC leadership conference called "Is DEI Dead?" The title alone should say it all. "Diversity," "equity," "inclusion," "empowerment," "intersectionality," "privilege," "allyship," "systemic oppression," and "representation"—these are all buzzwords that have carried weight and spurred corporations, governments, and individuals to focus on race-based disparities and initiatives to help narrow the gaps. They have fostered meaningful conversations, raising awareness and driving action around social justice issues. Each term carries crucial meanings for addressing inequalities and advocating for systemic change. However, these same terms are losing their appeal and power today. In some circles, they have become kryptonite for advancing the concepts they stand for. Language is powerful, and words matter, but they can also be a distraction and create barriers to opportunity. Regardless of the language, we must be driven by the data. Understanding and using data analytics to identify racial and economic disparities is one of the most crucial tools for promoting equity and social justice.

By analyzing statistics related to income, education, health-care access, housing, and other factors, organizations and policymakers can pinpoint areas where disparities exist and develop targeted interventions to address them. Data can support critical investments for residents who live in a food desert and need a grocery store nearby that carries affordable, fresh produce. Data can support providing access to a pharmacy or mental health services in neighborhoods statistically lacking these critical resources. We are talking about providing economic mobility and quality jobs to people in all neighborhoods so they can thrive and patronize businesses where they live. Period. The consensus at the panel was that the words don't matter as long as the work continues. As long as the racial wealth gap persists, the work must be done to end it.

Pulling apart a city's history and data and listening to the personal stories of those impacted, positively and negatively, empower us to do better. It enables us to move forward without repeating harmful patterns, to bridge divides, and to make decisions with a broader lens. It also allows us to understand the whole narrative, to connect the past to the present. As much as it is a reckoning, it is an opportunity.

I want to emphasize that what is good for displaced communities, what is prosperous for Black and Hispanic communities, is good for business overall. It's been proven, time and again, that racial (and gender) diversity is an economic and competitive advantage for a city—and for individual companies, for that matter—and that economic equity leads to widespread prosperity. The opposite is also true, that economic inequity hurts everyone. The cost of inaction is a reality. In the technology sector, research finds that gender and racial disparities in innovation fields *inhibit* GDP growth per capita by 2.7 percent, according to research from Michigan State University and a 2019 report from the Washington Center for Equitable Growth. The same report pointed out that US GDP would be *up to 4.4 percent higher* if more women and African Americans received STEM training and worked in related fields. Achieving equity in the technology sector is a win-win for everyone.

Ignoring the wealth gap facing Black residents in Austin will harm the city's future. The wealth gap harms every city's future, and we can't afford indifference. According to *The Road to Zero Wealth* report published by Prosperity Now and the Institute for Policy Studies, if things continue as they are, it will take 228 years for the average Black family to reach the level of wealth of a white family today. Not only that, but the median wealth (net worth) of Black Americans will fall to zero by 2053. In other words, median household wealth for Black families, which is currently under $2,000 and has dropped yearly since 2013, will bottom out in about thirty years. (By comparison, the median household wealth for white families has increased year after year and is predicted to be $132,000 by 2053; median wealth for Latino families will drop to zero by 2073.) The racial wealth gap is hollowing out the middle class in our country, particularly for Black and Latino families. If this national downward trend continues, the divide between asset-poor and asset-strong/upper-class households will diminish the middle class, leading to economic instability for many families. This outlook may impact Austin's Black lower-wealth and longstanding residents the most. And in that scenario, everyone loses. The Austin metro area officially became a majority-minority metro in 2020, with the percentage of the population identifying as "Non-Hispanic White alone" falling below 50 percent. The future economic prosperity in the city will depend on communities of color.

Knowing this should create a sense of urgency to address the racial wealth divide. Collaboration among economic developers, public and private sector leaders, and philanthropic organizations is essential. We need to reimagine the systems by which we create a dynamic economy. We cannot afford to ignore the threat to our collective economic well-being.

Comprehensive change is required. And that change is rooted in the *authentic* secret sauce ingredients: *talent, innovation, and place.* Our mindset, our behavior, what collaboration looks like, the policies we adopt, and the narrative that drives our thinking—all these must be reexamined. If we're willing to do that, the impact could be revolutionary. As a pacesetter, Austin could become the first city with a thriving tech ecosystem that closes the racial wealth gap of all its residents. That's a vision we can all share and actively participate in achieving.

We know what is not working. But we must also learn from what *is* working. The tale of two Austins—one in which some Black residents are not thriving, and one in which some Black residents are making important strides—tells us that while there are shadows there are also bright spots. A 2021 McKinsey report, *The State of Black Residents: The Relevance of Place to Racial Equity and Outcomes,* found that Black residents do best in high-growth hubs, such as Austin. The city clearly has the ingredients to start tipping the balance so the tale of two Black Austins becomes a single narrative of prosperity and inclusion.

Austin attracts people. And many of the people who move here become ambassadors of the city. In the nineties, I recruited my brother, sisters, and mom to move to Austin (my first talent attraction effort), and they settled in East Austin. One still lives there today. In 2015, my next recruitment event was David (partner) and Jordan and Juwan (my bonus sons), who love Austin. My dad—who went by Coach Aramious McDaniel—is in a heavenly place today; however, my special memories of him in Austin are connected to his community leadership and mentorship. He attended all the Texas Relays track and field events, supporting athletes he coached, and as founder of Waco Southern Panthers Youth Football and Cheer he attended many tournaments and many beloved family gatherings. These memories will hold a place in my heart forever. East Austin and Central East Austin still represent a blend of cultural vibrancy, community, and personal growth for me. They hold memories that shaped my past and will impact my future.

Onward!

Practical Solutions to Close the Racial Wealth Gap and Preserve Culture

Austin's history offers several lessons to any city or region determined to close inequity gaps and position itself as a pacesetter.

Policy:

- *Balance environmental preservation policies with the protection of under-represented communities.* Austin's efforts to protect its waters and green spaces are admirable and account for a considerable aspect of the city's ability to attract young workers and technology companies. But it has come at the expense of minority populations on the east and central-east side of the city. Protection in one area means development in another, and development that is highly concentrated in any location—particularly in neighborhoods that are majority Black or Hispanic—will inevitably change the identity and makeup of that neighborhood. Efforts must be made to make preserving at-risk communities as much of a priority as the environment.

- *Policymakers of all levels must implement anti-displacement measures.* Policies that foster inclusive development, stabilize communities of color and low-income communities, and address housing affordability and price increases are a must. Measures should also ensure that housing supply anticipates and meets the demands of low-income residents and communities of color.

Talent and Workforce:

- *Balance national talent recruitment efforts with local outreach and training to retain longtime residents.* Today, we see a tremendous push to bring and retain newcomers to a region. But it's equally important to turn an eye toward longstanding residents and discover their needs and preferences to ensure they stay and thrive. Many longtime residents are older and have roots that go back several generations. They have anchored the neighborhood for decades and spent years contributing to a sense of place, mainly if they are small-business owners or patrons who regularly support businesses, schools, and churches. They are the foundation for the next generation, for their children and grandchildren. The more stability provided for older generations, the easier it is for younger and future generations to thrive.
- *Develop affordable and livable conditions to attract tech talent.* This is important for all racial groups, as not all tech salaries—or those in tech-adjacent fields—can stretch far enough for a highly competitive housing market.
- *Support the development of workforce housing.* Likewise, employment opportunities beyond the tech sector are critical to any city's equitable growth, and improving availability and affordability across housing types for all income levels, including at-risk residents, helps narrow economic gaps.
- *Support equitable investment in early childhood and primary school education.* Acquiring core skills—academic, STEM, cognitive, social, and emotional—sets one on a course for success early in life. A city and state's commitment to its very youngest pays enormous dividends throughout

the child's lifespan, resulting in a resilient and prepared workforce. This begins with increasing access for all income levels to programs prioritizing early childhood development and improving outcomes for children.

- *Establish innovative tech training programs and nontraditional training delivery methods*. Looking outside the usual pathways helps residents find employment opportunities in high-growth, high-demand, and emerging industries. Consider nonprofits, churches, and school collaborations (like tech meetups) with employees who look like the members of the community being targeted. Promote tech jobs that do not require a bachelor's degree to remove barriers to opportunities. Consider partnering with national nonprofits like Cyversity, which works toward consistently representing women, underrepresented populations, and veterans in the cybersecurity industry. They offer scholarships, mentorship, and workforce development.
- *Advocate for increased support for reentry programs to ensure returning residents can access work and business opportunities*. Cities like Austin—robust and vibrant—are well-positioned to attract reentering residents. Efforts to re-welcome these residents through training and providing affordable housing can help restore communities.

Community, People-Centric, and Place-Based Engagement:

- *Resist tokenizing or burdening people of color. Instead, outreach strategies should be developed to bring diverse perspectives from the community.* Sometimes, an organization will ask a person of color (or a woman or member of the disabled or LGBTQ+ communities) to step into a role of visibility to illustrate a commitment to diversity, but without making changes toward inclusion. This is called tokenizing, and it is not inclusive engagement. In other instances, a person of color is put in a position to represent the voice of all people in a community and may not be adequately informed on the real issues (or even live in the neighborhood being discussed). I understand the impulse, but the most beneficial way to offer inclusion is to bring voices to the table (in person or virtually, providing opportunities to meet people where they are) who understand the target community, including its challenges and desired opportunities.
- *Make the local community and the public sector a strategic partner in the planning decisions of the business recruitment and retention strategies*

early on. Implement broad-based community engagement and empowerment with local nonprofit organizations that facilitate ways for the residents to participate. Maintain partnerships between local and diverse chambers of commerce, business associations, and regional and state economic agencies to develop and improve programs to recruit and retain businesses.

- *Understand the importance of place*. A 2021 McKinsey report, *The State of Black Residents: The Relevance of Place to Racial Equity and Outcomes*, found that Black residents with the best outcomes were those living in suburbs and exurbs (aka prosperous areas beyond the suburbs) and high-growth hubs, such as Austin. (Outcomes included life expectancy, income, and being in a management role.) The problem: Black residents are underrepresented in the very places where their outcomes are the highest. On the other hand, Black residents are overrepresented in places where outcomes are poorer, places like megacities (New York, Atlanta, and Washington, DC, where costs of living are higher) and rural counties. The solution may be twofold: attract and retain Black residents in places where they are proven to thrive—and provide support in ways that increase parity—and improve the factors in megacities that are known to affect outcomes, such as housing affordability, access to insurance, and commuting time and cost. The goal in inclusive placemaking is a commitment to longtime residents and businesses to create affordable options for them to remain, and to preserve the uniqueness of neighborhoods and commercial districts by creating opportunities to learn and promote the history and culture of diversified communities. A spotlight also needs to be shone on the financial penalties that can occur due to one's zip code. For example, premiums for auto, home, and rental insurance are higher in zip codes considered high-risk, resulting in disparities in wealth accumulation. A 2017 study by Consumer Reports and ProPublica, an investigative reporting nonprofit, found that auto insurers not only charge more in high-risk neighborhoods, they also charge more in predominantly minority neighborhoods compared to nonminority high-risk neighborhoods. Advocating for policies that promote fair pricing—regardless of your zip code—is one way to help change discriminatory practices.
- *Use place-based data to inform policymakers and residents in order to create a more equitable community*. To identify the true needs of a community, look to local data and the lived experiences of those who are

affected. Organizations such as Measure Austin provide research-based information to help community engagement have the most beneficial impact. Educating both policymakers and the people who live with the disparities will help lead to real solutions to reduce the financial penalties. For example: providing financial literacy training (i.e., how to increase credit scores to seven hundred or above and identifying financial assistance programs) and improving full economic participation. Operation Hope is one such program. Founded by entrepreneur and financial expert John Hope Bryant, the organization's free workshops educate participants in how to manage money, raise credit scores, budgeting, and more. Let the data lead you so that your initiatives are quantitative and qualitative.

Innovation and Entrepreneurship:

- *Create business hubs targeting underrepresented founders by providing low-cost and flexible space in growth centers.* If your goal is *not* to create yet another tech-bro theme park, make economic, gender, and racial diversity a part of the blueprint from day one. Designate low-cost and affordable office and retail space for solopreneurs of color when planning a tech hub. This creates an environment that will nurture the next generation of business owners. This could include pop-up retail space or a market-style space where vendors rotate in and out quarterly. The Jackson Tech District in Jackson, Mississippi, launched by STEM entrepreneur Nashlie Sephus, PhD, is an innovative model for how to do this. The project will transform abandoned buildings downtown into a hub that includes residential space, a grocery store, commercial space, an event space, a tech incubator lab, and more—all aimed at lifting Black-owned businesses and families and furthering STEM opportunities for people of color. It's a live-work-play ecosystem. Sephus is also the founder of the Bean Path, a Jackson-based nonprofit devoted to technical upskilling and exposure in the community, and she has woven the foundation's mission into the hub plan.
- *Tech and innovation* hubs should support local businesses by creating a "buy local" initiative, procuring goods, services, food, etc. from the community. This way, local entrepreneurs can continue to prosper along with the tech companies.

- *Create a tech consortium* of underrepresented groups that brings together founders, startups, anchor companies, and educators committed to driving progress, innovation, and closing the racial wealth gap. The nonprofit Austin Urban Technology Movement (AUTMHQ), founded by social entrepreneur Michael Ward, is doing this work, connecting Black and Hispanic community members—high school students, small-business owners, and college students—with the technology companies and resources needed to close the digital equity gap. AUTMHQ facilitates internships, apprenticeships, mentorships, job placement, industry networking events, and corporate education.

CHAPTER **SEVEN**

Upsetting the Apple Cart

Innovation and Disruption

We all know how pervasive the conversation around innovation and disruption has become. Once rarely mentioned in business and economics, the terms are now so overused they have become objects of parody. "Word 'Innovate' Said 650,000 Times at SXSW So Far," one *Onion* headline read during South by Southwest (SXSW). "People are saying the word 'innovate' at a rate of 8.2 times per second," the article went on, quoting a fictitious SXSW official, "and at that pace we can estimate it will be uttered approximately 24 million times before the festival ends." *The Guardian* dubbed "disruption" to be "Silicon Valley's emptiest buzzword;" *Fortune* implored it was "time to retire" the word; and *Forbes* argued it was "lazy and wrong terminology" co-opted by every startup under the sun, who were utilizing it in ways Clayton Christensen, author of *Innovator's Dilemma,* himself had not intended. Usage continues unabated, however, as even a cursory browsing of a SXSW event program can confirm.

When overuse strips words of their meaning, it's hard to return to how they were first used, how they were first received. Both *innovation* and *disruption* have historically been treated with a healthy dose of skepticism, representative of challenges to the social order. Trying new things (innovating) was inevitably disruptive, potentially causing more harm than good. Trying something new when what you have in place is working threatens the existing process and entails risk that many feel is unnecessary. When we take the idea of disruption out of its trendy SXSW context, who would wish for it? Aren't we already stressed enough without welcoming more disruption in our lives? Of course, these are now watchwords employed by entrepreneurs convinced their ideas will revolutionize (another tired word) the market. SXSW provides a forum for that excitement. We claim to welcome the turmoil, at least as long as we are not personally threatened by the changes. And the city of Austin, host to the international festival, invites innovation and disruption, if not always in practice, certainly in spirit. We're "weird," after all.

A more recent, and more relevant, understanding of these concepts is present in Joseph Schumpeter's midcentury ideas surrounding "creative destruction"—the eternal process of dismantling (or destroying) old production methods to make way for updated, innovative ones. These ideas prefigure Christensen's argument in *Innovator's Dilemma* regarding "disruptive innovation" (innovations which create a new market and eventually replace the traditional market). The economic framework helps us understand how imperative invention and reinvention is to an industry's survival, even while they implicitly reveal that disruption comes at a cost. We can see how lethal it is to ignore innovation, even at its most disruptive. The list of well-known firms who, due to disruptive innovations, either have disappeared or are merely hanging on is long.

Silicon Valley, of course, staked the original claim to tech innovation. While innovation was never restricted exclusively to "technology," there is no doubt that the rapid unfolding of Moore's Law (that the number of transistors on a microchip doubles about every two years) and the processing speed of the computer chip would quickly upend entire industries. That Austin was among the early adopters of this explosive change had everything to do with Kozmetsky, as we saw in chapters 1 and 3. Yes, Silicon Valley realized the economic benefits of tech innovation first and most dramatically in the growth of venture capital. Kozmetsky, however, was seeking more than just capital. He wanted innovation to be seen in a larger social context. By including innovation in the name of IC^2, and by imploring the city to embrace the concept, he dramatically extended its implications beyond the private sector. He understood that innovation in the public and academic sectors, as well, yield the greatest benefits for everyone involved. This open mindset, this connectivity between the triad of public-private-academic, encouraged all parties to shoulder the risks of disruption together and enjoy the successes together, and it set the stage for Austin's future wins (and, yes, a few losses—more on that later). Kozmetsky's vision for innovation just so happened to dovetail with the Stanford Research

Institute (SRI) suggestion in their 1985 report that Austin create a "climate for science and technology innovation and entrepreneurial activity by nurturing new startups, creating business incubators, encouraging spinoffs, and increasing venture capital availability." Together, these visions ensured that innovation and its offspring—disruption—would be built into Austin's DNA for decades to come. These timely, consequential prescriptions for growth and development also set the stage for one of Austin's defining features, the annual festival whose entire theme is innovation: South by Southwest Interactive.

SXSW: From Innovation to Disruption and Beyond

SXSW—the supersized annual festival that started with live music and then morphed into interactive and film—didn't spring up as some small grassroots musicians' collective and organically evolve into the giant it is today. And it certainly didn't happen in a vacuum. It came together strategically and collaboratively and in an environment that had been seeded and nourished for decades by thought leaders committed to innovation and unafraid of disruption. It happened in a city where all the elements of success were in place for it to explode: a well-established and burgeoning music scene, and a broad-minded private sector player—the Austin Chamber of Commerce—which had embraced Kozmetsky's vision for collaboration between industry, academia, and the public sector.

It's hard to overstate the importance of the Austin Chamber of Commerce's posture when describing the inception and meteoric rise of SXSW, so I'll begin there. By the 1980s, Austin's chamber had evolved in three directions that paved the way for SXSW to take hold and for the tech industry to explode (and which would later find its own way into SXSW's universe). First, the chamber was chaired by the visionary Vic Mathias, who held the title for twenty-six years, beginning in 1956. With Mathias at the helm, the chamber had adopted a decidedly forward-thinking stance. Mathias, whose name has, since 2014, adorned the east lawn of the municipal park where each year so many SXSW musicians perform (at Vic Mathias Shores, or Auditorium Shores), was instrumental in pivoting Austin's economy from one that revolved primarily around agriculture, the University of Texas, and the state capital to one of manufacturing—but not in the oil-and-gas image of Houston. In 2003, a reflective Mathias noted that electronics manufacturing—forward-looking, innovative—was the ticket, as it was a "clean" industry and not a "smokestack" one. Austin, in other words, would actively resist any appearance of a Gulf Coast skyline. Pike Powers, a fixture at the chamber for decades, reiterated this point. "Early on we decided we were not going to take on companies or groups that polluted the air or water," he said in a 2012 interview. "Having clean air to breathe and clean water to drink was a valuable community asset." The "clean" ethos Mathias and his team had embraced in the 1950s had helped advance ideas of supporting technology firms which was being borne out. But as of yet, artistic industries, such as the music sector, hadn't yet seen a boost from the "clean" ethos, a fact which was on the minds of many chamber members.

The second way the chamber had changed: It had begun to take "quality of life" very seriously in its efforts to shape the city's future. Quality of life, however defined, had been an obvious component of Austin's self-image since its inception. Political ecologist Paul Robbins, who in the early aughts interviewed Mathias, noted that the former Austin chamber president had observed how quality of life was one of the things he believed attracted technology companies to the city in the first place. Robbins wrote, too, of how IBM, which had had a presence in the city since the late 1930s, but not yet a manufacturing one, sent one of its representatives to Austin on a site-selection mission in 1966. Among the selector's criteria were the usual suspects—infrastructure, cost of doing business, and so on—and a more novel one: quality of life. The chamber started to awaken to the notion that the city's quality of life was not a mere accessory but an engine, a powerful instrument for attracting and keeping people and industry alike.

Speed was the third change taking place inside the chamber. Whereas the institution "had traditionally propounded a slow-growth policy," wrote Barry Shank, who chronicled the rise of Austin's music scene in *Dissonant Identities*, it had by the mid-1980s "developed into a fast-growth, pro-development advocate." Susan Engelking, an economic developer and green transit advocate with whom I worked briefly and whose thoughts mirrored my own, noted this sense of urgency when in 1994 she wrote of the city's development over the previous fifteen years. "At the heart of Austin's approach to economic development policymaking is the "high value . . . placed on the ability to mobilize quickly and act on opportunities."

These three cards—a refocus on "clean" industry, a recognition of quality of life's indispensableness, and an urgent posture—were all finally in play when musician Ernest Gammage first approached the chamber in the early 1980s, full of ideas about how to put Austin on the map not just as a technopolis, but also as an entertainment powerhouse. Gammage, a University of Texas finance graduate and president of the Texas Music Association's Austin chapter, had played in numerous bands since arriving in Austin in 1963 and was a fixture in the city's iconic music venues in the 1970s. In a stroke of luck, David Lord, whom the chamber had recently hired to head its tourism bureau, was there when Gammage came knocking. Lord was interested in turning Austin's music scene into more than simply a lure for itinerants. He played an important role in placing Gammage and his ideas within SRI's framework, and also in synthesizing them with the chamber's newer identity as an institution teed up for "clean" industry clusters, mindful of quality of life and geared for fast-paced growth. Lord was also the person who gets credited for Austin's catchy slogan, rooted in an estimate of the city's impressive number of live-music venues per capita: "The Live Music Capital of the World." While Austinites have long debated who coined the slogan, and whereas the city council would only officially adopt it more than five years afterward, Lord was the first to get it into print, in a 1985 *Billboard* magazine ad.

It was with these players in place and in this milieu that in 1985, the chamber—excited by Gammage and Lord's vision—created the Austin Music Advisory Committee (AMAC) to take advantage of Austin's already-burgeoning live music scene and expand it into ancillary (and profitable) elements such as production and management. AMAC's mission, according to its founding initiative, *Austin Music: Into the Future* (1985), was to "identify and describe the Austin music industry's current status; to identify and define problems facing the industry; [and] to develop possible solutions and recommendations for those problems."

The report itself reads as if could have been written by Michael Porter, the Harvard professor and proponent of industry clusters. "Austin's pool of performing talent is extraordinary for a city of its size," it read. "However . . . the industry's ancillary components—record companies, production facilities, etc.—have not developed at the same pace. This absence of an adequately developed support structure has forced many local musicians to leave Austin." How might Austin cultivate another kind of "clean" cluster, the AMAC seemed to have been wondering, one of music production, one that might rival the likes of New York, Los Angeles, and Nashville?

It's important to note that, on a parallel track, SRI was delivering its blueprint for technology-centered growth and development for Austin. So, occurring simultaneously were grand plans rooted in the two innovative fields that eventually defined Austin worldwide—technology and music. This was no coincidence. SRI's report had explicitly recommended greater support of the city's young music industry, and clear in the AMAC report's language was SRI's influence: "The music industry offers Austin its most fertile ground for developing an 'opportunity economy,'" the report read, employing a term Stanford had used in its own report's title, "simply because so many of the necessary ingredients are already in place."

The assorted contributors to the AMAC report—Gammage, Mike Tolleson, and Phyllis Krantzman among them—knew those ingredients well. Tolleson, an entertainment lawyer, was cofounder of the Armadillo World Headquarters, which, though now shuttered, had spread Austin's signature "progressive country" sound nationwide via *Austin City Limits,* the longest-running television music series (and producer of Austin's *other* giant music festival, ACL). Krantzman had written her UT master's thesis on Austin's entertainment industry and in the process had surveyed hundreds of performers to capture an impression of the "average Austin musician."

Despite the unverifiable claim that Austin was "the live music capital of the world," live music played a comparatively smaller role in the AMAC's planning than did recorded, produced music. That's because, at the vision's core, was an image of Austin with a "support structure," a cluster, similar to those of other music cities like Nashville and Los Angeles, with major labels, studios, and so on. Economically, this focus on produced music made greater sense in the predigital era, before anyone could accurately predict how, and how soon, the internet would bring the recorded-music industry to its knees and thereby make live music more important than ever. And—spoiler alert—even with the eventual support of the city council, which had originally been uncharacteristically slow to move on AMAC's ideas, the effort to transform Austin into a music city akin to others ultimately failed. "By the late 1990s," wrote urban geographer Eliot Tretter, "it was apparent that no viable music industry full of recording studios, labels, lawyers, and

A&R representatives had emerged in Austin . . . [and] that nothing of that scale was probably ever going to materialize." Yet without the chamber's forward-looking and innovative stance, the efforts of Gammage and team may have stalled, the chamber may never have formed AMAC in the first place, and SXSW may have taken years longer to materialize, if at all.

That the dream of rivaling Nashville or Los Angeles never became reality was in fact fortunate. Free online music-sharing platforms changed the landscape beyond what anyone could imagine. Austin's "music industry" would likely have fallen victim to that disruption. The efforts of Gammage, Lord, and the AMAC, however, were not at all in vain. "An opportunity economy begins with an abundant local resource," the AMAC report had read. "Through mutual cooperation and planning, this resource is developed to its maximum potential." That "abundant local resource" was of course the city's deep talent pool of musicians, and in Austin, that "mutual cooperation"—that spirit of creative collaboration—was itself an abundant local resource, one harnessed certainly since Mathias's time but before it, too. From those same cooperative principles emerged SXSW, which debuted two years after the AMAC report was inked, and which drew heavily from the report's findings.

While SXSW was not a chamber initiative, the willing embrace by the broader community spoke volumes. This acceptance by the city and the chamber was further evidence that an "ecosystem"—a cluster of internal support and mutual reinforcement—was deeply rooted in Austin. A festival and conference that is today well known as a forum for creativity, innovation, and (yes) disruption was rooted in those same values. Roland Swenson, a band manager and *Austin Chronicle* staffer, was part of that ecosystem. Swenson had contributed—as had Gammage, Tolleson, and Krantzman—to the findings of AMAC report, *Austin Music: Into the Future*. But whereas Lord was busy imagining a "Live Music Capital of the World" built around music production, Swenson seemed driven by a more literal interpretation of the slogan. In 1986, the chamber had sponsored a booth at the New Music Seminar in New York City to highlight Austin's music scene; soon afterward, an attempt to establish an Austin offshoot of the event failed. Seizing an opportunity, however, Swenson—along with *Austin Chronicle* cofounders Louis Black and Nick Barbaro and others—decided they didn't need New York. They could put on a conference themselves, and what emerged the next year—the first SXSW—was an event primed not only to resist the tech disruptions soon to hit the music-production industry (digitization), but to celebrate them, to even become stronger because of them.

As with so many complaints about "the way things used to be" we would be remiss if we didn't join in the lament about missing the early days of SXSW. Armbands at ten dollars rather than $1,000. Johnny Cash or Willie Nelson at the Continental Club for the price of two beers. Listening to Mike Judge, Richard Linklater, and Quentin Tarantino talk movies without having to wait for hours to get in. But, as with so much of Austin's history, that's the inevitable price of success.

Seven years later, in 1994, the number of music venues at SXSW had doubled, artists showcased nearly tripled, and workshops and panels more than quadrupled. A major development in conference programming had occurred, too, one that brought the event back full circle to the discussions in the 1980s about both music and technology innovation—the inauguration of the festival's first dedicated interactive component.

In the 1990s, many innovations highlighted at SXSW Interactive now seem quaint—CD-ROMs and so on. Yet as the World Wide Web flourished, discussions of piecemeal innovations began to take a backseat to those of full-scale, industry-wide disruptions. Not until SXSW 2000, however, once Napster—which stoked fear into the music-production industry—emerged from an Austin-Bergstrom International Airport terminal to debut its MP3 digital file-sharing technology, which would compete with the live music shows, did the event's conversations on innovation and disruption truly begin to accelerate. "It was fascinating," reported the *A. V. Club*, noting a palpable change since the previous year's conference, "to see the topics of panel discussions shift from 1999's 'Downloading On the Upswing: Trouble for the Music Industry?' to 2000's 'What's My Business Model?' during which representatives of dotcom companies such as the bandwidth-sucking, MP3-distributing rogue Napster imparted marketing wisdom."

Easy to forget now is how radical Napster really was, introducing free, instant, unlimited tracks to everyone with an internet connection. "The enormous influence of Web music on the music segment of South by Southwest," wrote *The New York Times* in 2000, "exposed the ferocious effects of new technology on the record business." One SXSW festivalgoer, a music journalist, captured the atmosphere well: "It's chaos out there right now. . . . This was going to revolutionize the music business. I wanted front-row seats." Because Austin had inadvertently failed to avoid turning itself into a music-production mecca like Nashville or New York, however, as envisioned fifteen years earlier, neither the chaos nor ferocity of the digital revolution left many in the city's music establishment bothered: The annual *Austin Chronicle* "Best Of" poll in 2000 named the "Napster fracas" one of the year's best music events.

Since Napster, startups began eyeing SXSW as a launchpad. Twitter (now X) in 2007 had been live for months without much success, for instance, but marketing it at SXSW gave it a second coming. SXSW, said cofounder Evan Williams in 2011, "just chose to blow it up." Knowing that "hallways were where the action was," Williams and team paid $11,000 to showcase the social-media platform via the Austin Convention Center's countless flat-panel TVs. Festivalgoers could not get enough: "When you're down at [SXSW Interactive] zipping to and from different venues, what's the best way to stay in touch with your friends?" reported *Wired* magazine. "This year . . . it's Twitter."

Eventually, of course, disruptors get disrupted themselves. Napster, whose user base once topped sixty million, filed for bankruptcy in 2002, a year after a legal injunction precipitated by a complaint by musical group Metallica ordered the company offline. (Afterward, the platform struggled to find a viable business model, was eventually absorbed into another musical service, and has since virtually disappeared.) Foursquare (the location app), Highlight (a social networking app), and Meerkat (a mobile livestreaming app)—all launched at SXSW—suffered similar fates. X, meanwhile, is valued in the billions of dollars and is intricately entwined with another Austin newcomer, Elon Musk.

None of this is to suggest that we should be dismissive of Napster. It was a radical platform. It afforded us the opportunity to rethink everything we thought we knew about the way music existed in our lives—and not only from a business perspective. The concept of "recorded" music was reimagined. Instead of being dependent on a device wedded to a storage medium that could play it back, it became possible to "stream" music. In short, the idea that music was not dependent on a traditional physical thing that we kept in a sleeve or in a plastic case was a radical transformation. The impact of this thinking, long in the making but without a business model, exploded at SXSW. The line between music and technology began to blur.

It is now unthinkable for musicians not to consider social media outlets for their creative output. The disruption is now the norm.

Decades after its inception, SXSW itself has become ripe for disruption. The event has "lost its community of innovation," said one executive in 2018, explaining why his company stopped sending people there. "There is no uniqueness. It's like the same bland shopping mall on every corner." I was also among the advocates for change. SXSW "can't continue to grow and have the same kind of dynamic that has made it really attractive in the past," I told the *San Antonio Express-News* in 2015. "You'd really compromise that ability and turn it into something it wasn't intended to be." It would be wise, I suggested, for the event to choose alternatives for its staging. By way of example, I contrasted it with two very different festival styles I'd seen in Germany. If SXSW wanted to get back to its roots, it could look to the contemporary art festival held every five years in Kassel, which had resisted becoming "too corporate," as critics have suggested SXSW had. Or it could go the Oktoberfest route—an annual extravaganza whose unifying theme is beer and that keeps growing while primarily focused on profit and attendance. There was a certain snarkiness in that comparison, but it struck a chord. Is SXSW just a party, an excuse to hang? Or is it of enduring cultural significance? Evidence of an expanded model is already taking shape. In 2023 and 2024, SXSW was hosted in Sydney, Australia. In economic terms, the ultimate export.

Criticism is hardly new to the organization. Its website notes the growing "resistance" to the conference. Ten years ago, in 2012, a self-aware panel titled "Social Media Is a Bubble and SXSW Is a Fad" had many, reported *The Irish Times,* talking about how they "wanted SXSW to go back to the way it used to be years ago, when it was a laidback spring break for developers and designers in a cool city in Texas." In 2014, Managing Director Roland Swenson, still with the event nearly thirty years since the *Austin Music: Into the Future* report, remarked on its own future: "If SXSW doesn't keep changing and evolving, it will wither and die." In other words, if there isn't a commitment to innovation—and even disruption—the city's most defining and successful cultural event in decades could become just another feature of the city that we take for granted without giving it a lot of thought, the tech equivalent of Austin's Sixth Street, known for bars and drunken frat parties.

This is not an incidental observation. It is no exaggeration to say that SXSW has been a major contributor to Austin's international reputation. It has also had a transformative effect on the city itself. In 2019, before the pandemic, the economic impact of SXSW on Austin was calculated to be over a third of a billion dollars. Beyond those numbers, however, was the growing sense that Austin's "openness" had moved to a different level. The city was no longer a place to be discovered—both in the sense that you had found something others weren't aware of and also in the sense that you could be discovered there. It now was a place on the global cultural map for musicians, filmmakers, tech startups, and innovative thinkers. Bars and hotels suddenly took on an air of sophistication previously unimaginable. After the remodel of the Four Seasons (once Texas-themed), the Driskill remains the only longstanding hotel with a distinctively local flavor. (Newer hipster hotels such as the San Jose and the Hotel Magdalena—both on trendy South Congress Avenue—are gilded, unironically, with nostalgic Austin music-themed decór.) From Rainey Street (a hipper, breezier alternative Sixth Street) to Mueller (a beautiful mixed-use, urban-style community at the site of the former Austin airport) to the Domain (think Fifth Avenue shopping meets upscale condo living), Austin has entered the realm of urban chic that gives longtime Austin residents pause. SXSW has everything to do with that change.

SXSW has, in effect, become as synonymous with Austin's identity as its heritage institutions: the university and the Texas capitol. Its connection to the city's traditional music scene (of which *Austin City Limits* was a major part) and to the tech sector are baked into its formula. Regardless of which direction SXSW takes, its identification with Austin is as powerful a marketing message as any community could hope for. SXSW is a brand, pure and simple.

Behind every brand is a formula, and for Austin's SXSW, the idea of "creativity" is perhaps a better characterization than the appropriately mocked notions of innovation and disruption. I see it each time I go, beginning with my move to Austin in 1994, the same year the Interactive portion launched. One SXSW adviser captured this spirit well when he said the conference "was meant to bring creators together and spark cultural fires that would last long after the event itself." A Professional Convention Management Association executive, the kind of person who makes conferences their business, was quoted in *USA Today* describing what made SXSW "unusual" among its peers: The conference, she said, is "much more about figuring out how to get people to talk to each other and learn from each other." The term "cross-pollination" is sometimes bandied about, too, to describe the intellectual and practical magic that occurs there each year.

This "unusual" trait makes the challenges facing SXSW's future good ones to have. How to be creative and how to grow, how to do so while preserving what made something promising to begin with, and how to mitigate or reverse the developments that over time may have threatened or diluted those promises—these are difficult questions to answer. Yet as tricky as they are, for organizations and cities alike, they are simpler than questions of where to even begin or how to make up for ground lost to inaction. Perhaps most important and challenging question of all: How can cities best tap the resources unique to them? These local raw materials—whether it's a pool of talented artists or an industry cluster of businesses—not only make innovation possible, they also equip cities with the tools necessary to absorb or adapt to the disruptions, technological and social, that will face them in any case.

The desire to emulate Austin, to find the magic formula that will ensure growth and prosperity on a par with Austin's, is understandable. While there is no secret that, once revealed, will transform a city that is losing population to one that becomes a talent magnet, there are lessons to be learned. The answer to "Why Austin?" may be best approached by understanding the forces that work *against* innovation and creativity. SXSW could not easily take root in a community resistant to change. This is what I learned in a very roundabout way in Racine, Wisconsin.

Some years ago, I turned on my garbage disposal and recoiled at the metallic screech that followed. A spoon had slipped down the drain and been chewed up. Nothing unusual, and easily forgotten. But by an odd coincidence I was soon to meet the very company whose product mauled my spoon.

We were working on a project in Racine, Wisconsin—a project that at its core was about innovation in manufacturing. As all consultancies do, we conducted one-on-one interviews with major employers in the region, companies that included S. C. Johnson, Modine, and Twin Disc. Another of those major employers was InSinkErator, a division of Emerson since the 1960s, and the world's leading producer of garbage disposals.

After our general questions were answered—questions regarding workforce availability, regulatory concerns, and logistics—I couldn't resist asking one of the company's engineers, "Why did my spoon need to be chewed up? Wasn't there a way that could have been prevented?" I had been thinking about my mangled spoon and wondered why a relatively simple sensor could not have solved that problem. To my surprise, the engineer took my personal question seriously. Via email, we continued to explore the topic—until word arrived from senior management that this exchange had reached an end.

It was an abrupt stop to what I thought was a promising discussion about innovation. Was it possible that to pursue such an improvement would be unwelcome for reasons having nothing to do with its practicality? As I delved deeper into the question of garbage disposals, a different picture began to emerge.

Changing the design features of something as mundane as a garbage disposal could upset a delicate balance. Might it expose the firm to market threats from larger companies better equipped to deliver such a feature? Would it be more logical to control the existing production processes and supply chain, and maintain the status quo, than to upset the business model through product improvements?

The company still exists—and flourishes—despite what seemed to be an oddly defensive mentality. There was a lesson to be learned here, one that needs to be given further thought. The first part of the lesson is the difference between corporate innovation and entrepreneurial innovation. If I'm in the garbage disposal business—a well-established profit center residing in a large consumer products corporation—what does innovation do for me? Yes, the consumer might be better served by a new design with technological improvements, but with what benefits to shareholders? Resistance to change, it must be noted, is at least as common as the desire to innovate. Not only is change difficult, it entails very specific business risks, not the least of which is that when we open the door to new technology we may put our own business at risk. This may well have been the case with InSinkErator. Once you introduce even a small improvement into an existing device, you open yourself to unexpected risk. And in this case it turns out that there is much more at stake. The United States is the only country with widespread use of garbage disposals in their kitchens. There are reasons for this, each of which poses a fundamental threat to the existing business model.

Why, for example, do we not compost? Why do we tolerate clogged drains resulting from the misuse of this "appliance"? Why do we sometimes chew up our silverware? Why, in other words, are we willing to pay for something whose "convenience" is outweighed by its disadvantages? From the point of view of the company, these questions needn't be answered. Consumers rarely pay directly for garbage disposals; they are part of a series of amenities that represent only a rounding error in the cost of a home. A company producing such an amenity (or failing to produce one!) isn't dependent on anything more than the buyer's tacit acceptance of the status quo. The larger point is that innovation often entails threats not only to our current business model but also to our social framework. This pattern is not unique to InSinkErator. I discovered it at other companies as well. VPs for research are quick to acknowledge that a company's multitude of patents (and much of its intellectual property) would probably never see the light of day.

It would be wrong to single out Racine, or southeastern Wisconsin, as particularly resistant to innovation. The difficulty of building out an entrepreneurial ecosystem based exclusively on corporate risk-taking is universal. In other words, you can't rely on corporations to willingly innovate and take on the risks of disruption. InSinkErator—and scores of other companies—do not necessarily benefit from the disruption that new technology brings in its wake. In fact, such innovation and disruption could spell their end; knowing that, many companies that do risk innovation and disruption fortify themselves through market strategies. When we think of companies most closely associated with disruption, we see that as soon as they have profited from that disruption they move rapidly to close the market not only to competitors, but also to disruption from within. And this shouldn't surprise us. Being enamored of disruption is to ignore market realities on the one hand and the social costs on the other. The goals of a corporation are not the same as those of the entrepreneur.

My experience in Racine, Wisconsin, is not only of interest to understanding how businesses succeed or fail. The interaction between innovative businesses and the communities in which they operate is central to successful economic development. The success of an entrepreneurial ecosystem—which is made up of both creative, innovative individuals and corporations with sizable market access—rests on that understanding. We build models on certain assumptions and then build an entire infrastructure to reinforce those assumptions. And they continue to work for us. Until they don't. Nevertheless, innovation is essential not only to the survival of businesses but also to how those businesses relate to the communities in which they operate. And as the InSinkErator example makes clear, it also requires us to think about how "disruption" complicates the picture.

I understand the hesitations of civic leaders resistant to innovation and disruption, just as I understood the hesitations of the firm that built my kitchen's garbage disposal. Ambitious collective undertakings of all kinds warrant a degree of caution. The long-term costs of stepping into uncertain territory can seem steep compared to the immediate benefits of clinging to the known. And it is true that even institutions that have embraced innovation have fallen. Sears, for instance, exited Austin in 2018 after more than fifty years in Texas' capital, citing, along with its bankruptcy announcement, a hope that by thinning its retail outlets nationwide it would be "better able to compete with Amazon." It first appears to be a typical story of a brick-and-mortar incumbent bested by a high-tech entrant, yet it is easy to forget that Sears attempted very early on to enter the digital arena. "Prodigy," *CBS News* reported, referring to the now-defunct online portal created in 1984, "was a joint venture between Sears, IBM, and CBS, eleven years before Jeff Bezos founded Amazon. It was just a little ahead of its time."

Sears did not fail, however, because of one smart yet premature experiment in innovation. The company ultimately "needed to reinvent themselves in a really disruptive way," said Don Katz, author of a book on the firm, when commenting on its downfall. "It just didn't happen." Sears is not unique in this regard, either. A small, nimble player with a powerful tool can take out a giant, as thought leaders have long told us, and never is that truer than when the giant, resting on his laurels, takes his gifts and his position for granted. Mike D of the Beastie Boys noted such a dynamic when interviewed by the filmmakers behind *Downloaded*, a 2013 documentary that chronicled Napster's own rise and fall. "Big innovations rarely come from the big companies that are already dominating the game," he said. "The music business is a great, great example of that—of just complacency being a total death sentence." Urbanist Jane Jacobs captured the phenomenon, too, when in *Cities and the Wealth of Nations* she quoted an MIT social scientist who found remarkable the "innovative capacity" of smaller firms, a capacity, the scientist said, "only a few exceptional giant firms . . . have so far been able to achieve on a grand scale."

Yet despite how historically innovative Sears was, it has not proven to be one of these "exceptional giants," and the problem with its Prodigy venture was not necessarily that it was too soon; it was that it was too little. Innovation, as I stress to cities resistant to it, is not a mere event, a singular failed experiment, nor is it a mindset that once developed and proven fruitful in the past can endure forgotten or mismanaged into the future. It is a process, not an achievement; a way of being more than one of doing; a value more than a behavior, though it is that, too; an organism rather than a stone.

Jacobs, who championed the dynamic interaction of people, and Karl Popper—who believed that open-mindedness is critical to a community's ability to thrive—are often cited together, and for good reason. An open society, like a "commercial" one, welcomes "strangers and aliens," and calls to mind Kozmetsky's model. Welcoming outsiders and turning them into insiders is a virtue, yes, and is a stopgap at preventing population and economic decline. But even more instrumental is a community's ability to facilitate innovation. Open societies are innovative societies, where deeply held assumptions are regularly questioned and where disruption is both inevitable and—ultimately—embraced. And like companies that cling too long to a predetermined model, closed societies will be disrupted.

Indeed, the more open a society, the more it primes itself for creative collaboration, the kind that spawned the growth and development of Austin as both a technological and artistic hub. It is little wonder, then, why creativity was the third term, along with innovation and capital, that George Kozmetsky ultimately adopted to name his institute. In fact, it seems as if Kozmetsky considered the progression from creativity to innovation a path-dependent one: Creativity, according to biographer Monty Jones, meant to Kozmetsky the "invention of ideas or methods," whereas innovation meant the "application of those inventions to problem-solving."

As cities become more open, creative, and innovative—and as they export the fruits of their creativity and innovation—the faster they grow. And it is at this point that the question of how to deal with the social disruptions borne by technology becomes paramount. As we will see in a later chapter, the most profound and far-reaching economic effects include the threat to the traditional employment model. What are "jobs" for if they can be performed better by automation or done away with completely through AI? We can see this as an abstract discussion, or as one to be dealt with on a national policy level, or as a distinct and specific challenge for a community. Will the city ignore disruptions to the job market (along with other disruptions that include energy, transportation, and all the other things challenged by AI) or will it make itself resilient to them? To borrow from Nassim Nicholas Taleb, the famed Lebanese philosopher, trader, and risk analyst, will a city go even further and become more "antifragile"? That is, will it become more than resilient to the disruptions caused by its own industries, and thus stronger because of them?

I say it is a question, a choice, because while a city's openness, creativity, and innovation may catalyze disruption, those things do not guarantee resilience or antifragility in disruption's wake. Or, they may guarantee it, but for a few, and not the many.

What should matter, then, from a civic and economic-development standpoint is, first, how open, creative, and innovative a city is to begin with, because those same conditions and forces that lead to disruption also equip a city to deal with its less-than-desirable consequences. Second, how many of a city's residents are equipped to withstand or resist disruption's downsides—among them displacement, higher costs of living, traffic congestion, environmental threats, and the unrest and division that income- and education-based stratification often engenders among a populace. And third, how many could not only withstand or resist such downsides, but experience a net benefit—grow stronger—because of the opportunities disruption brings?

Yes, Austin may score well in its response to the first question—it is inarguably open, creative, and innovative by many important measures. The second and third are more problematic, that is withstanding disruptions and even becoming stronger because of them. Since the late 1970s, Austin has struggled with its evolution from "sleepy college town" to technopolis. George Kozmetsky and his fellow University of Texas colleagues David Gibson and Raymond Smilor predicted these struggles when they wrote about a possible "shattering of the consensus that originally made the technopolis possible" in their prescient 1989 paper, *Creating the Technopolis*. They wrote, too, of how, "With each new economic development activity there [will] likely to be some community group that [feels] the loss of some, from their view central, aspect of Austin that made the city unique, desirable, and affordable. Such a list of 'losses' might include more days when Barton Springs Pool, the city's best swimming location, is closed because the spring-fed pool is too full of silt from runoff at construction sites; the loss of landmarks, such as the Armadillo World Headquarters, where music greats and yet-to-be greats performed in a casual, intimate setting; and the loss of affordable land and housing."

The debate about the risks and rewards of technology is constant and contentious. Contributors to the 2012 book *Inequity in the Technopolis,* which explored the impact of social and economic disruptions in Austin since the 1980s, found the above quote to be dismissive of groups resisting growth. Based on my conversations over the years with both Kozmetsky and Gibson, they in fact cared deeply for all those things—the environment, music culture, affordability, and so on—and there is little reason to believe that whatever "dismissiveness" that could be inferred was the result of callousness or indifference. More likely is that their attitude was rooted in an optimism for what technology, when developed and deployed by institutions both public and private, could accomplish. The essayists writing in *Inequity* touched on this optimism, too: "The three professors argued," they wrote, referring to Kozmetsky, Gibson, and Smilor, that "individuals working together in the new economy would alleviate social ills."

Gibson, in 2013, wrote of how the wealth generated in Austin during the preceding decades had, in fact, alleviated some of those ills, "in terms of financial gifts to UT Austin and other regional educational institutions, providing angel funding for new waves of entrepreneurs in emerging industries, and other charity and philanthropic contributions." Citing the *Inequity* contributors, however, he recognized, too, how the "growing economic and educational divide is an increasingly important challenge for the Capital City in particular and for Texas in general."

Critics may argue that philanthropy and charity are not enough and that systemic, regulatory change must also occur in order to address those growing economic challenges Gibson and the contributors to *Inequity* refer to, and to address them quickly. Indeed, there are many policy changes on which "market entrepreneurs" and "urban entrepreneurs," as Anthony Orum might call them, would agree, especially when it comes to housing affordability. In Austin, for instance, new housing developments are more expensive to build than in Houston or Dallas and are held up weeks longer in Austin's onerous planning restrictions.

Already in 2006, a study showed that Austin housing was overpriced by at least 7 percent because of what it dubbed "the planning penalty," and a 2015 paper by a University of Texas graduate student concluded that renters could save upwards of $720 annually if regulatory delays were reined in and approval time for development were cut in half. Renters are particularly disadvantaged in that the landlords of the multifamily properties in which they reside do not enjoy the same homestead-exemption tax relief as single-family homeowners do, which means that when property values skyrocket, as they have in Austin, property-tax increases are necessarily passed on to tenants through higher rents. All this in an era when renting is on the rise: In 2019, *Governing* magazine, using census data, found that metros of at least one hundred thousand residents had shown a median renting-population increase of 31 percent between 2000 and 2017, whereas ownership had increased by only 7 percent. In Austin, the number of renters had increased 46 percent during the same time period, ten points higher than the city's increase in home ownership. As renting and ownership in the urban core become less feasible for anyone but those with means, populations are displaced to the outskirts, which leads to a host of further disruptions, including sprawl, traffic congestion, automotive pollution, greater impervious cover of Austin's prized landscape, and more geographic stratification along income lines.

Revising land-development and tax codes in a way that safeguards funding for public schools, maintains environmental protections, promotes density in the city's core, and makes living within city limits more affordable are challenging but not impossible civic innovations, ones that do not require technology—they are innovations that advantage many and that anyone but the most diehard not-in-my-backyarders can agree to pursue.

How exactly Austin mitigates these problems—how it makes more of its citizens resilient or antifragile in the face of social and economic disruption—is the preeminent challenge for the city. The focus on social justice that took shape with the Black Lives Matter movement after the death of Trayvon Martin in 2012, and the movement's acceleration in 2020 following the death of George Floyd, signaled a radical shift of priorities.

Austin remains in an advantageous position: New industries, entrepreneurship, and an outward-facing posture foster resiliency. Embracing innovation is essential to the growth of any community. Being resistant, or fearful, to acknowledge the inevitable disruption engendered by new ideas is to be at an economic disadvantage—a disadvantage that quickly turns to out-migration and a decline in the tax base.

CHAPTER EIGHT

JENNIFER TODD-GOYNES

According to Plan

The Chattahoochee River flows south along half of Georgia's western border with Alabama, continues through Florida, and eventually empties into Apalachicola Bay as part of the Apalachicola River. My perception of nature, public waterways, and how people interact with them was shaped by the Chattahoochee River, a physical and cultural reminder of my community's shared connection to nature and history in the suburb of Atlanta where I grew up. I have memories of playing near the Chattahoochee's riverbank and walking on park trails near the river, but swimming and wading were usually neither allowed nor advisable. The river was often polluted by runoff and sewage, creating a remarkable stench and a generally unsafe environment. Subsequent moves to mid-Atlantic cities as an early adult brought more of the same—rivers that were unsafe for swimming and so cloudy that you couldn't see the bottom. My first visit to Austin to see the University of Texas to better inform my decision on where to attend graduate school provided a stark contrast. I was struck by the pristine waters of Barton Springs, nearby swimming holes with clear water, and the Barton Creek Greenbelt's extensive trail network and abundant wading opportunities. Austin was the first city I visited with swimmable water and a close connection to nature. I knew I had found the place for me to live and learn more about the world of community planning and economic development.

Over the years, as both a resident and city planner, I discovered that the natural beauty that first attracted me to Austin had a unique and sometimes complex relationship with the city and its residents. I would also discover that other elements I valued—a sense of community, an entrepreneurial spirit, economic opportunities for growth and expansion—were shaped by the advocacy and decision-making of nonprofit organizations, the city council, business alliances, and community groundswell. In any city, the trajectory of the community's character and growth can be a force of its own, regardless of the guardrails put around it; this trajectory can result in prosperity for some, but rarely for all. City planning is an attempt to provide those guardrails by shaping the way that a community looks, feels, and functions through regulations that influence what can be built, where it can be built, and how much can be built. What these regulations cannot fully account for are the people and identity of a place—the characters that fill a city's buildings and streets, its beloved community and cultural institutions, and the activity patterns that create the fabric of individual and collective experience. In Austin, the desire to preserve the city's natural beauty, laid-back character, history, creative vibe, and nostalgia for the place that Austin once was—while also spurring and accommodating the city's transformation from a big small town to a small big city—has become its defining challenge.

Austin's natural environment includes extraordinary features few other communities can claim. One is hard-pressed to think of other major cities with comparable access to nature. Portland's Forest Park comes to mind, but there are no swimming holes along the trails and no springs in which to swim. The hot springs elsewhere in the Cascades are hours away. The role these natural assets continue to play in attracting young people to Austin—and creative people of all ages—cannot be overstated.

The ability to easily engage with nature at a moment's notice, to feel like you are not in a city at all, has an enduring charm. Austin's extensive network of trails through preserves and along a river in the middle of town, a system of creeks and rivers, small parks sprinkled along the water's edges, and prominent green spaces are the envy of other cities. The preservation of these natural features was, of course, one of the major challenges in Austin's growth. Austin residents never wavered in their desire to keep these areas pristine. Community leaders emerged as strong advocates, and policymakers had no choice but to follow their lead. While preservations of Austin's expansive waterways and green space was not executed perfectly—it did not fully consider the effect of development and gentrification in some areas of the city, particularly the east side—it is still a shining model of how a city prioritized the natural resources that have become a defining characteristic of its attraction, quality, and livability.

The city's network of natural preserves began in the 1930s with the establishment of Zilker Park, which was gifted to the city from Andrew Jackson Zilker. In many ways, Zilker is Austin's Central Park. But unlike Central Park, it is in the center of a network of trails that extend along creeks and bluffs throughout the city. Once part of a ranch, the park is now a center of public life offering more than 350 acres with land- and water-based recreation, a sculpture garden, a botanical garden, and the annual Austin City Limits Music Festival (ACL).

ACL began as a one-weekend event in 2002, expanding in 2012 to a two-weekend event attracting thousands of festivalgoers and generating millions in economic impact for the city. Along with musical and cultural events such as SXSW, ACL—an outdoor music festival in the heart of the city, surrounded by greenery, water, and buildings—became yet another reason to visit Austin and be part of the continuing music scene.

Not every part of Austin's natural environment is so extensively programmed with activities and populated by visitors. Quieter enclaves can be found in the one thousand-acre Barton Creek Greenbelt that extends through western and southern Austin. The Greenbelt has miles of trails for walking, running, and biking, multiple swimming holes, waterfalls, opportunities for kayaking, and areas for rock climbing. A visit to the Mayfield Park and Nature Preserve in Northwest Austin might include an encounter with free-roaming peacocks, and a journey further to the northwest to the Balcones Canyonland Preserve provides thousands of acres of undeveloped habitat for endangered animal species, native plants, and human exploration. The decision to conserve these natural areas was generational, with a growing commitment to improving the quality of air and water, not only for current residents, but also for future generations.

Is Austin's commitment to preserving undeveloped land a template for other communities? Some candor is required here. Not every city has springs, escarpments, and creeks flowing into a meandering river. Not every community has rolling hills and endangered golden-cheeked warblers to protect. But every city makes choices about what is worth preserving and what is needed to support industry, to house its people, and to find transportation options.

And yes, the creeks and rivers. This book begins with that theme, and it is echoed in every attempt to explain what makes Austin Austin. The city's growth and development continue to be shaped by water—the need to protect, conserve, and recreate in or around it. Lady Bird Lake runs through central Austin, part of a string of lakes along the Colorado River that provide the city with drinking water, recreation, energy, and flood mitigation. The lake is a central part of life in Austin, connecting the city's largest downtown park (Zilker) with smaller parks and enclaves along the ten-mile Ann and Roy Butler Hike-and-Bike Trail loop, and providing year-round opportunities for water-based recreation. While swimming has been banned in the lake since the 1960s, the shoreline is dotted with rental companies for kayaks, canoes, standup paddleboards, and electric boats, as well as ramps that allow individual users to launch their own vessels. Austin's history, however, includes episodes in which the river was more threat than refuge.

Austin, and Central Texas generally, are known as flash flood alley. Several bridges and overlooks along Lady Bird Lake's hike-and-bike trail denote historic highwater marks, an ongoing reminder of the area's history of flooding. Chapter 2 describes the dams built along the Colorado River to control episodic flooding. The most recent project was the Longhorn Dam, built in the 1960s at the eastern end of the river to create a cooling pond for the (now decommissioned) Holly Street Power Plant. The secondary effect of this dam was to create Town Lake, renamed Lady Bird Lake in 2007, an important name change that signifies the work of Lady Bird Johnson—the former first lady and wife of President Lyndon B. Johnson—in shaping the city we know today.

Early photos of Lady Bird Lake show a body of water seemingly neglected and ignored by the built environment along its shores. The city appears to have its back to the water, a legacy of moving development further inland and away from areas that might flood. As a mostly undervalued area, the lake was known for its polluted and trash-filled water and muddy, unrefined banks defined by past floods. In 1968, the future of the lake began to change with the adoption of the Comprehensive Plan for the Development of Town Lake, which focused on the city's need for additional outdoor recreation space. This work was carried forward in part during the 1970s by a group of citizens led by Lady Bird Johnson, Ann and Roy Butler, Roberta Crenshaw, and others who formed the Town Lake Beautification Committee. The goal of the committee was to improve the shoreline with vegetation and construct features that might attract people to the area. The group successfully planted thousands of trees, shrubs, and flowers to stabilize and beautify the shoreline. Their efforts were supported by city investments in park space at Festival Beach, representing one of the earliest public-private initiatives led by citizen engagement.

Subsequent planning efforts to leverage the lake include a Town Lake Comprehensive Plan in 1988, which recommended that the lake and surrounding park space "project beauty, serenity, and naturalness," and reflects the beautification efforts that began twenty years prior. This plan is one of the earliest and most ambitious examples of city council policy prioritizing a carefully planned, programmed, and preserved natural environment. The next comprehensive planning effort was completed in 1999, introducing a plan for capital improvement projects along the shore of Lady Bird Lake; this master plan was expanded in 2009 with stakeholder feedback and has guided implementation to the present day. Lady Bird Lake has evolved to become a second park space in its own right, and a critical part of the open space infrastructure of Austin.

Real estate development in Austin has always had to work within the limitations set by the city's creek and river networks, which are both beautiful and prone to flooding. An early attempt to leverage this resource was in the 1976 *Austin Creeks* booklet put together by a committee of Austinites, including Sinclair Black, who has supported many of Austin's transformative projects, including successfully advocating for a city Great Streets program, developing retail on Second Street in downtown, relocating I-35 below street level and covering it with a "cap" of park space and development, and contributing to landmark developments such as the Seaholm power plant redevelopment, located just steps from the river and which is now a hub of walkable restaurants and shops. *Austin Creeks* called for a network of pedestrian and bicycle trails along creeks and rivers, creating an extensive nonvehicular transportation system throughout the city. This plan would establish a mechanism for access to undevelopable floodplains and provide greater access to the city's waterways. Achieving this vision required acquiring land over three years at an estimated cost of $1.2 million dollars, an investment that seems trivial in hindsight. While the full scope of the plan has not been achieved, enough of the original vision has remained intact and is one of Austin's greatest amenities.

Subsequent years brought more active stewardship of Austin's waterways. A large-scale development over the Barton Creek watershed spurred citizen action and the establishment of an organization now known as the Save Our Springs Alliance (SOS). SOS has become a major force in Austin's development trajectory. While SOS has raised public awareness of the importance of preservation, the alliance has often emerged as an opponent of development and faced criticism for the critical tone and content of its messaging about proposed projects. In contrast, the Waterloo Greenway, a public-private partnership, is working in coordination with development trends to create a transformative 1.5-mile park system along Waller Creek, which runs from the University of Texas and through downtown, ending at Lady Bird Lake. The size and scope of this public-private project is a prime example of the expansive partnerships that have enabled Austin to become a major city, characterized by world-class public spaces, with an estimated cost of $265 million. To date, Waterloo Greenway has completed several major projects such as an eleven-acre urban park, a five thousand-seat indoor amphitheater, and a 350-seat open-air theater; future projects include additional creek restoration and a trail running through most of downtown from the University of Texas to Lady Bird Lake.

When we at TIP first began thinking about "how Austin became Austin," the temptation was to focus on those features most appealing to a growing artistic and tech-savvy population. Austin, as Richard Florida noted early on, was a kind of model city for his "creative class." That perspective, however, was always skewed. It effectively ignored how different communities within the city were affected by growth. And it ignored the high price imposed on Black and Hispanic neighborhoods.

In fact, the evolution of Austin's built environment, especially around the city's green spaces and waterways, is a story of racial discrimination. In 1928, the Austin City Council adopted a master plan that segregated the city, pushing Black people east of East Avenue, the predecessor of I-35 (chapter 6 covers much of this uprooting in detail). The plan stated that "the negroes are present in small numbers, in practically all sections of the city, excepting the area just east of East Avenue and south of the City Cemetery. This area seems to be all negro population. It is our recommendation that the nearest approach to the solution of the segregation problem will be the recommendation of this district as a negro district; and that all the facilities and conveniences be provided the negroes in this district, as an incentive to draw the negro population to this area."[1] The effect of this plan was to deny services to Black and Hispanic people who lived west of East Avenue. Unsurprisingly, East Austin suffered from a lack of investment in infrastructure and community amenities. In addition, undesirable projects and land designations that would not be accepted in other parts of town were placed in these neighborhoods.

One of the most well-known and egregious environmental injustices in East Austin was the tank farm, a fifty-two-acre petroleum storage facility and industrial site. Located in close proximity to residential neighborhoods, residents soon suffered from health issues, including asthma, skin conditions, and lung disease. Carcinogenic water, soil, and air pollution from the facility was well documented. Property values decreased in an area already struggling under the legacy of redlining in the 1928 plan. When a proposal was put forth in the 1990s to expand the tank farm, the community successfully fought back. Under the leadership of the East Austin Strategy Team and People Organized in Defense of Earth and Her Resources (PODER), they successfully lobbied to have the tank farm closed and relocated. The legacy of pollution and low property values, however, has been a heavy one. Not until a new office development began in 2022 did the land redevelop. When complete, the site is slated to include two office buildings, green space, stormwater mitigation, and approximately $7 million in community benefits for local affordable housing and community development groups.

Each of the City of Austin's comprehensive planning efforts have been affected by and linked to the 1928 plan. It wasn't until 1979 that another comprehensive plan, Austin Tomorrow, was adopted on the heels of efforts to beautify and improve Lady Bird Lake. Austin Tomorrow was an early acknowledgement that Austin's growth pattern was not congruent with the citizenry's goals for environmental protection, managing growth, and minimizing urban sprawl. The plan remained in place through the early 2000s and was one of the earliest efforts to guide Austin's rapid growth, resulting in enhanced environmental protections and the ability to develop with a mix of uses. After its inception, Austin Tomorrow received periodic updates to ensure its relevancy.

Growth and the associated pressures caused by decreased housing affordability, increased commute times, and more frequent traffic weren't limited to Austin—the surrounding towns and communities were also experiencing population growth, prompting a convening between community, environmental, business, and government leaders from Bastrop, Caldwell, Hays, Travis, and Williamson counties to discuss creating a united vision for the future of the region. The group formed Envision Central

Texas (ECT) in 2001 and hired Fregonese Calthorpe Associates (FCA) to manage a visioning process focused on the nexus of transportation, environmental preservation, social equity, and economic goals to create a sustainable regional economy. Early efforts in the ECT process centered around community workshops during which FCA asked people to show what they wanted future development to look like by manipulating development patterns on maps. ECT used this community input to develop four future land-use scenarios in which population growth remained constant while patterns of land use, transportation, and open space preservation varied. The four scenarios were to continue current development trends, concentrate growth along major transportation corridors, share growth between existing and new communities, or concentrate growth in existing communities. A post-analysis community survey revealed a preferred scenario in which the region would concentrate growth in existing areas while accommodating limited growth in new areas.

Over the approximately twenty years since ECT, a lack of policy direction and monetary investment has resulted in a region that has not developed according to the preferred growth scenario. While a few of ECT's predictions, such as the ability of the region to support major nodes outside of downtown, have come to fruition, the region's growth has been generally characterized by sprawling low-density developments with a lesser priority on investing in transit or infill development that would further densify and build out the urban core. The effects of this growth pattern have been acutely felt by the Austin community as well; increased numbers of commuters enter and exit Austin every day, housing has become less affordable, and traffic has become more frequent.

Inevitably for a city that doubles in population every twenty years, Austin is experiencing some effects of inadequate planning, such as more traffic on the city's north-south highways, I-35 and Mopac, housing costs increasing at a faster rate than wages, and the dislocation of neighborhoods—especially in East Austin—that accompanies rapid growth. The regional ambition of ECT and a desire to influence Austin's future growth led to an entirely new comprehensive planning process dubbed Imagine Austin. In planning exercises with city staff, participants consistently identified a future growth scenario that prioritized infill and redevelopment with minimal development on previously undeveloped land; this vision echoes Austin Tomorrow's focus on "directed expansion and inner-city development" and the ECT preferred scenario of concentrating growth in existing communities with limited growth in new areas. Within the context of Imagine Austin, this notion of creating balanced growth was expressed as "complete communities," creating places where people from ages eight to eighty would be able to live within a fifteen-minute walk, bike ride, or transit trip for their daily needs. The plan also created goals around livability, environmental sustainability, mobility and connectivity, economic prosperity, good governance, arts and culture, and education in support of a vision where all Austinites would have access to the amenities, transportation, services, and opportunities to fulfill their material, social, and economic needs. The plan was unanimously approved by council in 2012.

The dream of a development pattern that creates more walkable communities, as set forth in Imagine Austin, met stiff opposition in planning commission and council meetings. Zoning cases frequently become contentious between city staff and developers; distrust was the order of the day. Compromise was difficult as land development code language was often vague, allowing for subjective and inconsistent staff decision-making. Layers of zoning regulations and interpretations, some of which were governed only by unpublished administrative memos, made communication problematic at best. Many of Austin's political and community leaders saw these issues as symptomatic of a confusing and outdated land development code from the 1980s. In response, the city council directed city staff to undertake a rewrite of the land development code, an effort known as CodeNEXT.

Austin was one of the first cities to launch a complete rewrite of its land development code. Due to the complexities created by decades of overlapping regulations, and the potential controversy ignited by proposals to change development standards, many cities have historically chosen incremental or small-area approaches to code updates. Such approaches allow cities to engage with changes on a smaller scale, correcting issues over time and deciding whether to expand the new rules to a wider area. Rather than taking a more piecemeal approach, Austin's leaders chose to pursue a wholesale updating of regulations for virtually everything: zoning, parking, building design, water quality, utility alignment, transportation standards, affordable housing, and more. These code changes would impact how Austin looks, feels, and functions. Much of what you see and experience in a place is directly related to its zoning and site development standards.

A reduction in parking requirements, for example, allows more space for building and landscape development; at scale, increased density can also create more transit-supportive locations. An increase in allowable heights or building façade design standards can change the experience of a person walking down the street—how much sunlight they have access to, whether landscape can grow, and if the building frontage is welcoming and active with windows and signage or a bleak blank wall.

CodeNEXT's launch in 2015 coincided with a very tight housing market, rapid development, and increasing unaffordability. Austin's predominantly suburban development patterns meant that growth was experienced as a negative force creating additional traffic, environmental degradation, and overcrowded places with less mobility; such growth was also contrary to the community preferences for growth communicated in past planning efforts. Code restrictions left little room for incremental growth that might be implemented through single-family to duplex conversions, the addition of accessory dwelling units, or small neighborhood-scale commercial buildings. The negative impacts of growth within this system left many community members feeling overwhelmed and unable to envision a different path forward—one that favored multimodal connectivity, greater housing choice in building form and price points, and traditional development patterns not centered on a car. Scenario planning by Fregonese and Associates illustrated the necessity of code changes that would preserve housing units and create new opportunities for housing through redevelopment. Despite the potential benefits associated with a code update, the CodeNEXT process quickly became toxic. Vocal opponents cultivated misinformation that led to mistrust in city staff and the process, which was made worse by vague direction from political leaders, who rarely took a strong stand on hot-button issues. Turnover within city staff frustrated by the political environment and unclear direction also stymied progress. In 2018, council voted to suspend CodeNEXT.

The disintegration of CodeNEXT is one of the most prominent chapters in the Austin community's conversation about the city's future, and it is part of a larger narrative about how the city should develop. Concern with how the city will look, feel, and function are not new; neither are grand ambitions about the future. In 2005, Austin Mayor Will Wynn called for increasing the number of people living downtown from five thousand to twenty-five thousand over ten years. This ambition was rooted in the past work of Sinclair Black, who advocated for residential and retail development downtown, the scenario analysis of ECT, and conversations with venture capitalist and Zappos CEO Tony Hsieh, who was focused on transforming downtown Las Vegas. At the time of Mayor Wynn's announcement, a major investment in residential was seen as a tremendously ambitious (and perhaps unattainable) attempt to spur development downtown. The Great Recession prevented Mayor Wynn's goal from being realized within the stated timeline, but his ambition did contribute to changing the tenor of conversations about downtown Austin's growth and set the city on a path of investment in downtown residential.

My arrival in Austin was just a few years after Mayor Wynn's proclamation. I remember a downtown mostly empty at night, filled with mostly empty parking lots and garages, and only truly active during festivals such as South by Southwest. This is in stark contrast to the Austin of today and its skyline dominated by high-rise buildings, restaurants, and cranes supporting new construction. This change happened in part because of Wynn's vision, but also because of hard-fought policy change that would accommodate growth. Increasing allowable heights, removing parking requirements, and improving public park space all played a part in realizing that vision.

Austin's downtown and major corridors are often seen as the logical—and least contentious—places to handle growth. During CodeNEXT, for example, Mayor Steve Adler sought a "grand bargain" that would not add density to neighborhoods in exchange for adding increased density and housing along major corridors or in the major activity centers designated in the city's comprehensive plan. This approach sought a difficult balance between maintaining a dispersed suburban character that does not have the density to support walkable, transit-supportive development with urban benefits such as mixed-income housing, mixed-use buildings, and transit. It is emblematic of Austin's ongoing growth dilemma, wherein growth and change must be balanced with nostalgia for what the city once was and the culture that has made Austin into a top destination.

A few miles from downtown, in Northeast Austin, lies a successful example of this type of balancing act: The Mueller development sits on the former Robert Mueller Municipal Airport (RMMA) site, just east of the major corridor of I-35. It is a pedestrian-oriented base for anchor stores, local retailers, office buildings, mixed-income housing, green spaces, and a vibrant farmers market. Portions of Mueller are still under development, but its journey began in the early 1990s when the Base Realignment and Closure Commission designated Austin's Bergstrom Airforce Base for closure. This provided an opportunity to relocate the airport to a new location farther from residential areas, and in 1999 the new Austin-Bergstrom International Airport opened southeast of downtown. A vision for redeveloping the seven hundred-acre old airport site began as early as the mid-1980s, continued through the late 1990s, and resulted in an approved plan in 2000. Community groups, the City of Austin, the Catellus Development Corporation, and nonprofits all contributed to the vision for a walkable, mixed-use, mixed-income community. Mueller has developed in phases to ensure financial viability, compatibility with surrounding neighborhoods, and revitalizing East Austin are in balance.

Mueller is a special case where implementing walkable density was made easier by building on an abandoned site; by contrast, most of Austin's development has historically been suburban in nature with additional density in the central core. A side effect of prioritizing development downtown is that job opportunities are consolidated in one place, creating condensed commuting patterns rather than disseminating activity throughout the city. Over time, Austin's policymakers and developers have worked to rectify this by taking advantage of large-scale development and redevelopment opportunities. The Domain in North Austin is one of the largest new developments and is sometimes referred to as Austin's "second downtown." In contrast to Mueller, which is the result of a public-private partnership between the City of Austin and Catellus, The Domain is a private-development home to hundreds of retail stores, thousands of residential units, and more than three million square feet of office space.

Austin's rapid growth has resulted in landmark developments such as Mueller and The Domain, the recruitment of major employers, nationally-recognized festivals, and a spot on numerous top ten places to live lists. These developments occurred outside of what was anticipated by a comprehensive plan. The efforts of an earlier planning initiative—Envision Central Texas—were never formally adopted. Unmanaged growth continues to plague the region in the form of increased traffic with longer commute times, fewer housing choices at higher price points, and crowded public spaces. These externalities fuel a toxic community dialogue around planning for the future, which further stymies progress. The cycle continues to play out, and solutions are typically makeshift. Bolder initiatives—such as light-rail extensions—have met voter approval but are slow to start. As a further reflection that Austin does not live in a vacuum, that it can't escape being the capital of a very conservative state, the light-rail extension is being challenged by Attorney General Ken Paxton.

Progress, however incremental, is being made. Local government has been reorganized to emphasize equity in planning and historic preservation, institutionalizing the need to correct discriminatory injustice and racism. The city council has also revisited needed adjustments to the land development code (however piecemeal). Recently, regulations around the development of accessory dwelling units have become more flexible to allow for tiny homes and RVs, and the Home Options for Mobility and Equity (HOME) initiative would allow up to three homes on single-family lots. Another amendment to the land development code removed off-street parking requirements, creating an opportunity to use space for housing that would otherwise have been reserved for cars. Upcoming amendments include an effort to update rules around equitable transit-oriented development, affordable housing, and supporting live music venues and creative spaces.

Census population estimates from the early 2020s indicate that Austin's growth rate is slowing. If this trend holds true, it may allow Austin to catch up to the rapid expansion of years past and place additional focus on creating accessible opportunities for people of all ages, abilities, incomes, and cultural backgrounds to thrive. Urgent attention is still needed to increase access to financially attainable housing. In addition, the displacement of entire communities must be addressed. Austin is on the precipice of major transportation investments through Project Connect, a transit initiative to improve the rail and bus networks, and the expansion of I-35. In particular, the expansion of the highway creates an opportunity to reconnect neighborhoods through "cap and stitch" road construction over sunken parts of the highway.

A more thoughtful pattern of growth should include incorporating Austin's past into its future with culturally rooted art, storytelling, and policymaking. When I first visited Austin, I was struck by the confluence of Western, Southern, and Mexican cultures in the city's architecture, the names of streets and parks, in the restaurants and businesses, and in the history of people I met. The region has a rich history built on the traditions of Native American tribes, Mexican, German, and Czech immigrants, and settlers from other parts of the United States. Over time, the integration of different people and traditions organically created a unique culture of tolerance and acceptance in Austin. The city's rich musical tradition grown in old Czech and German dance halls evolved into new venues such as the Armadillo World Headquarters that attracted "outlaw" musicians such as Willie Nelson and Waylon Jennings. Austin became a place for cultivating creativity, where artists from different genres could play at the same venues and have an opportunity to make something entirely new together. It was also the kind of place that Leslie Cochran, a homeless political advocate known for cross-dressing and outrageous outfits could be dubbed the "Queen of Austin" with his own line of paper dolls at the local bookstore. This ability to "keep it weird" is not something that can be fabricated, and it's threatened by Austin's growing homogenization, economic segregation, and unaffordability. The city's famous slogan risks becoming nothing more than a bumper sticker.

People were once attracted to Austin because it was a place that offered a reasonable cost of living in a beautiful place with a vibrant creative economy; this is still what attracts newcomers. The creative community is a huge driver of Austin's success, yet this community does not benefit proportionally. Many of Austin's creators, makers, and low- to middle-income workers are pushed to surrounding communities, creating growth challenges in surrounding cities and towns, and leaving Austin without some of the people who helped to make it "The Live Music Capital of the World." Addressing the big issues of affordability, transportation, and the environment that supersede political boundaries requires regional cooperation and dedication. Envisioning a future where the impossible becomes possible is, after all, in the community's DNA. While Austin has not lived up to the complete, connected community goals of Envision Central Texas or Imagine Austin, the vision has not been lost. Regional policymaking is never easy. The sheer pressure of future growth, however, will keep open the door of an Austin intimately connected with its extraordinary creeks and topography.

CHAPTER NINE

The Future of Jobs

Candidates for every major public office in the United States—politically left, right, or center—routinely promise how, once elected, they will bring more jobs to their constituents. President Barack Obama promised in 2008 to create five million "green" jobs; President Donald Trump guaranteed in 2016 that he would be "the greatest jobs president that God ever created." And in June of 2021, President Joe Biden declared, "We have now created over two million jobs in total since I took office—more jobs than have ever been created in the first four months of any presidency in modern history, triple the rate of my predecessor, eight times the rate of President Reagan."

Politicians campaign as if their careers depend on job creation, regardless of how low the unemployment rate might be. Whether these jobs should be created by the public or private sector is often treated as a technicality, left for debate between Keynesians and supply-siders. The idea that Americans need more jobs is a deep-seated one.

Traditionally, the field of economic development has operated with the same mindset. Ask someone in the profession to define *economic development* and job creation is always in the mix. The primary—and often only—metric by which success is judged is, in fact, jobs. And for the longest time, manufacturing jobs were by far the jobs most sought-after. Recruiting corporations to a city or region through the use of incentives (often in the form of tax abatements) has long been the primary mechanism used to accomplish all this. Incentives, of course, reduce a company's cost of doing business. In addition to direct monetary advantages, incentives may shorten the timeline to production through expedited regulatory oversight. Also in the mix may be funding for infrastructure improvements (in the form of roads, sewer, and water lines) or reduction in utility rates. Finally, there are various forms of employment assistance for job and skills training. This form of incentive is so widely baked into every state's business model that it rarely functions as a distinguishing advantage.

For most practitioners of economic development, job creation via corporate recruitment is still the overriding objective. Crafted in their efforts are incentive "packages" that combine some mix of the financial and regulatory components described above. What politicians accept when they approve or condone these packages is that a corporation will create jobs whose benefits ripple throughout the wider economy. In theory, any revenue lost from tax breaks will be made up through more jobs and greater overall tax revenue in the future. Despite how many tax breaks and subsidies we provide, the reasoning goes, it will all be worth it in the long run.

I have painted this situation reductively, but in decades past, this process sometimes worked out for both community and corporation. Today we face a different reality. As workplace automation and AI advance, as the gig economy (e.g., independent contractors, often enabled by digital platforms) expands, and as the traditional relationships between employees and corporations dissolve, the idea of using public funds to incentivize job creation does not make the same sense it once did. Nevertheless, most economic development organizations and municipal leaders still cling to the idea. In doing so, however, they often fail to bring lasting value to the communities they serve—and inadvertently line the pockets of corporations that are, naturally, more than happy to take a handout.

I am not new to this topic. In the mid-1990s, Fort Worth—Dallas's smaller, more laid-back sister city—was determined to bring the Texas Motor Speedway to a plot north of the city's downtown. In exchange for the racing facility—which would seat upward of 120,000, have an estimated yearly economic impact of $160 million, and bring hundreds of jobs to the community—Fort Worth exempted the Speedway Motorsports corporation from all property taxes. This arrangement disgruntled many, and not just the 125 families who were uprooted from their community to make room for speedway parking lots. The Northwest Independent School District (NWISD) was also less than pleased. Because Texas doesn't collect a state income tax, abatements like the one given to Speedway Motorsports are felt most keenly by local schools, which receive significant funds from corporate taxes. NWISD estimated it was losing about $1.5 million annually thanks to the abatements offered up to Speedway Motorsports, so it decided to sue Speedway Motorsports (and by extension, NASCAR, whose events it hosted).

Few in Texas' economic development world wanted to help NWISD in its legal battle. I, however, did want to, though my cause was deemed radioactive by many of my colleagues, as it would be a full-frontal attack on tax breaks generally. I decided to take the gamble anyway and support a fight against what seemed to me an ill-thought-out arrangement. As with so many lawsuits, the outcome was ambiguous, but we did force concessions on behalf of the school district—precisely because we were able to show that the types of jobs promised (racing-industry specific) would fail to materialize.

When I wrote a piece in *The Dallas Morning News* in 1996 about the controversy, I caused a stir. I said, in part:

> The reality of abatements is that they are risky and may actually be harmful to the local economy. Since economic development corporations measure their success by new business recruitment and new jobs created (regardless of pay levels or longevity), they have little inclination to determine whether the company would have located in the community without the abatement, or whether it will provide benefits equal to the cost of abatements.

In the process of making this argument publicly on behalf of NWISD, I gained a reputation as someone willing to challenge traditional economic development practices—and I also met many who quietly shared my feeling that the way cities use tax incentives in the service of job creation was often ineffective and, at worst, counterproductive. That this subject remains controversial is an understatement. Looking back on the development that occurred around the Texas Motor Speedway, it can easily be argued that the economic impact—in jobs and capital investment—was easily met (and exceeded). But that fact obscures the equally important question of whether the incentives were necessary in the first place, or if they simply served to sweeten an already done deal whose major beneficiary was the billionaire NASCAR hall-of-famer and Speedway owner Bruton Smith.

More than twenty years later, this same issue would enter the national discourse in a new but similar form through a high-profile announcement by the largest online retailer in the world. In the wake of the announcement, two Texas cities—Austin and Dallas—would reveal their contrasting approaches to corporate incentives and job creation as they vied for consideration. There is no better example to illustrate this difference than the development process associated with the Mueller development discussed in chapter 8.

In September 2017, when Amazon announced it was seeking candidates for the location of a second North American headquarters—its "HQ2," as it became known—local governments scrambled. The announcement was extraordinary: Amazon released along with it a request for proposals (RFPs) to all cities in the US and Canada. Included in the RFP was a comprehensive list of what the company was seeking, what its expectations were, and which requirements cities must meet to be considered. Typically, corporate site selections are quiet affairs. Companies balance their expansion needs against their existing location, closely examining a host of factors and comparing different communities in their ability to deliver. Labor availability, transportation access, infrastructure, business climate—it is a long list and quickly verges on the esoteric. Sometimes consultants—"site selectors"—are brought in, but it is not unusual for the analysis to be done in-house. And most often the site selection is done with limited fanfare. But Amazon's search was national news, rippling far beyond the usual local political environment of corporate expansions.

Collaborating with economic development firms, more than two hundred cities created elaborate bid packages carefully detailing why they would make the ideal home for HQ2 and what they were prepared to offer, from generous tax breaks to fast-tracked construction approvals to infrastructure upgrades. Much effort and strategy went into these pitches. Chicago, perhaps playing directly to Amazon founder Jeff Bezos's reported *Star Trek* fandom, enlisted William Shatner to record the voice-over on its Super Bowl-worthy advertisement, which encouraged the online retailer to choose it for its headquarters. The competition's winning prize was substantial: Amazon estimated its second headquarters would employ fifty thousand workers, a major win for any community. And that number did not take into account the ancillary service jobs that would be created by these highly paid "knowledge workers." Austin, on the other hand, showed little interest in this competition. The local economy did not need tech incentives to grow.

As I watched the HQ2 story unfold—and even as my firm was pulled into the process on behalf of Quicken Loans founder Dan Gilbert and the City of Detroit—two thoughts occurred to me. First, this all seemed oddly familiar. The almost-desperate-seeming competition to throw public money at a corporation in exchange for jobs was exactly what I had warned against in 1996. Here the scale was even grander with the story getting major media coverage. My second thought was that some tectonic change was happening in the way that cities and corporations would interact in the future. I wondered whether Amazon, having profoundly and permanently disrupted the retail market, would now do the same not just to the site-selection process but also to the fundamental relationship between cities and the major employers that ultimately provide the tax base and the employment opportunities that help those cities grow and stay alive.

Impassioned, high-profile arguments for and against incentivizing Amazon were daily news. While many (not only politicians) argued that any city would be foolish to ignore the chance at serving as HQ2's home, others were dismayed at the idea of offering cash benefits to a company with the largest market value in the world, portraying incentives as a form of corporate welfare and questioning whether the promised jobs would, in fact, offer the promised benefits to the community. In the best of cases, such as contingent incentives based on performance or tax rebates only after development was complete, would the investment be justified? Would it provide what could have been provided by a host of smaller, more scalable developments?

When Amazon announced a surprise split deal for HQ2—they would build two headquarters, one in Arlington, Virginia, and another in Queens, New York—the backlash among residents and politicians in Queens was so strong that the company ultimately took New York City off the list. Activists decried the $3 billion in "tax breaks" that Amazon would receive in exchange for a supposed twenty-five thousand jobs and pointed to potential housing unaffordability, transportation gridlock, and displacement of local residents due to the new headquarters. Real estate website Zillow estimated that area rents could rise by more than $200 per year.

Queens-based Congresswoman Alexandria Ocasio-Cortez, a darling of the left since her 2018 election, was a prominent anti-Amazon voice; when the company killed its plan to set up shop in Queens, she took to Twitter to praise the community that "defeated Amazon's corporate greed, its worker exploitation, and the power of the richest man in the world."

Months later, she told her constituents at a community board meeting that there was "very little proof that [Amazon's] promises were rooted in reality." Attendees applauded when she said, "We shouldn't be inviting bullies to our neighborhood." Clearly, Ocasio-Cortez and the many who shared her position felt that the potential for future jobs was not, in fact, worth the price.

In Texas, few Austinites lost any sleep when Amazon passed the city over, despite Austin having landed on the short list of top twenty cities. "Austin is . . . already seeing very strong growth, with a significant amount of immigration, and a city that is already trying to keep up with that growth," University of Texas economics professor Julia Coronado told the *Austin American-Statesman* shortly after the announcement. "It didn't need [HQ2] per se." For a city with an infrastructure already groaning under a massive influx of people and experiencing skyrocketing housing costs, landing another corporate behemoth was not a make-or-break situation. Mayor Steve Adler made this clear when he took the stance that Amazon and its fifty thousand jobs were welcome—but only if the company were willing to bring its resources to bear on solving Austin's transportation and mobility issues. This attitude was starkly different from that of Dallas, where Mayor Mike Rawlings had eagerly participated in courting the company and was willing to do what it took to put his city atop Amazon's list of 238 candidates. "This is about taking care of a customer . . . and what do you like? Blue? Red? You like something that is slimming?" he was quoted as saying. Dallas, like so many other Amazon wooers, and like most growth-hungry cities, was willing to do nearly anything to win over what they saw as the ultimate creator of jobs—a big, successful technology company. The city developed an incentives package that would last ninety-nine years.

Dallas and Austin's divergent attitudes reflected both the different on-the-ground realities in each city and the changing views on traditional economic development practices. Dallas's approach was in keeping with decades-long tradition, whereas Austin's ambivalence reflected a general skepticism about whether diverting public funds to corporations ultimately paid off. Regardless of where one falls on this particular debate—whether one believes that Queens would or would not have ultimately benefited from HQ2's presence—the broader issue of corporate incentives and job creation is becoming more fraught. In other words, one does not have to be a democratic socialist—or a MAGA crusader against corporate welfare—

to recognize that the model of shelling out tax abatements to companies in exchange for job creation requires reevaluation. At the very root of this issue lies a simple question with a complex answer: What is a job?

In preindustrial societies, no one had a "job." People worked, of course—in fact, a greater percentage of the population engaged in work then than now (in part because children worked)—and they had skills they honed over their working lives, but in no sense did they have what we think of as a job. No punching in, no paternalistic relationship with a business entity, no middle manager keeping them in line. The arrival of the Industrial Revolution brought with it the concept of the corporation as we know it now, and it is within that framework that we picked up the idea we now have about what a job is. Factories needed people to work according to specific schedules, enter into relationships with their employers, and develop skills that complemented the corporation's other moving parts. In the ensuing decades, this model of going to a certain place, performing a specific function over certain hours, and abiding by a set of rules became second nature. Many of us have lost sight of how all this is an historical anomaly, one now losing ground to a new conception of work that reveals a shift just as large as that from preindustrial to industrial.

Since the 1880s, factory-line workers have been slowly replaced by increasingly sophisticated machinery. Automation played a key role in the steady decline of Detroit and the automobile industry mid-century and into the 1980s, and many working in industries like mining and trucking today watch as their occupations threaten to be automated out of existence. As innovation proceeds apace, we're now making a quantum leap forward into AI and machine learning, developments that promise to drastically expand the types of jobs affected by technology. AI expert Kai Fu Lee predicted that somewhere around 50 percent of the world's jobs would be fully automated by 2027. The idea of jobs being replaced by machines is hardly a new one, and a jobless future has been long predicted even as new occupations emerge.

But what is true is that we are rapidly approaching a world where our idea of a "job" is markedly different than it was during most of the twentieth century. With the rise of the 1099 or gig economy, accelerated by COVID-19, we are already well on our way: An NPR/Marist poll found that one in five US jobs is held under contract. The researchers estimated that by 2028, "freelancers and contractors could make up half of the American workforce" and noted, correctly, that "policymakers are just starting to talk about the implications."

When the COVID-19 pandemic hit the US in the spring of 2020, still more assumptions about the nature of jobs—what a job entails—began to emerge. The first of these was whether one's job required one to be at a specific place in order to perform it. Work-from-home became surprisingly efficient, but of course only for those who were not required to interact with other people in person (the service sector, including hospital and emergency personnel) or to work in factories or on farms (manufacturing). Likewise, many small businesses, everything from automotive repair shops to HVAC technicians, couldn't execute their trades from the comfort of their couches or home desks. The larger economic shift towards those who could work from home (including professional services) was hardly new; now it became starkly apparent. It was as if a giant beta test were being conducted to see if remote work was feasible. The professional class passed with flying colors. In the context of our discussion of what a job actually entails, a stark line was drawn.

No question, the decline of the traditional job in the twentieth-century sense, a decline hastened by both technology and contract arrangements, is having and will continue to have profound social and economic consequences. In this regard, the COVID-19 pandemic simply accelerated an existing trend. In an article I authored for the *Economic Development Journal*, I wrote, "The prevailing view of work—that the ultimate objective is to enter into a fixed relationship with a corporation by getting a 'job'—is rendered obsolete. It is replaced by a vision of work as a means of meeting the individual's needs: financial, personal, and creative." Younger workers' views of meaningful employment involve much more than fitting into a corporate niche.

While economic developers stick to the objective of bringing traditional jobs to communities via large employers, the younger workforce and many large employers have moved on. They see how people are contributing economic value outside of the nine-to-five in-office paradigm—and they are acting accordingly.

Reflected in all this is a rather uncomfortable truth for economic developers: A healthy economy does not necessarily require job creation in any traditional sense. Even as recent labor force participation rates have declined, productivity rates continue to grow. The same phenomenon can be seen from a slightly different angle. Notwithstanding a sharp dip in 2008, our gross domestic product has increased while job creation shows only modest growth.

When jobs, in the twentieth-century sense of the word, are the primary focus of economic development, we miss several important realities. First is that jobs are not necessarily what the economy needs, especially during periods of near full employment (by standard measurements). The main issue is not the jobs themselves but the supply of competent and creative people to fill them. In addition, the old "job creation" model assumes that corporate benefits will be local. With the combination of "gig workers," contractors, and remote workers, an employer with an office in one community might employ many people from across the country, or the world. Perhaps most importantly, the old model assumes that businesses will continue to create jobs as they seek to grow. We can sum up this fallacy in a simple mantra: *Business is not in the business of creating jobs.* If a corporation sets up shop in one community but then finds that it can increase its productivity and profits without increasing its greatest cost—labor—it will absolutely do so. As technology moves forward, the opportunities for businesses to do more with a smaller payroll will only grow. It is more than a little revealing that public officials have a great deal of trouble coming to grips with this most obvious of insights.

Again, given all this, why do we still offer gargantuan sums of taxpayer funds in exchange for traditional jobs?

By any measure, the sum of money transferred each year from public coffers to businesses' balance sheets is staggering—and all in the name of job creation. The Brookings Institution puts that number at between $45 billion and $90 billion, depending on how you define and measure the expenditure. "That's more than the federal government spends on housing, education, or infrastructure," noted Derek Thompson in *The Atlantic* in 2018. "And since cities and states can't print money or run steep deficits, these deals take scarce resources from everything local governments would otherwise pay for, such as schools, roads, police, and prisons." Texas itself accounts for much of the annual sum of public money that goes to corporations in economic development deals. Through its Chapter 313 program alone—just one of many of the state's economic development programs—Texas handed corporations $7 billion in tax credits between 2002 and 2016. The program was expected to balloon to $1 billion annually by 2022.

The uncomfortable truth for economic developers is that the majority of these corporate enticements may be unnecessary, and that is certainly true for Chapter 313. University of Texas scholar Nathan Jensen examined that specific program. Because of its structure, which includes supplemental payments that hinge on whether tax breaks are a factor in the company's decision to locate to Texas, Jensen could determine the effectiveness of the incentives:

> Although the credits were a determining factor for several companies that moved to the state, 85 to 95 percent of companies that received the credit would have relocated to Texas regardless of whether the program existed. This means the state gave away tax dollars—which otherwise could have been used for public services—to companies that were going to move to Texas anyway.

Indeed, tax incentives do not—at least at first—factor in when a corporation compiles a list of sites for a relocation. A typical initial survey by an expanding business may include up to fifty cities, with little conjecture over which will offer the most generous abatements. Only once the corporation uses its other criteria (the makeup of the workforce, suppliers located in the area, and so on) to narrow its list of candidates—usually fewer than ten cities—do tax incentives come into play. That is when the corporation begins to negotiate among candidate cities to get the best possible deal.

So while job creation through tax breaks is not exactly a zero-sum game, these economic development practices can give the illusion of job creation when *job relocation* would be more accurate. Tax-break programs "don't add to overall employment so much as they just shuffle jobs around," wrote Adam Davidson, cofounder of the *Planet Money* podcast, in *The New York Times Magazine* in 2011. "This helps explain [then-governor] Rick Perry's claim that more than one million jobs were created under his watch in Texas while the rest of the country lost more than two million." In other words, Perry's boast about new jobs was really just a relocating of those jobs from other states, not ground-up creation.

The most unscrupulous companies have been known to bounce around from city to city, soaking up tax breaks wherever they may be found. History's worst offenders have been call centers. In the 1990s, many cities wanted to attract these businesses. Call centers ping-ponged from region to region, taking advantage of tax breaks and offering very little of value in return, especially not lasting employment. Today most such firms have been outsourced to Mexico, India, and the Philippines, but the same dynamic is still in play with other businesses.

Even when communities can recover a portion of their incentive packages after a deal went wrong, more often than not the damage is already done. Take one of the most notorious site-selection catastrophes: Rhode Island's overture to the ill-fated video game company 38 Studios, founded by former Boston Red Sox pitcher Curt Schilling. Rhode Island offered to back a $75 million loan for 38 Studios, which promised 450 new jobs. Despite warnings from inside the state's own economic development community, Rhode Island forged ahead with the deal. As 38 Studios prepared to release its first game, *Kingdoms of Amalur: Reckoning*, it found itself pulled between the demands of the market and its promises to Rhode Island. "Mr. Schilling and his main investor found themselves at cross-purposes," reported *The New York Times*. "He needed to control costs, but the taxpayers had been promised more jobs, and jobs they got." Two years later, 38 Studios went bankrupt, the jobs disappeared, and state officials were left wondering whether to blow the state's budget by paying back the bonds or to default on them, putting at risk their credit rating. Lincoln Chafee, who became Rhode Island's governor shortly after the deal was final, called it "the worst investment that's ever been made . . . in the history of Rhode Island."

Thanks in some measure to HQ2, these dynamics have come to the attention of more policymakers, activists, and regular citizens than ever before. Many now question the wisdom of offering incentives in the first place. Mark Funkhouser, former Kansas City mayor, has gone so far as to propose a ban on such deals: "We need a national law that prohibits corporations from extracting bribes from state and local governments and bans governments from donating tax dollars to private entities—a sort of domestic equivalent of the Foreign Corrupt Practices Act, which prohibits American companies from bribing foreign governments." Why would New York City or Washington, DC, need to incentivize Amazon to move its jobs there when the company would have gone to either place anyway?

While banning such incentives might be easier for wealthier cities, it does not work for all. Indeed, not all cities are like Austin, which has the luxury of approaching economic development with plenty of its own cards to play. Aside from everything else, if job creation were the perfect yardstick for measuring a city's economic success, Austin would still excel. In the century's second decade, Austin's unemployment rate hovered at least two to three percentage points below the Texas average. In May 2018, unemployment was at a minuscule 2.6 percent. Beginning the third quarter of 2022, and despite the ravages of the pandemic, the unemployment rate is that low yet again. And the labor force participation rate (a more accurate indicator than unemployment rate) is the highest in the nation.

Austin has never been unduly focused on the tax-breaks-for-jobs model, however. This is in large part due to the advantage of long being a desirable place for high-skilled people and the companies that want to employ them. On December 9, 1966, an *Austin American-Statesman* headline declared, "IBM WILL BUILD HERE." In the article, IBM Vice President Gordon Moodie explained that the company looked at many other locations but that "Austin sold itself. . . . It offers a fine living and working environment, outstanding educational advantages and impressive recreational and cultural features. The kinds of people we need are here." IBM became one of the city's top employers, and seven companies soon moved to Austin to act as its suppliers. And as with similar economic-development deals from that time period, no huge outlays of taxpayer money were required. "Austin's success in the 1960s and 70s in making the transition from government to high technology manufacturing," wrote Austin historian David C. Humphrey, "was built on the traditional factors of relatively low-cost land, a high-skilled workforce at reasonable wages, and a desirable quality of life."

Former Austin Mayor Will Wynn said something similar not long ago when I spent several hours discussing Austin with him and Zappos founder Tony Hsieh, who was in town for SXSW. Looking out over the city blocks below the balcony on which we stood, Hsieh asked Wynn what Austin had done to put itself at the forefront of job creation. Wynn's answer was short on tax abatements and long on "quality of place."

Austin does not refrain entirely from offering incentives to businesses relocating to Central Texas, of course. These deals are not always perfect, but in my estimation the city does a better-than-average job of vetting and ensuring that the deals make good sense. In addition, there are a set of implicit agreements—along with explicit zoning restrictions—ensuring that no company, tech or otherwise, moves to the city thinking it will be allowed to develop over the Barton Creek Greenbelt. The City of Austin's web page for its business expansion incentive plan lists some of the more explicit criteria for companies seeking enticements: They should be creating jobs "at above-industry standard compensation, especially for middle-skill workers" and for people who are facing socioeconomic hardship, and companies should be able to show that they will create community benefits beyond tax revenue. A clear departure from the old "jobs at any cost" model.

Mayor Wynn's successor, Steve Adler, campaigned heavily on smarter approaches to job creation. He was explicit, for instance, about how incentives should be geared toward ensuring Austin gets the right kind of jobs. "We've shown we can bring lots of high-paying jobs to this city," he said at his victory party immediately following his 2014 election, "but are we clever enough and smart enough to bring enough middle-class jobs for the people that live here?" He went on, "We are losing people and communities, because it's unaffordable for many to live in this city." This echoes concerns articulated in Imagine Austin, a thirty-year plan for the city crafted in 2012 that Jennifer Todd-Goynes wrote about in chapter 7. Imagine Austin presented six key challenges and opportunities, one being "Promoting Prosperity for All." The plan's authors asked, "How do we help all Austinites find good jobs in our high-skill economy? How do we ensure that musicians, young families, and hourly workers aren't priced out of Austin? How can we help wage growth catch up to the rising costs of living, closing the affordability gap? How can we expand job opportunities and enhance the skills of our labor force?" The answers are complicated, and I offer a different perspective in chapter 10.

Another blind spot in traditional, jobs-focused economic development practice is indeed that the jobs created through typical tax-abatement deals are very often the ones that require the greatest tech skills and come in the lowest quantity. The higher wage occupations being sought (such as coders or even mechanics) are also the most vulnerable to technological innovation, particularly AI. By assuming that we can simply entice large corporations to our communities and expect them to create jobs, and thus prosperity, we may in fact be contributing to the hollowing out of the middle class.

Whenever I repeat the line that best summarizes the flawed central assumption of economic development—"Business is not in the business of creating jobs"—the reactions from different audiences fascinate me. As I have said, the statement often elicits gasps from economic developers and matter-of-fact shrugs from CEOs and human resources directors. Encapsulated in these two reactions is the deep disconnect between economic developers and corporations. To one the idea is heretical; to the other it is common sense.

No one suggests that corporations should work against their own economic viability. It would be foolish to expect a profit-seeking enterprise to employ workers who do not contribute to the efficient creation of products and services. Nevertheless, the tax-abatements-for-jobs model is built on this very assumption. In fact, the *compact* between businesses and cities is broken. It is in desperate need of revision *from both sides*. Currently, neither can hold up its end of the bargain—not the city, because of incentives that do not pay off; and not the companies, because they cannot guarantee numerous, well-paid, and long-lasting jobs, especially in an era of increasing automation. Amazon's HQ2's promise of fifty thousand jobs over ten years was itself quite a leap—even the wisest business leaders would have difficulty pinpointing how many jobs they could create in two years, let alone an entire decade. And in any case, communities have few tools for keeping their corporations accountable to such commitments.

Economic developers have operated almost exclusively in the space between corporations and their hiring practices in communities and the needs and desires of those communities where corporations set up shop. This means we must navigate between the Scylla of corporations' inherent drive to do more with fewer jobs and the Charybdis of communities' expectations that we will help bring stable jobs to them, along with economic security, health insurance, and a place to socialize and find meaning. Yet how long will economic developers continue to reward corporations for doing something not necessarily in their own interest—that is, creating more jobs?

And what is the alternative? For starters, expectations must be rethought. Civic leaders and the economic developers who work with them must take seriously the possibility that by handing out significant tax incentives they could be undermining their power to fund the very things that make the city attractive to talent and business alike—among them civic amenities, updated infrastructure, and good schools. Businesses, on the other hand, will need to be more transparent about the fact that their growth will not be employment-dependent.

Critical, too, is an acknowledgement that financial incentives, including both direct cash payment and tax rollbacks, are not the only available tools for economic prosperity. When cities do incentivize corporations, the deals should begin with a realistic assessment of whether the agreement will create both immediate and lasting value in the community. Secondarily, the talent question (skilled workers) must be a part of the agreement. Acres of land might be offered totally free to a corporation, but if local talent is not available, the deal should never go forward. This, of course, is more or less obvious, but it is perverted when the agreement requires that jobs be created—as if they exist separately from the business model that determines corporate profitability. And viability.

As economic developers and local civic leaders confront this new reality, we must become better students of our local and regional workforces. It is not enough to understand the composition of employees traditionally on the payroll in the region. Those data are the most readily available but form only part of a much larger picture. A labor market of entrepreneurs, freelancers, and people with side jobs and side businesses, for instance, is growing outside the realm of traditional employment measures. This cohort will continue to grow. For each new job created by an entrepreneurial firm, the firm often creates four to five outsourced jobs. Economic developers must understand this burgeoning "1099 economy" and find ways to tap into its value and its implications, as corporations are already doing so. Beyond the creation of more nine-to-five jobs, economic developers must ask themselves, how else might corporations contribute to the community?

Measuring the success of an economic development project by a metric other than job creation is a significant departure from tradition. Yet we have arrived at an inflection point. We are realizing that business has a fundamentally different relationship to labor than it has ever had. We are recognizing that people without traditional jobs add value to the economy, in some cases more so than people with traditional jobs. The adoption of a broader perspective on who is creating value within our local economies has never been more important. The relationships between cities and corporations, and between corporations and employees, are shifting rapidly and irreversibly. Cities must devise new, creative approaches if they are to build and maintain the vibrant, equitable, and prosperous cities of the future.

CHAPTER TEN

The Future of Austin

If we have given any clarity to the question of how Austin became Austin, does that better equip us to know what Austin can become? I think the answer is yes. Or rather, the answer has to be yes. The combined pressures of technology (AI), sustainability (climate change), and social equity have turned economic development on its head. And of course, it is not just the economic development world that is affected. A community without a vision for addressing these issues is one whose future is deeply compromised. For Austin, that vision has been long in the making. Its general outline was established at its origin ("seat of empire"), reinforced by the damming of the Colorado River and the creation of a "coastal culture" along its highland lakes, the embrace of a countercultural ethos encapsulated by "weirdness," and finally its transformation into one of the nation's premier technology centers. At the beginning of the twenty-first century, Austin emerged as a global destination for creative talent. SXSW Interactive was more than an add-on to a music culture. The most unlikely of institutions and corporations now seek a home in Austin, including even the Army Futures Command, a division focused on war-readiness and technology, established in 2018.

What Comes Next

Here's the thing about vision: Don't begin by limiting your ambitions. Austin in 2050 will look like what? If the answer is simply a bigger and more bloated version of its current self, is that a vision worth pursuing? Is it a vision at all?

Austin's future successes may not, in fact, lie with what we currently think of as our proudest accomplishments. The recruitment of major corporations, ever taller high-rises, huge population gains—will these be the markers of Austin 2050? What if we flip the narrative and ask what is best left *un*done, what can we avoid falling prey to, what is best left *un*developed. In other words, can we imagine a future where we can resist the temptations of overreaching?

One of the most surprising side effects of the COVID-19 pandemic was the relief we felt at not having to contend with traffic anymore. Austin's notorious congestion is enough to send even the calmest of people into a rage. Suddenly the roads and highways felt appropriate for the volume of cars passing over them. The air was cleaner, and it was noticeably quieter. The commute time for those without the luxury of being able to work from home was reduced dramatically. We suddenly had a vision of what a congestion-free future would look like. What might have followed from this experience was an imperative to not build more roads and accommodate more vehicles and to change the transportation paradigm altogether. Collectively, we had conducted a massive beta test to determine whether office jobs could be done remotely. It soon became evident that the test was successful. Here was a promise for a different future.

Now more than five years later, in 2025, that promise is clouded. While many workers were able to adjust their schedules to a less frequent commute, the surge of new residents more than offset that advantage. Rather than rethink the commute between home and work (which is the overwhelming source of traffic congestion), the old approach to the problem was the only one under serious consideration: build more roads. Supposedly creative solutions (bike lane improvements) were ill-conceived and remained oblivious to changing modes of personal mobility, which included not only electric scooters but also the emerging wave of e-bikes. A major bond initiative for light-rail passed, but the prospect of traffic reduction as a result remains something of a pipe dream. The budget has already skyrocketed, the timeline may be double what was anticipated, and the routes chosen do not reflect commuting realities.

This scenario, however, is not as bleak as it may seem. Commuting patterns are changing. Personal mobility is becoming a reality, and the promise of semiautonomous vehicles is no longer a fantasy. If we're to be optimistic, the combination of smart decisions in the past will outpace poorly conceived choices of the present. And what does that mean? It means that people have made choices based on their expectations for what the city can be: walkable, committed to green space, and not dominated by highways and arterials that divide neighborhoods. Sometimes the best planning is no planning at all. This is the lesson of Jane Jacobs and Christopher Alexander. It is also the vision of Sinclair Black and the planners at the City of Austin whom he has influenced. A city that protects green space in relation to the total population (and acts on it) is one with no need to "solve" the traffic problem. If the traditional solution to traffic congestion (build more roads!) has always failed, then perhaps the way out of the conundrum is to approach the question from an entirely different angle. What if, we might ask, no more roads could be built—then what would we do? There is a perverse logic to this approach, one that seeks solutions by redefining the problem entirely.

As Jennifer Todd-Goynes makes clear in her chapter on Austin's convoluted planning history, traffic is not the only point of contention in the city's growth. It does, however, remain a flash point in our conflicted views of whether we can accept even more transplants. It is no surprise that the Austin Chamber of Commerce has repeatedly identified traffic as "our most pressing issue." And while solving Austin's traffic problems is not the aim of this book, mobility is central to the idea of what the future may hold. In short, the future of roads, highways, and other forms of public transit will remain crucial to the larger vision of what Austin can become. The combined forces of technology, social equity, and climate change (affecting every aspect of the environment) will eventually overrun the existing debate over how many more lanes to add to I-35. If people are commuting less, if they live close to their place of work, and if new forms of mobility emerge, the old debate may finally be put to rest. A more holistic approach to the question of where we live in relation to where we work and where we recreate is both necessary and inevitable.

The other major change that coincided with the pandemic was the heightened attention to social equity. The murder of George Floyd in May of 2020 brought old issues of racial division to the fore. Like other cities across the United States, Austin responded with protests and demonstrations. The revulsion at what was so graphically evident quickly took on a broader perspective. As Tracye McDaniel's chapter starkly lays out, the divisions within the city have a long and painful history. Not that Austin's racial divide was a secret. When I moved to Austin in the spring of 1994, my realtor refused to take me to the east side of the city. Crossing the interstate, he said, was pointless. He maintained that there was no reason to look at properties in East Austin because nobody would want to live there.

A reckoning with the redlining of Austin was long overdue but had to wait almost another decade to be realized. And, many would argue, it was too late to make a difference. The "gentrification" of East Austin surged with the onset of the pandemic. The average home price in East Austin was "still" under $400,000 in 2019—seemingly reasonable compared to other trendy neighborhoods until you consider its steeper-than-average increase over the last twenty years compared to other areas of the city. By the fall of 2023 (despite rising interest rates) it was nearly $550,000.

The confluence of the pandemic with rapidly rising home prices east of the interstate had broader implications, ones directly tied to the sense of injustice set in motion by the widening protests. The displacement of longtime Black and Hispanic residents from East Austin around this time is well-documented by 2020 census data, as well as more current data between 2020 and 2023. The connection does not require sophisticated analysis. Rapidly rising demand for housing, accelerated by new residents and by apartment and condo dwellers looking for larger living spaces from which to work remotely, meant that the east side was increasingly an option. That trend is irreversible.

Remote work (and its implications for traffic) along with social equity issues (and their implications for housing) are not the only fallouts of the COVID-19 pandemic. As has become obvious to us all, these trends are now accelerating. The future was foreshortened. And while it may be trite to say that these forces open new opportunities, that may not be an exaggeration.

It has long been assumed that Austin's population would continue to increase indefinitely. But while growth has been continuous for over a century now, trends can sometimes slow or even reverse themselves. In 1971, Seattle had a billboard that read "Will the Last Person Leaving SEATTLE—Turn Out the Lights." And here in Austin, in 2024, we went from being the tenth-largest city in the country to eleventh. This raises a different kind of question, one that considers the city in the larger context of regional growth. After all, the Austin metropolitan area continues to grow at a prodigious rate. This was the question of Envision Central Texas more than twenty years ago: How do you accommodate an expanding *region*? That Austin, the capital city, will continue to be the magnet for countless people is obvious. Where in the region they will live, and what their commitment to the city of Austin will be is another question entirely. What we can hope for—and work toward—is a steady reinvention of the city, a reinvention that draws on the visionaries who saw in Austin something extraordinary, unbound by the conventions of their own time. Those elements point the way to Austin's future.

There is a straight line connecting the origin story of Austin to what it can become: Austin as a global city, a city taking its place among the great cities of the world. This acknowledgement—this continuation of a vision—must be baked into our civic leaders, our corporations, our universities, our people. In many respects, the framework is already in place: the University of Texas, where "what starts here changes the world." International tech companies that seek to grow not just in manufacturing or distribution, but also in R&D and design. Global connections to include a growing list of national and international flight destinations. Festivals and conferences that already have worldwide prominence. And most importantly, the talent that emerges in the city—those individuals whose fortune and future are themselves magnetic. We've seen that in my time in the city, in George Kozmetsky, in Michael Dell, and now even in Elon Musk, who chose to build his own vision of the future of transportation with the Model Y Tesla and Cybertruck factory in Austin.

So what does the future look like from 2026 and beyond? What are the factors that will come into play for Austin—and for other cities seeking to take their place as global centers of commerce and creativity? We could identify dozens of challenges, dozens of paths forward, but we can be confident of three that are nonnegotiable for Austin and, indeed, for cities across the world. They are environmental resiliency, social equity, and technological savvy.

1. The Environment

While the Colorado River, Barton Springs, and the creeks flowing into Lady Bird Lake have always been part of Austin's identity, the creation of the Highland Lakes transformed Austin. This transformation, however, invites a new perspective on the community. That perspective—that vision—was first articulated by Sinclair Black in 1973–74. Austin's creeks are integral to the city's identity. They are not a flooding nuisance that needs management. They are not incidental "runoffs" that can be built on top of. Austin's creeks are priceless assets that will increasingly define the city's geography and its development potential. In ways that were still not fully appreciated in the 1970s, they are also a crucial safeguard against the damaging effects of climate change.

2. Social Equity

Interstate highways that divide communities are certainly not unique to Austin. But reversing trends that separate the city between the haves and have-nots is a formidable challenge. As with so many cities, this challenge divides along racial lines, particularly for Black and Hispanic neighborhoods. If we fail to create opportunities for disadvantaged populations to participate in the reinvention of Austin, we will have a community for whom openness is no longer possible. We will have separated ourselves from the broader world that births new ideas and new solutions.

3. The AI Challenge

George Kozmetsky established a framework for understanding technology that has served Austin well. The dynamics, however, have changed more rapidly than anyone could anticipate. These are best understood as the complex (and evolving) effect of information technology—and AI in particular—on individuals, cities, and corporations. This is a complex topic, gyrating wildly between the promise of ever more remarkable solutions to some of humanity's most persistent problems (from transportation to communication to health) and the growing anxiety around privacy and "machines replacing humans." These concerns—and the promise of technological solutions—are not new. The particular challenge for our institutions, however, has never felt more fraught. We have to wonder whether economic development will be able to overcome a growing range of contradictions. The inadequacy of "job creation" as a metric is certainly at the top of that list, but it also includes weighing the benefits of commercial and industrial development against the effect on the environment. In the most general sense, we can't stop asking the question that weaves itself through this book and through our economic lives: What are the long-term consequences of unbridled technological growth?

Austin may well be in the bull's-eye of these issues, but in varying degrees every community will face similar challenges. I should like to think of this work—and that of my coauthors—as a call to action. And perhaps we can view these challenges in a way that every community leader and, indeed, every individual will feel invested in.

In this regard, Austin remains a model. The commercial real estate sector is as vibrant as any in the country. Growth in the surrounding counties has eased the price of Austin homes and rentals. Major tech corporations continue to seek out opportunities within the downtown and along Lady Bird Lake. The vision of Austin—one of creative collaboration between the city and tech companies—continues to insulate us against the more severe shocks that roil other communities. While Austin's resilience is particularly robust, and while the Austin story is unique, there are lessons applicable to other cities.

We have shied away from suggesting that there is a road map for others to follow. A map, after all, suggests that we know the lay of the land. We do not. As Boris Pasternak wrote in the poem "Hamlet," attached to *Doctor Zhivago* (mirroring a Russian proverb): "Life is not a walk across an open field." This has stuck with me. There is no map from where we are to where we are going. We can't see the destination because the destination is not yet determined. The future is always a blur. There are, however, lessons to be shared. In the case of Austin, we can identify those that other cities may find useful. Our work at TIP Strategies seeks to incorporate them in all of our thinking. And yes, they revolve around the three most pressing issues every community and every region must face: incorporating technology into the urban fabric, ensuring climate resiliency, and being willing to address social equity in ways that go beyond sloganeering and help close the wealth gap.

AFTERWORD

The future is unrolling in ways I could hardly have imagined when I first conceived of this book. A pandemic hardly anyone saw coming upended a wide gamut of economic and social norms. The commercial real estate market was upended. The retail sector was thrown into turmoil. Education suffered immeasurable damage. Supply chains were disrupted. And no sooner had we emerged from the worst of COVID-19 than we were struck with unprecedented natural disasters, from wildfires in Hawaii and California to hurricanes in Florida and throughout the Southeast (along with a devastating ice storm in Texas that stressed the power grid to the breaking point).

On top of these environmental shocks, we continue to be roiled by social justice issues that have become political flash points—from police shootings, to the dilemma of housing the homeless, to our position on immigration, both illegal and legal. "Diversity, equity, and inclusion" as a social agenda is being actively exorcised not only from academia but from federal programs overall. As the second Trump administration takes office, a trade war is in full bloom, and Biden's support for clean energy initiatives is being replaced by a renewed drive for fossil fuel extraction. It is no exaggeration to say that social and political divisions threaten to rend the fabric of our social compact. However this resolves itself, the needs of communities will continue to be heard. In fact, those needs will be more pressing than ever regardless of who is president or which party is in power. Economic development policy—and the public sector's response to the needs of the private sector—must adapt itself accordingly, but it cannot be passive in the face of these changes.

It is against this backdrop that Austin's future will take shape. And not just Austin's, but also those of aspiring cities across the country. The resiliency of those communities will be tested: environmentally and socially.

Where people move and why they move will continue to determine economic success. There is no "steady state" for American cities. The reasons for Austin's growth, and the way it will manage that growth, can be a model for other communities. What we have sought to do in this book is to highlight some of the reasons for Austin's success, along with the inevitable pitfalls that explosive growth entails. The unwillingness to preserve those qualities that first attracted people is a prescription for failure. No one wants to identify with a community that has lost its essential character.

We have argued that in Austin's case, a commitment to the *geography* of the region was essential to its success. "Geography is destiny," a quote attributed to Napoleon and many others, is relevant here. The hill on which Lamar declared Austin to be a seat of empire, the Colorado River, the springs and streams that flow through the city—this is geography. When you embrace it, when you preserve it, you maintain the most essential aspect of what it means to be a place. If there are lessons to be learned from Austin, this is the first and most important.

The trick, of course, is to define what commitment to place actually means. And in this challenge we see the seeds of Austin's expanding vision of a community that embraces innovation and creativity. The coastal culture created by the lakes, a downtown that actively encouraged residential development, a university whose mission was to change the world, and a cultural scene that took music and made it a universal platform of expression. Embracing technology and its role in benefiting the community is the only way forward. Every community charts its own course. This happens both by accident and by design. The essential elements of success, however, are available to us. The preservation of the unique identity of a community begins with its geography (a sense of place) and extends to an embrace of an open society. Austin's future rests on maintaining that commitment. The future of your community depends on it as well.

Acknowledgments

In many ways, acknowledging all those who helped bring this book to fruition is the hardest part of the job. It is hard for many reasons, beginning with the sense of loss I feel at those who passed away since I began this project. Pike Powers, John Aielli, and John Fregonese top that list. They were not only a constant source of inspiration, they were also dear friends. On the drive back to Austin from Houston, John Fregonese and I talked about how the story of Austin needed to be told, how it needed to reach a larger audience. And Pike, well, without him this book wouldn't exist. He provided unlimited access to all the facts and issues and themes that made him an indispensable part of the Austin story.

Other pivotal people featured throughout the book include Tim McClure. Tim is a friend and mentor from when we first met in the 1990s. Of course, his fame will forever be associated with the "Don't Mess with Texas" campaign, but his influence reaches far beyond that. In fact, I still blame him for delaying the book by a year or two. And I thank him at the same time. It was he who criticized an early draft by pointing out that I was omitting the history of East Austin. Of course, he was right—and it's still embarrassing that I needed to be reminded of the importance of that topic. Fortunately, Tracye McDaniel was able to fill that void. I also need to blame, and thank, Travis James for another delay caused by another omission on my part. When I outlined that same early draft for him, he wanted to know why I was giving short shrift to the entrepreneurial and startup scene in Austin. Elsie L. Echeverri-Carroll and Evan Johnston's chapter corrects that glaring oversight.

The number of people who generously gave hours and hours of their time to filling in the Austin story is extensive. Not only did Dave Gibson of IC^2 coauthor the definitive book on Austin's collaborative tech growth, but he also willingly sat through my pestering and persistent questions. Also at IC^2, Monty Jones, George Kozmetsky's biographer, filled in important gaps in my appreciation of George's thinking.

Glenn West, Greg Hartmann, Laura Kilcrease, Bill Stotesbery, Isaac Barchas, and Sandy Dochen all added to the Austin story from their unique perspectives. Steven Pedigo both reviewed the book and helped find a willing publisher in Texas A&M University Press. Thom Lemmons's willingness to take a risk on me is no small matter.

Sinclair Black's influence is well-documented in the book, and his visionary approach to the importance of Austin's creeks cannot be overestimated. Similarly,

Larry Speck's contribution to the architectural integrity of Austin needs to be acknowledged.

Anthony Orum was kind enough to discuss his underappreciated Austin history book *Power, Money & the People: The Making of Modern Austin*. It was through him that I learned to understand the importance of Austin's "coastal culture."

The number of individuals and organizations given only a passing reference—or not cited at all—is extensive. That list begins with Angelos Angelou, who made my transition to consulting possible and who is a key figure in Austin's tech evolution. John Sibley Butler, a distinguished professor at the University of Texas is both a personal friend and an inspiration to everyone who has had the pleasure of his company. It's a strange coincidence that he and I served together in the Americal Division in Vietnam, although we did not know each other then. Carol Thompson, Jim Skaggs, Josh Baer—the list goes on and I apologize in advance to those I have failed to mention.

Central to many of the themes in this book is the profound influence of Richard Florida. I first met Richard while serving on a panel with him in Wisconsin shortly after the publication of *The Rise of the Creative Class*. His willingness to tolerate my critiques—many of which he had already anticipated—speaks to his unwavering commitment to getting these topics right, a flexibility not many writers possess.

I would also be remiss if I didn't recognize Matt Patin, who helped organize my thinking, guided early drafts, and put up with my bursts of ill temper. And it was Tula Karras who finally brought the book to fruition. Her careful editing and thoughtful critiques were invaluable. This book might never have been completed without her.

My partners and colleagues at TIP Strategies also deserve more than a passing reference. Without the support of Tom Stellman, in particular, I would not have had the confidence to continue with this project. His enthusiasm for the book kept me going when I thought that I would never see light at the end of the tunnel. My coauthors, Jennifer Todd-Goynes and Tracye McDaniel, along with Elsie L. Echeverri-Carroll and Evan Johnston, are responsible for addressing topics I would have been unable to do justice to.

Finally, my love and appreciation to my wife, Jan. She suffered through my bleakest moments ("This will never get done. Why did I ever think this was a good idea?!") and then produced the bibliography, which may prove as valuable as anything that might be attributed to me.

Notes

CHAPTER ONE

1. The story of Holiday House echoes the very debate about growth and eccentricity that continues to roil the city. Holiday House was the restaurant where George Kozmetsky would meet friends for breakfast—usually at the ungodly hour of 5:00 a.m. After fifty years in business, it was forced to close when its new vegan landlord decided that its non-vegetarian fare should condemn it to oblivion. A fractured fairy tale in every sense.
2. It is no small irony that McLuhan's book *The Medium is the Massage* is invariably misread as "the medium is the message." McLuhan wrote this book to demonstrate that (among other things) technology mattered not just for what it delivered to us; the medium of technology was itself the "message." It massaged us into confusing the delivery with the product. It is a small step, according to his way of thinking, that the iPhone and other tech devices would become cult objects in their own right. His insights were well ahead of their time. They prefigured the media explosion that began with television and then morphed into the internet.

CHAPTER FIVE

1. Elsie L. Echeverri-Carroll is a senior research fellow at the LBJ School of Public Affairs at the University of Texas at Austin. Evan Johnston is a senior analyst at TIP Strategies. Many people provided helpful comments on the research summarized herein. We are particularly indebted to our collaborators at the IC^2 Institute, Professor David Eaton at the LBJ School, and Maryann Feldman. We are also grateful for the financial support of the Kauffman Foundation, the interviewers who gave more than one hundred hours of their time, and Capital Factory for its collaboration in two workshops. A total of ten students worked intermittently on this research, and all made important contributions to this project. However, we would like to highlight the dedication of Erica Mirabitur, who spent countless hours collecting and reviewing more than five hundred archival documents. Finally, this book's editor, Jon Roberts, edited it with patience and an exceedingly sharp pen. This manuscript reads differently because of his friendship and skills.
2. Jorge Guzman and Scott Stern, "The State of American Entrepreneurship: New Estimates of the Quality and Quantity of Entrepreneurship for 32 US

States, 1988–2014," *American Economic Journal: Economic Policy* 12, no. 4 (2020): 212–43.

3. Jim Clardy left Texas Instruments, where he worked for twenty-one years, to found Crystal Semiconductors in Austin in 1985. Three engineers—Nav Sooch, Jeffrey Scott, and David Welland—left CS to found Silicon Labs in Austin in 1996.
4. Elsie L. Echeverri-Carroll and William Brennan, "Are Innovation Networks Bounded by Proximity?" in *Innovation, Networks and Localities*, eds. Manfred M. Fischer et al. (Springer-Verlag, 1999), 28–49.
5. This includes documents from the 1960s onward, published at the *Austin American-Statesman*, the *Austin Business Journal*, the Austin Chamber of Commerce, and the IC^2 Institute.
6. Arnold C. Cooper, "The Role of Incubator Organizations in the Founding of Growth-Oriented Firms," *Journal of Business Venturing* 1, no. 1 (1985): 75–86.
7. As Enrico Moretti from the University of California at Berkley noted in *The New Geography of Jobs*, "One [direct] high-tech job generates 5 [indirect] local service jobs. In essence, he said, high-tech jobs are the cause of local prosperity, and doctors, lawyers, roofers, and yoga teachers are the effect." Enrico Moretti, *The New Geography of Jobs* (Houghton Mifflin Harcourt, 2013), 60. Austin exemplifies this employment dynamic. A 2022 Brookings Institution report notes that among 384 metropolitan areas in the US, only eight "superstars," including much smaller Austin, accounted for nearly half of the nation's technology sector job creation between 2015 and 2019. Mark Muro and Yang You, *Superstars, Rising Stars, and the Rest: Pandemic Trends and Shifts in the Geography of Tech*," Brookings Report (2022), https://www.brookings.edu/articles/superstars-rising-stars-and-the-rest-pandemic-trends-and-shifts-in-the-geography-of-tech/.
8. See the well-cited book among practitioners, academics, and the media with close to fifteen thousand citations in Google Scholar. AnnaLee Saxenian (a professor at the University of California at Berkeley), *Regional Advantage: Culture and Competition in Silicon Valley and Route 128*, (Harvard University Press, 1994).
9. These business scholars focus on "spin-offs," or independent startups founded by one or more individuals directly after leaving employment in an incumbent (parent company) that does not have ownership or decision-making power in the firm, to distinguish them from other new entrepreneurs whose founders did not leave an established firm to create a new startup. This spin-off process is especially important for entrepreneurial high-tech firms. Amar V. Bhide, *The Origin and Evolution of New Businesses* (Oxford University Press, 1999); Colin Mason and Ross Brown, "Entrepreneurial Ecosystems

and Growth-Oriented Entrepreneurship," paper prepared for the workshop organized by OECD LEED Programme and the Dutch Ministry of Economic Affairs, 2014; David Goss and Eugene Sadler-Smith, "Opportunity Creation: Entrepreneurial Agency, Interaction, and Affect," *Strategic Entrepreneurship Journal* 12, (2017): 219–36; Steven Klepper, "The Origin and Growth of Industry Clusters: The Making of Silicon Valley and Detroit," *Journal of Urban Economics* 67, (2010): 15–32.

10. Octávio Figueiredo, Paulo Guimaraes, et al., "Home-field Advantages: Location Decisions of Portuguese Entrepreneurs," *Journal of Urban Economics* 52, no. 2 (2002): 341–61.
11. Edward Glaeser and William Kerr, "Local Industrial Conditions and Entrepreneurship: How Much of the Spatial Distribution Can We Explain?" *Journal of Economics and Management Strategy* 18, no. 3 (2009): 623–63.
12. Jesper B. Sørensen and Magali A. Fassiotto, "Organizations as Fonts of Entrepreneurship," *Organization Science* 22, no. 5 (2011): 1322–31.
13. Arnold C. Cooper and William C. Dunkelberg, "Entrepreneurial Research: Old Questions, New Answers and Methodological Issues," *American Journal of Small Business* 3, (1987): 11–23; Ramana Nanda and Jesper B. Sørensen, "Workplace Peers and Entrepreneurship," *Management Science* 56, no. 7 (2010): 1116–1126; Peter Roberts et al., "Founder Background and Evolution of Firm Size," *Industrial and Corporate Change* 20, no. 6 (2011); Benjamin A. Campbell et al., "Who Leaves, Where to, and Why Worry? Employee Mobility, Entrepreneurship and Effects on Source Firm Performance," *Strategic Management* 33, no.1 (2012): 65–87; Michael S. Dahl and Olav Sorenson, "The Who, Why, and How of Spinoffs," *Industrial and Corporate Change* 23, no. 3 (2013): 661–88.
14. In a 2002 study of Silicon Valley startups, Diane M. Burton found that 93 percent of entrepreneurs worked for established firms. Diane M. Burton et al., "Coming from Good Stock: Career Histories and New Venture Formation," *Research in the Sociology of Organizations* 19, (2002): 229–62.
15. Arnold C. Cooper, "The Role of Incubator Organizations in the Founding of Growth-Oriented Firms," *Journal of Business Venturing* 1, no. 1 (1985): 75–86; Olav Sorenson, "Social Networks and Industrial Geography," *Journal of Evolutionary Economics* 13, (2003): 513–27; Jesper B. Sørensen, "Bureaucracy and Entrepreneurship: Workplace Effects on Entrepreneurial Entry," *Administrative Science Quarterly* 52, no. 3 (2007): 387–412.
16. Chistina Carias et al., "Entrepreneurship, the Initial Labor Force, and the Location of New Firms," *Small Business Economics* 60, no. 3 (2023): 865–90.
17. Vera Rocha et al., "Leaving Employment to Entrepreneurship: The Value of Co-worker Mobility in Pushed and Pulled-Driven Start-ups," *Journal of Management Studies* 55, no. 1 (2018): 60–85.

18. Paul Gompers et al., "Entrepreneurial Spawning: Public Corporations and the Genesis of New Ventures, 1986 to 1999," *The Journal of Finance* 60, no. 2 (2005): 577–614.
19. Edward, J. Malecki, "Entrepreneurs, Networks, and Economic Development," *Advances in Entrepreneurship, Firm Emergence, and Growth* 3, (1997): 58.
20. Daniel Isenberg, "When Big Companies Fall, Entrepreneurship Rises," *Harvard Business Review*, March 18, 2013, https: //hbr.org/2013/03/when-big-companies-fall-entrep.
21. Gompers et al., "Entrepreneurial Spawning," 577–614.
22. Edward J. Malecki, "Entrepreneurship and Entrepreneurial Ecosystems," Geography Compass 12, (2018): 1–21.
23. Mason and Brown, "Entrepreneurial Ecosystems"; Daniel J. Isenberg, "Applying the Ecosystem Metaphor to Entrepreneurship: Uses and Abuses," *The Antitrust Bulletin* 61, no. 4 (2016): 564–73; Colin M. Mason and Richard T. Harrison, "After the Exit: Acquisitions, Entrepreneurial Recycling and Regional Economic Development," *Regional Studies* 40, no. 1 (2006): 55–73; Ben Spiegel and Richard Harrison, "Toward a Process Theory of Entrepreneurial Ecosystems," *Strategic Entrepreneurship Journal* 12, no. 1 (2018): 151–68.
24. Mason and Brown, "Entrepreneurial Ecosystems"; Mason and Harrison, "Entrepreneurial Recycling"; Ben Spigel, "Developing and Governing Entrepreneurial Ecosystems: The Structure of Entrepreneurial Support Programs in Edinburgh, Scotland," *Journal of Innovation and Regional Development* 7, no. 2 (2016): 141–60.
25. They also considered the possibility that the ecosystem weakened in the third phase, a situation that does not apply to Austin at this moment or in the foreseeable future.
26. Isenberg, "Entrepreneurship Rises."
27. The MIT Cartography Project demonstrates the utility of using new business filings from secretary of state offices to measure the birth of new entrepreneurial startup firms over time. Guzman and Stern, "The State of American Entrepreneurship."
28. For an explanation of the TSOS data, see: Elsie L. Echeverri-Carroll and Maryann P. Feldman, "Chasing Entrepreneurial Firms," *Industry and Innovation* 26, no. 5 (2019): 479–507.
29. Jeffery C. Susbauer, "The Technical Entrepreneurship Process in Austin, Texas," in *Technical Entrepreneurship A Symposium*, eds. Arnold C. Cooper and John L. Komives, (Purdue University, 1972); Raymond W. Smilor et al., "Creating the Technopolis: High-technology Development in Austin, Texas," *Journal of Business Venture* 4 (1989): 49–67.
30. Margaret P. O'Mara, *Cities of Knowledge: Cold War Science and the Search for the Next Silicon Valley*, (Princeton University Press, 2005).

31. Since 1945, Applied Research Laboratories has been involved in military-sponsored research, https://www.ece.utexas.edu/research/groups/applied-research-laboratories.
32. Susbauer, "Technical Entrepreneurship," 33.
33. Raymond W. Smilor et al., "University Spin-Out Companies: Technology Startups from UT-Austin," *Journal of Business Venture* 5, (1990): 63–76.
34. Over the course of its forty-year history, Tracor spun off more than twenty companies, including Austron, Radian, Pinson Associates, Melster Engineering, Weed Instrument, Texas Research International, Galaxy Microsystems, SGE, Zycor, Continuum, Nova Graphics International, and McBee's Research Applications. Diana J. Kleiner, "Tracor: A Pioneer in Defense and Commercial Electronics," in *Handbook of Texas Online* (Texas Historical Association), August 1, 1995, https://www.tshaonline.org/handbook/entries/tracor.

    See also fig. 5 in Raymond W. Smilor et al., "The Austin/San Antonio Corridor: The Dynamics of a Developing Technopolis," The IC² Institute, University of Texas at Austin, 1987. https://repositories.lib.utexas.edu/items/a12ace02-d5a7–4ffe-864b-035229b6e722.
35. Smilor et al., "Creating the Technopolis."
36. Smilor et al., "Creating the Technopolis"; William H. Cunningham, *Texas Way: Money, Power, Politics, and Ambition at the University,* (The Dolph Briscoe Center for American History, University of Texas at Austin, 2018), 325.
37. Amy K. Glassmeier, "Factors Governing the Development of High-Tech Industry Agglomerations: A Tale of Three Cities," *Regional Studies* 22, no. 4 (1988): 287–301.
38. Including Hewlett Packard, Apple, Applied Materials, Compaq, Silicon Labs, Intel, Maximum Integrated Circuits, Lamb Research, Qualcomm, Google, Bizzard, and large foreign corporations such as Tokyo Electron (Japan), Samsung (South Korea), Nokia (Finland), Xplore Technologies (Canada), and Bioware (Canada).
39. Jonathan Miller "Regional Case Study: Austin, Texas, or How to Create a Knowledge Economy," *Angelou Economic Advisors, Inc.* (1999): 3.
40. Miller, "Austin, Texas," 4.
41. Guzman and Stern, "The State of American Entrepreneurship," 226. Guzman and Stern, at the business schools at Columbia and MIT, respectively, propose that a business's decision to incorporate as a for-profit corporation in Delaware, which offers favorable incorporation and tax advantages, provides a good, measurable proxy for high-growth, innovative startups, because they are more likely to patent, receive venture capital, go public, or experience fast growth. It is unlikely that a founder with no intention to grow would incur the yearly expense (around $1,000) to maintain a registration in Delaware.

42. Gompers et al., "Entrepreneurial Spawning."
43. Jesper B. Sørensen, "Closure and Exposure: Mechanisms in the Intergenerational Transmission of Self-Employment," *Research in the Sociology of Organizations* 25, (2007): 83–124; Gompers et al., "Entrepreneurial Spawning;" Sørensen and Fassiotto, "Organizations as Fonts."
44. "Trilogy Software—the biggest tech mafia you've never heard of," Contrary (blog), November 25, 2020, https://www.contrary.com/blog/trilogy-software.
45. Kirk Ladendorf, "Software firm moves to Austin: Trilogy cites labor pool, high-tech firms," *Austin American-Statesman*, October 1, 1992.
46. Lori Hawkins, "Can Austin tech industry follow Trilogy's example to replenish talent pool?" *Austin American-Statesman*, September 1, 2012.
47. Kozmetsky and Smilor report that there were only three capital venture institutions in Austin in 1983: Business Development Partners, FSA Capital, and Rust Capital. George Kozmetsky and Raymond W. Smilor, "Transforming Texas and the Nation: Productivity Through Entrepreneurship and Risk-Taking," IC² Working Paper, WP-1983–09–01, University of Texas, 1983. https://repositories.lib.utexas.edu/server/api/core/bitstreams/db06f586-e536–4fa0–9ed2-a4ce50feadb9/content.
48. Elliot Tretter, *Shadows of a Sunbelt City* (University of Georgia Press, 2016), 16.
49. Austin Ventures not only seeded many generations of entrepreneurs but was also the anchor for the attraction of other financial service providers from more advanced regions—California, in particular. Two venture banks from California, Silicon Valley Bank and Imperial Bank, established their Austin-based loan production offices in 1996. These banks provided funds only to startups that had already secured angel or venture capital from Austin Ventures or other venture capital firms. Austin Ventures also spins off other venture capital firms, such as LiveOak. See Melissa Gaskill, "Banks Competing with VC Firms for Big Deals," *Austin Business Journal*, January 23, 2000.
50. See dealroom.co/guides/austin
51. Sandy Yu, "How Do Accelerators Impact the Performance of High-Technology Ventures?" *Management Science* 66, no. 2 (2020): 530–52.
52. Saxenian, "Regional Advantage," 32, for example, mentioned how the Wagon Wheel Bar, in Mountain View, California, a popular watering hole, where engineers met to exchange ideas and gossip, was termed "the fountainhead of the semiconductor industry."
53. Tretter, *Shadows of a Sunbelt City*, 66.
54. Gibson and Rogers, *R&D Collaboration on Trial*, 123.
55. Pike Powers, "Building the Austin Technology Cluster: The Role of Government & Community Collaboration in the Human Capital," *Proceedings of Rural And Agricultural Conferences, Federal Reserve Bank of Kansas City*, May 2004, 56.

56. Michael Frontain, “The Impact of Microelectronics and Computer Technology Corporation (MCC) on the U.S. Tech Landscape,” in *Handbook of Texas Online* (Texas State Historical Association), updated August 2, 2020, https://www.tshaonline.org/handbook/entries/microelectronics-and-computer-technology-corporation-mcc.
57. Gibson and Rogers, *R&D Collaboration on Trial,* 483; Diana J. Kleiner, “SEMATECH: Pioneering Semiconductor Manufacturing in the U.S.,” in *Handbook of Texas Online* (Texas State Historical Association), July 1, 1995, https://www.tshaonline.org/handbook/entries/sematech.
58. Joshua Long, “Sustaining in the Creativity Archetype: The Case of Austin, Texas,” *Cities* 26, no. 40 (2010–2019): 39.
59. “Texas Enterprise Fund,” Texas Public Policy Foundation, September 22, 2020, https://www.texaspolicy.com/legeenterprisefund/.
60. Nathan Jensen and Calvin Thrall, “What Are They Hiding? What Firms Don’t Want Us to Know About Their Economic Development Incentives,” *Promarket: Stigler Center for the Study of the Economy and the State,* September 15, 2021. https://www.promarket.org/2021/09/15/firms-economic-development-incentives-transparency-research-texas/.
61. Nathan Jensen, “The Bait and Switch of Austin’s Economic Development,” *UT News,* July 9, 2019. https://news.utexas.edu/2019/07/09/the-bait-and-switch-of-austins-economic-development/.
62. Saxenian, “Regional Advantage,” 20.
63. See “Starting Teledyne” in Monty Jones, *A Civic Entrepreneur—The Life of Technology Visionary George Kozmetsky* (Dolph Briscoe Center for American History, 2018), 114.
64. Cooper’s 1973 research shows that in Palo Alto, 97.5 percent of new technology companies founded in the 1960s had one or more founders who were previously working in a local firm.
65. Alec MacGillis, “Rick Perry’s Texas Giveaways,” *ProPublica,* January 3, 2017. https://www.propublica.org/article/rick-perrys-energy-grants-in-texas.
66. Eva Ruth Moravec, “Texas Emerging Technology Fund Still Benefiting Life Science Startups,” *Silicon Hills,* October 21, 2015. https://www.siliconhillsnews.com/2015/10/21/texas-emerging-technology-fund-still-benefiting-life-sciences-startups/.
67. Bureau of Transportation Statistics, *T-100 Segment Airline Traffic Data.* Washington, DC: US Department of Transportation.
68. Hector Aguilar, “Partnerships as a Major Strategy for Community College Improvement: A Case Study of a Community College Program” (Ph. D. diss., University of Texas at Austin, 2004).
69. Austin-Bergstrom International Airport is the second-fastest growing, mid-sized airport in the United States. Austin-Bergstrom International

Airport, "Austin-Bergstrom International Airport growing with Austin," FlyAustin.com. https://www.austintexas.gov/sites/default/files/files/Airport/AUS% 20Fact% 20Sheet% 20-% 20last% 20update% 2041823.pdf.

CHAPTER SIX

1. President, TIP Strategies, Austin, Texas.
2. All dollar figures are adjusted for inflation in 2022.
3. The word Hispanic is used throughout this chapter to mean "people descended from Spanish-speaking countries." The exception is if a cited source, such as a survey or study, uses the terms "Latino" or "Latina" or "Latinx," which means someone descended from a Latin American country.

CHAPTER EIGHT

1. Koch and Fowler Consulting Engineers, *A City Plan for Austin, Texas, 1928* (City of Austin Department of Planning, reprinted 1957), p. 57.

Bibliography

PREFACE

TIP Strategies, Inc. "TIP Strategies: Economic Development, Strategic & Workforce Planning." Accessed January 14, 2025. https://%40Jon@tipstrategies.com/.

TIP Strategies, Inc. "TIP Strategies: Economic Development, Strategic & Workforce Planning." Accessed January 14, 2025. https://%40john.karras@tipstrategies.com/.

CHAPTER ONE

Anders, Helen. "Holiday Bizarre: Walking Through a Wonderland of Austin Weirdness." *Austin American-Statesman*, September 27, 2018. https://www.statesman.com/story/news/2012/09/21/holiday-bizarre-walking-through-a-wonderland-of-austin-weirdness/9865104007/.

Austin Area Research Organization (AARO). "Who We Are." Accessed January 15, 2025. https://aaroregion.com/who-we-are.

Austin Technology Incubator. "About Us." Accessed January 31, 2025. https://ati.utexas.edu/about/.

Barry, Courtney. "Spreading the Wealth; In Silicon Hills, Making Good On Vows of High Tech Profits." *New York Times*, November 12, 2001. https://www.nytimes.com/2001/11/12/giving/spreading-the-wealth-in-silicon-hills-making-good-on-vows-of-high-tech-profits.html.

Diffusion Research Institute. "Dr. Everett M. Rogers—Diffusion Research Institute." 2025. https://diffusion-research.org/leadership_team/everett-rogers/.

Findell, Elizabeth, and Konrad Putzier. "Startup City Accelerated Growth Strains Austin." *The Wall Street Journal*, December 27, 2020. https://www.wsj.com/articles/start-up-city-accelerated-growth-strains-austin-11609093013?mod=mhp.

Frontain, Michael. "Microelectronics and Computer Technology Corporation [MCC]," in *Handbook of Texas Online* (Texas State Historical Association), September 13, 2007. https://www.tshaonline.org/handbook/entries/microelectronics-and-computer-technology-corporation-mcc.

Gibson, David V., and Everett M. Rogers. *R & D Collaboration on Trial: The Microelectronics and Computer Technology Corporation*. Harvard Business Press, 1994.

IC² Institute. "David Gibson—the IC² Institute." November 22, 2024. https://ic2.utexas.edu/people/david-gibson/.

IC² Institute. "George Kozmetsky—the IC² Institute." October 9, 2023. https://ic2.utexas.edu/george-kozmetsky/.

Inc. "These Are the 50 Best Places in America for Starting a Business." Accessed January 30, 2025. https://www.inc.com/surge-cities/best-places-start-business.html.

Jones, Monty. *A Civic Entrepreneur: The Life of Technology Visionary George Kozmetsky.* Briscoe Center for American History, University of Texas at Austin, 2018.

Kerr, Jeremy Stuart. *Seat of Empire: The Embattled Birth of Austin, Texas.* Texas Tech University Press, 2013. *Choice Reviews Online* 51, no. 05 (December 19, 2013): 51–2851. https://doi.org/10.5860/choice.51-2851. Accessed January 7, 2025.

King, Wayne. "The Talk of Austin; Texans Worry About Losing Nature's Touch." *New York Times,* March 26, 1985. https://www.nytimes.com/1985/03/26/us/the-talk-of-austin-texans-worry-about-losing-nature-s-touch.html.

Kleiner, Diana J. "Tracor," in *Handbook of Texas Online* (Texas State Historical Association), August 1, 1995. https://www.tshaonline.org/handbook/entries/tracor.

Lee, Adrienne. "UT Continues to Achieve All-Time Highs in Applications, Enrollment and Graduation Rates." *UT News,* September 19, 2024. https://news.utexas.edu/2024/09/19/ut-continues-to-achieve-all-time-highs-in-applications-enrollment-and-graduation-rates/.

Mackey, John P. "The Whole Story—John Mackey." Accessed January 7, 2025. https://johnpmackey.com/the-whole-story/.

Morelix, Arnobio, Robert W. Fairlie, Joshua Russell, E. J. Reedy, and Ewing Marion. "The Kauffman Index: Startup Activity Metropolitan Area and City Trends 2015." Ewing Marion Kauffman Foundation, 2015. ttps://www.kauffman.org/wp-content/uploads/2019/09/kauffman_index_startup_activity_metro_trends_2015.pdf.

Myerson, Allen R. "A New Breed of Wildcatter for the 90's." *New York Times,* November 30, 1997. https://www.nytimes.com/1997/11/30/business/a-new-breed-of-wildcatter-for-the-90-s.html.

Nodjimbadem, Katie. "The Trashy Beginnings of 'Don't Mess With Texas.'" *Smithsonian Magazine,* March 10, 2017. https://www.smithsonianmag.com/history/trashy-beginnings-dont-mess-texas-180962490/.

Omar L. Gallaga. "Did Austin Tech Doom Austin's Music Scene in 1984? Not so Much, It Turns Out." *Austin American-Statesman,* September 24, 2018. https://www.statesman.com/story/news/2017/05/10/did-austin-tech-doom-austins-music-scene-in-1984-not-so-much-it-turns-out/10174392007/.

Orum, Anthony M. *Power, Money & the People: The Making of Modern Austin.* Texas Monthly Press, 1987.

Overdeep, Meghan. "The History Behind Keep Austin Weird." *Southern Living*, March 1, 2024. https://www.southernliving.com/news/keep-austin-weird-history.

Popper, Karl R. *The Open Society and Its Enemies*. Princeton University Press, 2020.

Potrafka, Kris and David Hughen, hosts. *The Leadership Trap*, podcast, episode 18. "Laura Kilcrease, CEO of Alberta Innovators, founder of Triton Ventures, Austin Technology Incubator, Startup Advisor and Investor." May 15, 2022, https://theleadershiptrap.org/laura-kilcrease-ceo-of-alberta-innovates-founder-of-triton-ventures-austin-technology-incubator-startup-advisor-and-investor/.

Reedy, E. J., Robert W. Fairlie, Joshua Russell, Arnobio Morelix, and Ewing Marion Kauffman Foundation. "The Kauffman Index of Startup Activity: Metropolitan Area and City Trends 2016," 2016. https://www.kauffman.org/wp-content/uploads/2019/09/kauffman_index_startup_activity_metro_trends_2016.pdf.

San Antonio Current. "Keep San Antonio Lame." April 20, 2009. https://www.sacurrent.com/news/keep-san-antonio-lame-what-it-is-2377201.

Schwartz, John. "Austin Proud of Eccentricity Loses a Favorite." *New York Times*, March 10, 2012. https://www.nytimes.com/2012/03/10/us/austin-proud-of-eccentricity-loses-a-favorite.html.

Smilor, Raymond W., David V. Gibson, and George Kozmetsky. "Creating the Technopolis: High Technology Development in Austin, Texas." *The Journal of Business Venturing* 4, no. 1 (1989). https://www.sciencedirect.com/science/article/abs/pii/0883902689900335?via%3Dihub.

Spence, Jeremiah P, Zeynep Tufekci, and Joseph D Straubhaar, eds. *Inequity in the Technopolis: Race, Class, Gender, and the Digital Divide in Austin*. University of Texas Press, 2012.

Thorpe, Helen. "Austin, We Have a Problem." *New York Times*, August 20, 2000. https://www.nytimes.com/2000/08/20/magazine/austin-we-have-a-problem.html.

University of Texas at Austin. "Ben Streetman | Texas ECE - Electrical & Computer Engineering at UT Austin." Accessed January 18, 2025. https://www.ece.utexas.edu/people/faculty/ben-streetman.

Wassenich, Red. "How Austin Became Weird: The Story of a Slogan." *The End of Austin*, May 24, 2016. https://endofaustin.com/2016/05/24/how-austin-became-weird-the-story-of-a-slogan/.

CHAPTER TWO

American Society of Civil Engineers. *Infrastructure Report Card*. 2020. https://www.infrastructurereportcard.org/cat-item/dams/.

Barnes, Michael. "Revering Austin Patron Saint Robert Reed Crenshaw." *Austin*

American Statesman, September 25, 2018. https://www.statesman.com/story/news/2018/04/18/revering-austin-patron-saint-roberta-reed-crenshaw/10099959007/

Blackstock, Peter. "Austin Music Census Finds City at Tipping Point as Live Music Capital." *Austin American-Statesman*, October 24, 2017. https://www.statesman.com/NEWS/20171024/Austin-Music-Census-finds-city-at-tipping-point-as-Live-Music-Capital.

Chicago Tribune. "One Day in a War: My Lai and the Horrors We Need to Remember." November 13, 1989. https://www.chicagotribune.com/1989/11/13/one-day-in-a-war-my-lai-and-the-horrors-we-need-to-remember/

Clark-Madison, Mike. "Did SOS Matter?" *Austin Chronicle*, August 9, 2002. https://www.austinchronicle.com/news/2002-08-09/99629/.

Erard, Michael. "Anthony Orum on Austin." *Austin Chronicle*, May 23, 2003. https://www.austinchronicle.com/books/2003-05-23/160965/.

Florida, Richard. *The New Urban Crisis: How Our Cities Are Increasing Inequality, Deepening Segregation, and Failing the Middle Class—and What We Can Do.* Basic Books, 2017.

Greater Killeen Chamber of Commerce. "Major Employers Listing Greater Killeen Area (Includes Killeen, Fort Hood, Harker Heights and Nolanville) as of January 2015." Killeenhttps://killeenchamber.com/assets/uploads/docs/Major_Employers_Listing_-_January_2015.pdf.

GSD&M. "About." Accessed May 1, 2019. https://www.gsdm.com/about/.

Hattam, Jennifer. "Fight Freeport." *Mother Jones*, April 21, 1997. https://www.motherjones.com/politics/1997/04/fight-freeport/.

Hersh, Seymour. "The Massacre at My Lai." *The New Yorker*, January 14, 1972. https://www.newyorker.com/magazine/1972/01/22/coverup-my-lai-vietnam-war-seymour-hersh.

Largey, Matt. "Why Is Hippie Hollow Clothing-Optional?" KUT 90.5 (Austin NPR affiliate), July 31, 2017. https://www.kut.org/post/why-hippie-hollow-clothing-optional.

"Long, Walter Ewing," in *Handbook of Texas Online* (Texas State Historical Association), updated March 1, 1995. https://www.tshaonline.org/handbook/entries/long-walter-ewing.

Lower Colorado Regional Authority (LCRA). "Highland Lakes and Dams." https://www.lcra.org/water/dams-and-lakes/.

Neeley, Christopher. "One Million People Likely to Visit Barton Springs Pool Next Year, Drawing Concern from Officials." *Community Impact*, December 15, 2018. https://communityimpact.com/austin/central-austin/city-county/2018/12/05/one-million-people-likely-to-visit-barton-springs-pool-next-year-drawing-concern-from-officials/.

Orum, Anthony M. *Power, Money & the People: The Making of Modern Austin.* Texas Monthly Press, 1987.

Philips, Alberta. "How an Environmental Deal Led to Austin's Gentrification." *Austin American-Statesman*, November 17, 2017. https://www.statesman.com/news/20171117/phillips-how-an-environmental-deal-led-to-austins-gentrification.

Rahman, Fauzeya. "'Don't Mess With Texas' Lives on after 30 Years." *San Antonio Express-News*, February 20, 2016. https://www.expressnews.com/news/local/article/Don-t-Mess-With-Texas-lives-on-after-30-years-6844745.php.

Shea, Brigid, Bill Bunch, Mark Yznaga, David Butts, Gus Garcia, and Helen Ballew. "Memoirs of a Movement." *Austin Chronicle*, August 3, 2012. https://www.austinchronicle.com/news/2012-08-03/memoirs-of-a-movement/all/.

Sightlines. "Sinclair Black donates $5 million to UT School of Architecture for urban design studies." March 14, 2019. https://sightlinesmag.org/sinclair-black-donates-5-million-to-ut-school-of-architecture-for-urban-design-studies.

Smyrl, Vivian Elizabeth. "Wooldridge, Alexander Penn," in *Handbook of Texas Online* (Texas State Historical Association), updated April 4, 2019. https://www.tshaonline.org/handbook/entries/wooldridge-alexander-penn.

Standifer, Mary M. "Kate Ward," in *Handbook of Texas Online* (Texas State Historical Association), September 1, 1995. https://www.tshaonline.org/handbook/entries/kate-ward.

Swearingen, William Scott Jr., *Environmental City*. University of Texas Press, April 2010.

CHAPTER THREE

Barry, Courtney. "Spreading the Wealth; In Silicon Hills, Making Good On Vows of High Tech Profits." *New York Times*, November 12, 2001. https://www.nytimes.com/2001/11/12/giving/spreading-the-wealth-in-silicon-hills-making-good-on-vows-of-high-tech-profits.html.

Bloomberg, Michael. "Cities Must Be Cool, Creative, and in Control." *Financial Times*, March 27, 2012. https://www.ft.com/content/c09235b6-72ac-11e1-ae73-00144feab49a.

Bracken, David. "RTP Begins Updating Its Master Plan." *News & Observer* (Raleigh, NC), September 4, 2019, via WayBack Machine. https://web.archive.org/web/20101012050104/http://www.newsobserver.com/2010/09/04/663597/rtp-begins-updating-rules.html.

Dreher, Christopher. "Be Creative—Or Die." *Salon*, June 7, 2002. https://www.salon.com/2002/06/06/florida_22/.

Eddy, Jill A. "Watts Riots of 1965." Encyclopaedia Britannica Online. Accessed March 1, 2019. https://www.britannica.com/event/Watts-Riots-of-1965.

Florida, Richard. "The Creative Class and Economic Development," *Economic Development Quarterly* 28, no. 3, (July 2014). https://doi.org/10.1177/0891242414541693.

Florida, Richard. *The Rise of the Creative Class*, rev. ed. Basic Books, 2012.

Florida, Richard and Martin Kenney. "Venture Capital and High Technology Entrepreneurship." *Journal of Business Venturing* 3, no. 4 (February 1988). https://doi.org/10.1016/0883-9026(88)90011-0.

Ibrahim, Darian M. "Financing the Next Silicon Valley." *Washington University Law Review* 87, no. 4 (2010): 723. http://openscholarship.wustl.edu/law_lawreview/vol87/iss4/1.

Jacobs, Jane. *Cities and the Wealth of Nations: Principles of Economic Life.* Vintage, 1984.

Jacobs, Jane. "Downtown Is for People." *Fortune*, April 1958.

Jones, Monty. *A Civic Entrepreneur: The Life of Technology Visionary George Kozmetsky*. Briscoe Center for American History, University of Texas at Austin, 2018.

Kickler, Troy L. "Research Triangle Park." *North Carolina History Project.* Accessed March 1, 2019. https://northcarolinahistory.org/encyclopedia/research-triangle-park/.

Kozmetsky, George, Frederick Williams, and Victoria Williams. *New Wealth: Commercialization of Science and Technology for Business and Economic Development.* Greenwood Publishing Group, 2004.

Newport, Frank. "Democrats More Positive About Socialism Than Capitalism." Gallup, August 13, 2018. https://news.gallup.com/poll/240725/democrats-positive-socialism-capitalism.aspx.

Orum, Anthony M. *Power, Money & the People: The Making of Modern Austin.* Texas Monthly Press, 1987.

Smilor, Raymond W., David V. Gibson, and George Kozmetsky. "Creating the Technopolis: High Technology Development in Austin, Texas," *The Journal of Business Venturing* 4, no. 1 (1989). https://www.sciencedirect.com/science/article/abs/pii/0883902689900335?via%3Dihub.

Thore, Sten, and Ruzanna Tarverdyan. *Diagnostics for a Globalized World.* Now Publishers, 2015.

CHAPTER FOUR

Carney, Kristen. "Vermont Cities by Population (2025)." Vermont Demographics by Cubit. Accessed January 25, 2025. https://www.vermont-demographics.com/cities_by_population.

"City of Austin Population History: 1840 to 2016." AustinTexas.gov, citing the US Census Bureau. https://www.austintexas.gov/sites/default/files/files/Planning/Demographics/population_history_pub.pdf.

Crawford, Caroline, and Dana Schmidt. "Alumni Retention in United States Metropolitan Statistical Areas," *Cornell Policy Review*, June 29, 2017. http://www.cornellpolicyreview.com/alumni-retention-in-united-states-metropolitan-statistical-areas/.

Despart, Zach. "UVM's Incoming Class Has Fewer Vermonters." *Burlington Free*

Press, September 28, 2015. https://www.burlingtonfreepress.com/story/news/education/2015/09/28/uvms-incoming-class-has-fewer-vermonters/72566076/.

Donoghue, Mike. "Essex Officials Relieved Plant Will Stay Open." *Burlington Free Press*, October 21, 2014. https://www.burlingtonfreepress.com/story/news/local/2014/10/20/essex-officials-relieved-plant-will-stay-open/17630969/.

Florida, Richard. "The U.S. Cities Winning the Battle Against Brain Drain." CityLab.com, March 15, 2016. https://www.citylab.com/life/2016/03/which-metros-are-best-at-keeping-their-college-graduates/473604/.

Gomez, Rose. "Former Essex Jct. IBM Plant Marks a Milestone." WCAX.com (Burlington, VT, CBS affiliate), August 9, 2017. https://www.wcax.com/content/news/Former-Essex-Jct-IBM-plant-marks-milestone-439428613.html.

Herrera, Sebastian. "Amazon Opposites: Austin, Dallas Took Very Different Approaches to Wooing Retail Giant." *Austin American-Statesman*, November 16, 2018. https://www.statesman.com/news/20181116/amazon-opposites-austin-dallas-took-very-different-approaches-to-wooing-retail-giant.

Jones, Monty. *A Civic Entrepreneur: The Life of Technology Visionary George Kozmetsky*. Briscoe Center for American History, University of Texas at Austin, 2018.

Kimmelman, Michael. "Amazon's HQ2 Will Benefit from New York City. But What Does New York Get?" *New York Times*, November 12, 2018. https://www.nytimes.com/2018/11/12/arts/design/amazon-hq2-long-island-city-costs-benefits.html.

McCullum, April. "Vermont Will Pay Remote Workers $10,000 to Move Here." *Burlington Free Press*, May 31, 2018. https://www.burlingtonfreepress.com/story/news/local/vermont/2018/05/31/vermont-pay-remote-workers-move-incentive/659553002/.

Moreau, Erin. "Flatlanders in Vermont." Vermonter.com. Accessed March 20, 2019. https://vermonter.com/flatlanders/.

Old Citizen. "Passing Away: The Old Land-Marks Going." *Austin Daily Statesman*, October 5, 1884. Accessed January 25, 2025, at Newspapers.com. https://www.newspapers.com/image/364610378/?match=1&clipping_id=163924267.

Olson, Elizabeth. "What States and Cities Are Doing to Help Small Businesses." *New York Times*, March 3, 2010. https://www.nytimes.com/2010/03/04/business/smallbusiness/04help.html.

Porter, M. E. *The Competitive Advantage of Nations*. New York: Free Press, 1990. (Republished with a new introduction in 1998.)

Reisinger, Don. "IBM Celebrates 50 Years with the Selectric Typewriter." CNET, July 27, 2011. https://www.cnet.com/news/ibm-celebrates-50-years-with-the-selectric-typewriter/.

Rockwell, Lilly. "Timeline: IBM in Austin." *Austin American-Statesman*, July 28, 2017. https://www.statesman.com/news/20170728/timeline-ibm-in-austin.

Savage, David G. "The Public Ivys: A Guide to America's Best Public Undergraduate Colleges and Universities." *Los Angeles Times*, October 6, 1985. https://www.latimes.com/archives/la-xpm-1985-10-06-bk-5533-story.html.

Smilor, Raymond, David V. Gibson, and George Kozmetsky. "Creating the Technopolis: High-Technology Development in Austin, Texas." *Journal of Business Venturing* 4, no. 1 (January 1989). https://www.sciencedirect.com/science/article/abs/pii/0883902689900335?via%3Dihub.

Torre, Melanie. "Austin Growing by 35 People a Day, Hays and WilCo Growing by 120." *CBS Austin*, January 19, 2019. https://cbsaustin.com/news/local/austin-growing-by-35-people-a-day-hays-and-wilco-growing-by-120.

Torre, Melanie. "Some Visitors Come for SXSW, Leave as Future Home Buyers." *CBS Austin*, March 15, 2019. https://cbsaustin.com/news/local/some-visitors-come-for-sxsw-leave-as-future-home-buyers.

Winooski. "Vermonters Overwhelmingly Oppose US Border Wall, Support Vermont Border Wall." (satire), January 29, 2019.

Woolf, Art. "Vermont's Fastest-Growing Towns: A Look at Where and Why." *Burlington Free Press*, June 7, 2018. https://www.burlingtonfreepress.com/story/money/2018/06/07/vermonts-fastest-growing-towns-2017/657495002/.

Woolf, Art. "Vermont Paradox: While School Enrollment Falls, Costs Go Up." *Burlington Free Press*, April 25, 2018. https://www.burlingtonfreepress.com/story/money/2018/04/25/vermont-school-enrollment-falls-costs-go-up-art-woolf/547894002/.

Woolf, Art. "Why Vermont's Population Is Unlikely to Grow Anytime Soon." *Burlington Free Press*, December 26, 2018. https://www.burlingtonfreepress.com/story/money/2018/12/26/vermont-population-census-figures-show-why-growth-not-occurring/2414349002/.

World Population Review. "Burlington, Vermont Population 2024." Accessed January 25, 2025. http://worldpopulationreview.com/us-cities/burlington-vt-population/.

Wynn, Jonathan R. "'Welcome to Austin, Don't Move Here': Why Local Backlash Won't Stop SXSW." *The Guardian*, March 14, 2016. https://www.theguardian.com/culture/2016/mar/14/south-by-southwest-austin-residents-backlash.

CHAPTER FIVE

Aguilar, Hector. "Partnerships as a Major Strategy for Community College Improvement: A Case Study of a Community College Program." PhD diss., University of Texas at Austin, 2004.

Austin-Bergstrom International Airport. "Austin-Bergstrom International Airport growing with Austin." https://www.austintexas.gov/sites/default/files/files/Airport/AUS%20Fact%20Sheet%20-%20last%20update%2041823.pdf

Bhide, Amar V. *The Origin and Evolution of New Businesses*. Oxford University Press, 1999.

Burton, Diane M., Jesper B. Sørensen, and Christine M. Beckman. "Coming from Good Stock: Career Histories and New Venture Formation." *Research in the Sociology of Organizations* 19, (2002): 229–62.

Campbell, Benjamin A, Martin Ganco, April M. Franco, and Rajshree Agarwal. "Who Leaves, Where to, and Why Worry? Employee Mobility, Entrepreneurship and Effects on Source Firm Performance." *Strategic Management* 33, no. 1 (2012): 65–87.

Carias, Chistina, Steven Klepper, and Rui Baptista. "Entrepreneurship, the Initial Labor Force, and the Location of New Firms." *Small Business Economics* 60, no. 3 (2023): 865–90.

Cunningham, William H. and Monty Jones. *The Texas Way: Money, Power, Politics, and Ambition at The University.* The Dolph Briscoe Center for American History, University of Texas at Austin, 2018.

Cooper, Arnold C. "The Role of Incubator Organizations in the Founding of Growth-Oriented Firms." *Journal of Business Venturing* 1, no. 1 (1985): 75–86.

Cooper, Arnold C., and William C. Dunkelberg. "Entrepreneurial Research: Old Questions, New Answers and Methodological Issues." *American Journal of Small Business*, 3 (1987): 11-23.

Contrary. "Trilogy Software- the biggest tech mafia you've never heard of." Blog, November 25, 2020. https://www.contrary.com/blog/trilogy-software.

Dahl, Michael S., and Olav Sorenson. "The Who, Why, and How of Spinoffs." *Industrial and Corporate Change* 23, no. 3 (2013): 661–88.

Dealroom. "Austin." dealroom.co/guides/austin.

Echeverri-Carroll, Elsie L., and Maryann P. Feldman. "Chasing Entrepreneurial Firms." *Industry and Innovation* 26, no. 5 (2019): 479–507.

Echeverri-Carroll, Elsie L., and William Brennan. "Are Innovation Networks Bounded by Proximity?" In *Innovation, Networks and Localities,* edited by Manfred M. Fischer, Luis Suarez-Villa, and Michael Steiner. Springer-Verlag, 1999.

Figueiredo, Octávio, Paulo Guimaraes, and Douglas Woodward. "Home-field Advantages: Location Decisions of Portuguese Entrepreneurs." *Journal of Urban Economics* 52, no. 2 (2002): 341–61.

Frontain, Michael. "The Impact of Microelectronics and Computer Technology Corporation (MCC) on the U.S. Tech Landscape," in *Handbook of Texas Online* (Texas State Historical Association), updated August 2, 2020. https://www.tshaonline.org/handbook/entries/microelectronics-and-computer-technology-corporation-mcc.

Gaskill, Melissa. "Banks Competing with VC Firms for Big Deals." *Austin Business Journal,* January 23, 2000.

Gibson, David V., and Everett M. Rogers. *R&D Collaboration on Trial: The Microelectronics and Computer Technology Corporation.* Harvard Business School Press, 1994. 123–483.

Glaeser, Edward, and William Kerr. "Local Industrial Conditions and Entrepreneurship: How Much of the Spatial Distribution Can We Explain?" *Journal of Economics and Management Strategy* 18, no. 3 (2009): 623–63.

Glassmeier, Amy K. "Factors Governing the Development of High-Tech Industry Agglomerations: A Tale of Three Cities." *Regional Studies* 22, no. 4 (1988): 287–301.

Gompers, Paul, Josh Lerner, and David Scharfstein. "Entrepreneurial Spawning: Public Corporations and the Genesis of New Ventures, 1986 to 1999," *The Journal of Finance* 60, no. 2 (2005): 577–614.

Goss, David, and Eugene Sadler-Smith. "Opportunity Creation: Entrepreneurial Agency, Interaction, and Affect." *Strategic Entrepreneurship Journal* 12 (2017): 219–36.

Guzman, Jorge, and Scott Stern. "The State of American Entrepreneurship: New Estimates of the Quality and Quantity of Entrepreneurship for 32 US States, 1988–2014." *American Economic Journal: Economic Policy* 12, no. 4 (2020): 212–43.

Hawkins, Lori. "Can Austin tech industry follow Trilogy's example to replenish talent pool?" *Austin American-Statesman*, September 1, 2012.

Isenberg, Daniel J. "Applying the Ecosystem Metaphor to Entrepreneurship: Uses and Abuses," *The Antitrust Bulletin* 61, no. 4 (2016): 564–73.

Isenberg, Daniel. "When Big Companies Fall, Entrepreneurship Rises." *Harvard Business Review*, March 18, 2013. https://hbr.org/2013/03/when-big-companies-fall-entrep.

Jensen, Nathan. "The Bait and Switch of Austin's Economic Development." *UT News*, July 9, 2019. https://news.utexas.edu/2019/07/09/the-bait-and-switch-of-austins-economic-development/.

Jensen, Nathan, and Calvin Thrall. "What are they hiding? What firms don't want us to know about their economic development incentives." Promarket, Stigler Center for the Study of the Economy and the State, September 15, 2021. https://www.promarket.org/2021/09/15/firms-economic-development-incentives-transparency-research-texas/

Jones, Monty. *A Civic Entrepreneur—The Life of Technology Visionary George Kozmetsky*. The Dolph Briscoe Center for American History, 2018.

Kleiner, Diana J. "SEMATECH: Pioneering Semiconductor Manufacturing in the U.S.," in *Handbook of Texas Online* (Texas Historical Association), July 1, 1995. https://www.tshaonline.org/handbook/entries/sematech.

Kleiner, Diana J. "Tracor: A Pioneer in Defense and Commercial Electronics," *in Handbook of Texas Online* (Texas State Historical Association), August 1, 1995. https://www.tshaonline.org/handbook/entries/tracor.

Klepper, Steven. "The Origin and Growth of Industry Clusters: The Making of Silicon Valley and Detroit." *Journal of Urban Economics* 67 (2010): 15–32.

Kozmetsky, George, and Raymond W. Smilor. "Transforming Texas and the Nation: Productivity Through Entrepreneurship and Risk-Taking." IC[2] Working Paper, WP-1983-09-01, University of Texas at Austin, 1983. https://repositories.lib.utexas.edu/server/api/core/bitstreams/db06f586-e536-4fa0-9ed2-a4ce50feadb9/content

Ladendorf, Kirk. "Software firm moves to Austin: Trilogy cites labor pool, high-tech firms." *Austin American-Statesman*, October 1, 1992.

Long, Joshua. "Sustaining in the Creativity Archetype: The Case of Austin, Texas." *Cities* 26, no. 40 (2010–2019): 39.

MacGillis, Alec. "Rick Perry's Texas Giveaways." *ProPublica,* January 3, 2017. https://www.propublica.org/article/rick-perrys-energy-grants-in-texas.

Malecki, Edward J. "Entrepreneurship and Entrepreneurial Ecosystems." *Geography Compass* 12, (2018): 1–21.

Malecki, Edward J. "Entrepreneurs, Networks, and Economic Development." *Advances in Entrepreneurship, Firm emergence, and Growth* 3, (1997): 57–118.

Mason, Colin M., and Richard T. Harrison. "After the Exit: Acquisitions, Entrepreneurial Recycling and Regional Economic Development," *Regional Studies* 40, no. 1 (2006): 55–73.

Mason, Colin, and Ross Brown. "Entrepreneurial Ecosystems and Growth-Oriented Entrepreneurship." Paper prepared for the workshop organized by OECD LEED Programme and the Dutch Ministry of Economic Affairs, January 2014.

Miller, Jonathan. "Regional Case Study: Austin, Texas, or How to Create a Knowledge Economy." Washington, DC: European Commission Delegation, 1999.

Moravec, Eva Ruth. "Texas Emerging Technology Fund Still Benefiting Life Science Startups." *Silicon Hills*, October 21, 2015. https://www.siliconhillsnews.com/2015/10/21/texas-emerging-technology-fund-still-benefiting-life-sciences-startups/.

Moretti, Enrico. *The New Geography of Jobs*. Houghton Mifflin Harcourt, 2013.

Muro, Mark, and Yang You, "Superstars, Rising Stars, and the Rest: Pandemic Trends and Shifts in the Geography of Tech," *Brookings Report,* March 8, 2022. https://www.brookings.edu/articles/superstars-rising-stars-and-the-rest-pandemic-trends-and-shifts-in-the-geography-of-tech/.

Nanda, Ramana, and Jesper B. Sørensen. "Workplace Peers and Entrepreneurship." *Management Science* 56, no. 7 (2010): 1116–26.

O'Mara, Margaret P. *Cities of Knowledge: Cold War Science and the Search for the Next Silicon Valley*. Princeton University Press, 2005.

Powers, Pike. "Building the Austin Technology Cluster: The Role of Government & Community Collaboration in the Human Capital." *Proceedings of Rural And Agricultural Conferences, Federal Reserve Bank of Kansas City* (May 2004): 53–71.

Roberts, Peter, Steven Klepper, and Scott Hayward. "Founder Background and Evolution of Firm Size." *Industrial and Corporate Change* 20 no. 6 (2011): 1515–38.

Rocha, Vera, Anable Carneiro, and Celeste Varum. "Leaving Employment to Entrepreneurship: The Value of Co-worker Mobility in Pushed and Pulled-Driven Start-ups." *Journal of Management Studies* 55, no. 1 (2018): 60–85.

Saxenian, AnnaLee. *Regional Advantage: Culture and Competition in Silicon Valley and Route 128*. Harvard University Press, 1994.

Smilor, Raymond W., David V. Gibson, and George Kozmetsky. "Creating the Technopolis: High-Technology Development in Austin, Texas." *Journal of Business Venture* 4, (1989): 49–67.

Smilor, Raymond W., David V. Gibson, and Glenn B. Dietrich. "University Spin-Out Companies: Technology Startups from UT-Austin." *Journal of Business Venture* 5, (1990): 63–76.

Smilor, Raymond W., George Kozmetsky, and David V. Gibson. "The Austin/San Antonio Corridor: The Dynamics of a Developing Technopolis." WP-1987-03-01, IC^2 Institute, University of Texas at Austin, 1987. https://repositories.lib.utexas.edu/items/a12ace02-d5a7-4ffe-864b-035229b6e722.

Sørensen, Jesper B., and Magali A. Fassiotto. "Organizations as Fonts of Entrepreneurship." *Organization Science* 22, no. 5 (2011): 1322–31.

Sørensen, Jesper B. "Bureaucracy and Entrepreneurship: Workplace Effects on Entrepreneurial Entry." *Administrative Science Quarterly* 52, no. 3 (2007): 387–412.

Sørensen, Jesper B. "Closure and Exposure: Mechanisms in the Intergenerational Transmission of Self-Employment." *Research in the Sociology of Organizations* 25, (2007): 83–124.

Sorenson, Olav. "Social Networks and Industrial Geography." *Journal of Evolutionary Economics* 13, (2003): 513–27.

Spigel, Ben. "Developing and Governing Entrepreneurial Ecosystems: The Structure of Entrepreneurial Support Programs in Edinburgh, Scotland." *Journal of Innovation and Regional Development* 7, no. 2 (2016): 141–60.

Spiegel, Ben, and Richard Harrison. "Toward a Process Theory of Entrepreneurial Ecosystems." *Strategic Entrepreneurship Journal* 12, no. 1 (2018): 151–68.

Susbauer, Jeffery C. "The Technical Entrepreneurship Process in Austin, Texas." In *Technical Entrepreneurship A Symposium,* edited by Arnold C. Cooper and John L. Komives. Purdue University, 1972.

Texas Public Policy Foundation. "Texas Enterprise Fund." September 22, 2020. https://www.texaspolicy.com/legeenterprisefund/.

Tretter, Elliot. *Shadows of a Sunbelt City.* University of Georgia Press, 2016.

Yu, Sandy. "How Do Accelerators Impact the Performance of High-Technology Ventures?" *Management Science* 66, no. 2 (2020): 530–52.

CHAPTER SIX

Austin History Center. "Our Community Our Voice: Photographs from the Village Newspaper." Accessed June 2024. https://storymaps.arcgis.com/stories/4f4309e9d61147cd9fb82bf6b2daa4aa.

Austin Revitalization Authority. "About Us." Accessed June 2024. https://austinrev.org/about-us/.

Austin Technology Incubator, University of Texas at Austin. "About Us." Accessed June 2024 https://ati.utexas.edu/about/.

Austin Urban Technology Movement. "AUTMHQ Services." Accessed June 2024. https://www.autmhq.org/services.

Urban Technology Movement. "How Our Partners Work with Us." Accessed June 2024. https://www.autmhq.org/partnerinfo.

Badger, Emily. "Study: Austin is Most Economically Segregated Metro Area." *Texas Tribune*, February 23, 2015. https://www.texastribune.org/2015/02/23/austin-most-economically-segregated-metro-area/.

Barnes, Michael. "Clarksville and Wheatville Were Not Austin's Only Freedman Towns." *Austin American-Statesman*, June 21, 2014. https://www.statesman.com/story/news/2014/06/21/clarksville-wheatville-were-not-austin/6723726007/.

Barnes, Michael. "What You Don't Know About the History of East Austin." *Austin American-Statesman*, September 3, 2016. https://www.statesman.com/story/news/2016/09/03/what-you-dont-know-about-the-history-of-east-austin/10058269007/.

Bingamon, Brant. "The Long Story of East 11th and 12th Streets Takes a Turn." *Austin Chronicle*, October 18, 2019. https://www.austinchronicle.com/news/2019-10-18/the-long-story-of-east-11th-and-12th-streets-takes-a-turn/.

Brown, Jan Shelly, Matthew Finney, Mark McMillan, and Chris Perkins. "How to Close the Black Talent Gap." McKinsey Institute for Black Economic Mobility, February 3, 2023. https://www.mckinsey.com/bem/our-insights/how-to-close-the-black-tech-talent-gap.

Buchanan v. Warley, 245 U.S. 60 (1917), U.S. Supreme Court Center. Justia.com. Accessed June 2024. https://supreme.justia.com/cases/federal/us/245/60/.

Burnett, Colette Pierce, and Paul Cruz. *Mayor's Task Force on Institutional Racism and Systemic Inequities.* City of Austin, March 31, 2017. https://services.austintexas.gov/edims/document.cfm?id=274706.

Busch, Andrew M. "Crossing Over: Sustainability, New Urbanism, and Gentrification in Austin, Texas." *Southern Spaces*, August 19, 2015. https://southernspaces.org/2015/crossing-over-sustainability-new-urbanism-and-gentrification-austin-texas/.

Carlson, Kara. "Google's 'Future is Really Bright' in Austin, Company Executive

Says." *Austin American-Statesman,* August 13, 2021. https://www.statesman.com/story/business/2021/08/13/austin-google-exec-companys-future-really-bright-in-city-tx/5488231001/.

Charpentier, Marisa, and Audrey McGlinchy. *Two Paragraphs Forced Black Residents to East Austin. Exploding Real Estate Prices Forced Them Out.* KUT News, *Growth Machine podcast,* June 22, 2023. https://www.kut.org/austin/2023-06-22/two-paragraphs-forced-black-residents-to-east-austin-exploding-real-estate-prices-forced-them-out.

Choi, Laura, Violeta Gutkowski, Ana Hernández Kent. "Racial Equity Could Produce Widespread Economic Gains." Federal Reserve Bank of St. Louis, January 12, 2023. https://www.stlouisfed.org/publications/economic-equity-insights/racial-equity-labor-market-outcomes-economic-growth.

City of Austin. "Reflections Portrait Guide." Accessed June 2024. https://www.austintexas.gov/sites/default/files/files/Housing/AACHF/AACHF_Portrait_Guide_FINAL__5_3_13_-reduced.pdf.

City of Austin. "Welcome to the Equity Office Homepage." Accessed June 2024. https://www.austintexas.gov/department/equity-office.

City of Austin. "Anti-Displacement Task Force." Accessed June 2024. https://www.austintexas.gov/page/anti-displacement-task-force.

City of Austin. "Anti-Displacement Task Force: Recommendations for Action." November 2018. https://www.austintexas.gov/sites/default/files/files/Housing/Anti-Displacement_Task_Force_Final_Recommendations_and_Report.pdf.

City of Austin. "Anti-Displacement Funding." Accessed June 2024. https://www.austintexas.gov/page/anti-displacement-funding.

City of Austin. "Austin City Council Approves Economic Development Agreement with NXP." September 26, 2023. https://www.austintexas.gov/news/austin-city-council-approves-economic-development-agreement-nxp.

City of Austin, Neighborhood Planning and Zoning Department. "Chapter 4: Growth Management Addendum." Austin Tomorrow Comprehensive Plan, November 6, 2008. https://services.austintexas.gov/edims/document.cfm?id=123019.

Cook, Lisa D., and Jan Gerson. "The Implications of U.S. Gender and Racial Disparities in Income and Wealth Inequality at Each Stage of the Innovation Process." Washington Center for Equitable Growth, July 2019. https://www.congress.gov/116/meeting/house/110012/witnesses/HHRG-116-BA13-Wstate-CookL-20190924.pdf.

Contreras, Natalia E. "Austin Residents Displaced by Gentrification Could Own a Home Through a New City Program." *Austin American-Statesman,* April 18, 2022. https://www.statesman.com/story/news/2022/04/18/housing-program-set-help-low-income-austin-families-own-home/7318882001/.

Cronin, Mike. "By the Numbers: A Racial and Ethnic Breakdown of Austin's

Tech Workers." *Austin Business Journal*, September 14, 2017. https://www.bizjournals.com/austin/news/2017/09/14/by-the-numbers-a-racial-and-ethnic-breakdown-of.html.

Cyversity. "Partners." Accessed June 2024. https://www.cyversity.org/partners.

Daniel, David E. "The President's Viewpoint: Update on Project Emmitt." University of Texas at Dallas, October 2006. https://websites.utdallas.edu/past-presidents/daniel/documents/viewpoint-2006-10.pdf.

DOIT Software. "15 Top Tech Companies in Austin: Leaders, Innovators, and Market Overview." October 4, 2024. https://doit.software/blog/tech-companies-in-austin#screen17.

Echeverri-Carroll, Elsie. "Austin's Entrepreneurial Genesis." IC^2 Institute, University of Texas at Austin, September 1, 2017. https://ic2.utexas.edu/wp-content/uploads/echeverri-2017-austin-entrepreneurial-genesis-infographic.pdf.

Echeverri-Carroll, Elsie, and Michael Oden. "Preliminary Assessment of the Factors That Led Austin to Become a High-Tech Entrepreneurial City." The IC^2 Institute, University of Texas at Austin, July 31, 2016. https://ic2.utexas.edu/wp-content/uploads/echeverri-2016-austin-factors.pdf.

Equidad ATX. "Who We Serve." Accessed June 2024. https://www.equidadatx.org/programs.

Falcon, Russell. "Huston Tillotson University Announces Partnership with Tesla on Learning Initiatives Programs for Students." KXAN News, July 23, 2020. https://www.kxan.com/news/education/huston-tillotson-university-announces-partnership-with-tesla-on-learning-initiatives-programs-for-students/.

Gibson, Campbell, and Kay Jung, "Historical Census Statistics on Population Totals by Race, 1790 to 1990, and by Hispanic Origin, 1970 to 1990, for Large Cities and Other Urban Places in the United States." US Census Bureau, Population Division, Working Paper No. 76, February 2005. https://www.census.gov/content/dam/Census/library/working-papers/2005/demo/POP-twps0076.pdf.

Gilgore, Sara. "Google to Help Minority Entrepreneurs in Austin; Former Chamber Chief Involved." *Austin Business Journal*, May 5, 2017. https://www.bizjournals.com/austin/news/2017/05/05/google-to-help-minority-entrepreneurs-in-austin.html.

Gordon, Edmund T. "Racing Mapping Austin." Retelling Central Texas History. Accessed June 2024. https://ctxretold.org/black-communities/mapping-the-city/.

Greater Austin Black Chamber of Commerce. "GABC History." Accessed June 2024. https://www.austinbcc.org/our-office.

Hill, Sharon. "The Empty Stairs: The Lost History of East Austin." In *Intersections: New Perspectives on Texas Public History*, edited by Bonnie Tipton

Wilson. Texas State University, May 1, 2012. https://gato-docs.its.txst.edu/jcr:e08c7244-9193-49b1-b4d8-6cb3e4c4daab/The%20Empty%20Stairs%20The%20Lost%20History%20of%20East%20Austin.pdf.

Jackson Tech District. "Welcome To: JXN.TECH DISTRICT." Accessed June 2024. https://www.jxntechdistrict.com/.

Koch and Fowler Consulting Engineers. "A City Plan for Austin, Texas." Reprint of 1928 edition, 1957. https://repositories.lib.utexas.edu/items/f15262ac-77d6-4ef2-85bb-fa22c46085c7.

Larson, Jeff, Julia Angwin, Lauren Kirchner, Surya Mattu for ProPublica and Dina Haner, Michael Saccucci, Keith Newsom-Stewart, Andrew Cohen, and Martin Romm for *Consumer Reports*. "How We Examined Racial Discrimination in Auto Insurance Prices." April 5, 2017. https://www.propublica.org/article/minority-neighborhoods-higher-car-insurance-premiums-methodology.

Levin, Ethan. "An Economic Success, a Complicated Legacy: Austin's Smart Growth Initiative." *Harvard Urban Review*, March 30, 2019. https://harvardurbanreview.org/economic-success-complicated-legacy-austins-smart-growth-initiative/.

Linton, Alaya, Dan Shepard, and Xiomara Martinez-White. "Places Where Black Americans Thrive the Most (and Least)." LendingTree, August 28, 2023. https://www.lendingtree.com/debt-consolidation/thriving-black-americans-study/.

Magretta, Joan. "The Power of Virtual Integration: An Interview with Dell Computers Michael Dell." *Harvard Business Review*, March–April 1998. https://hbr.org/1998/03/the-power-of-virtual-integration-an-interview-with-dell-computers-michael-dell.

McKinsey Institute for Black Economic Mobility. "The State of Black Residents: The Relevance of Place to Racial Equity and Outcomes." February 1, 2024. https://www.mckinsey.com/bem/our-insights/the-state-of-black-resident-the-relevance-of-place-to-racial-equity-and-outcomes#/.

McQueen, Elizabeth, and Miles Bloxxon. "The Urban Music Fest and Homer Hill." *Pause/Play* podcast, episode 7, KUT Radio, December 22, 2020. https://www.kut.org/pause-play.

Mears, Michelle M. *And Grace Will Lead Me Home: African American Freedman Communities of Austin, Texas, 1865-1928*. Texas Tech University Press, 2009.

Mears, Michelle. "The Texas Hill Country Was Home to Freedmen." Hill Country Conservancy. Accessed June 2024. https://hillcountryconservancy.org/the-texas-hill-country-was-home-to-freedmen/.

Measure Austin. "About Measure." Accessed June 2024. https://www.measureaustin.org/.

Munn, Robyn. "In Memoriam: Pike Powers '65 'Godfather of Austin's Tech Boom' Passes Away." University of Texas School of Law, November 11, 2021. https://law.utexas.edu/news/2021/11/11/in-memoriam-pike-powers-65-godfather-of-austins-tech-boom-passes-away/.

National League of Cities. "City Profile on Racial Equity, Austin, Texas." 2018. https://www.nlc.org/wp-content/uploads/2018/03/REAL20Austin20City20Profile.pdf.

Noor, Adatia. "H-E-B Exec Champions Joe V's Smart Shop as Grocer Builds Another Value-Focused Store in Dallas." *Dallas Business Journal*, March 20, 2024. https://www.bizjournals.com/dallas/news/2024/03/20/joe-vs-smart-shop-heb-construction-orsak.html.

Operation Hope. "About Us." Accessed June 2024. https://operationhope.org/.

Pedigo, Steven. "How Austin Became the Human Capital." LinkedIn, May 1, 2018. https://www.linkedin.com/pulse/how-austin-became-human-capital-steven-pedigo/.

Prosperity Now. "The Road to Zero Wealth: How the Racial Wealth Divide is Hollowing Out the Middle Class." September 2017. https://prosperitynow.org/resources/road-zero-wealth.

Ramser, Chris. "Highlights from Census 2020." Austin Chamber blog, October 6, 2021. https://www.austinchamber.com/blog/10-06-2021-census-2020#.

Reconnect Austin. "History of the I-35 Corridor." Accessed June 2024. https://reconnectaustin.com/history-of-the-i-35-corridor/.

Reding, Shawna M. "Meet the 4 Black-Owned Austin Startup Companies Getting 100K from Google." KVUE News, September 23, 2021. https://www.kvue.com/article/money/economy/boomtown-2040/google-austin-startup-companies-black/269-c49ecaef-d284-4f37-946f-822b304dd236.

Richardson, Susan Smith. "Message From the Grassroots." *Texas Observer*, March 6, 2012. https://www.texasobserver.org/message-from-the-grassroots/.

Robbins, Paul. "The Town that Won the Pennant: A Short History of Austin's Economic Development." *Austin Environmental Directory*, 2013. https://environmentaldirectory.info/a-short-history-of-austins-economic-development/.

Santana, Steven. "A Look Back at Toyota's San Antonio Factory 20 Years Later." *San Antonio News Express*, October 25, 2023. https://www.mysanantonio.com/business/article/toyota-san-antonio-18445730.php.

Schaeffer, Katherine. "Decoded: 'What's the Difference Between Income and Wealth?' and Other Common Questions about Economic Concepts." Pew Research Center, July 23, 2021. https://www.pewresearch.org/decoded/2021/07/23/whats-the-difference-between-income-and-wealth-and-other-common-questions-about-economic-concepts/.

Smith, Amy. "Eric Mitchelle, RIP: Outspoken City Council Member Passes Away." *Austin Chronicle*, February 15, 2011. https://www.austinchronicle.com/daily/news/2011-02-15/eirc-mitchell-rip/.

Smith, Jordan. "Dorothy T. Goes Home." *Austin Chronicle*, April 22, 2005. https://www.austinchronicle.com/news/2005-04-22/267663/.

Solum, Anja. "Best Places for Black Entrepreneurs—2023 Edition." SmartAssets Data Studies. https://smartasset.com/data-studies/best-places-for-black-entrepreneurs-2023.

University of Texas at Austin, Office of Institutional Studies, "Statistical Handbook 1980-1981." Accessed June 1, 2024. https://utexas.app.box.com/v/SHB80-81Complete.

Swiateck, Chad. "H-E-B Donates $1 Million to Fund Two Affordable Housing Projects in East Austin." KUT News, December 3, 2024. https://www.kut.org/housing/2024-12-03/heb-donation-affordable-housing-east-austin-tx.

Tang, Eric, and Chunhui Ren, "Outlier: The Case of Austin's Declining African-American Population." Institute for Urban Policy Research and Analysis, University of Texas at Austin, May 8, 2014. https://services.austintexas.gov/edims/document.cfm?id=211081.

Tang, Eric, and Widelin Desir. "Those Who Stayed: The Impact of Gentrification on Longtime Residents of East Austin." Institute for Urban Policy, Research and Analysis, University of Texas at Austin, 2018. https://communitynotcommodity.com/wp-content/uploads/THOSE-WHO-STAYED-The-Impact-of-Gentrifcation-on-Longstanding-Residents-of-East-Austin.pdf.

University of Texas at Austin Athletics. "Darrell K Royal-Texas Memorial Stadium at Campbell-Williams Field." Accessed June 2024. https://texassports.com/sports/2013/7/24/facilities_0724133148.aspx.

University of Texas School of Law and Community and Regional Planning Program. "The Uprooted Project: A Snapshot of the Study." Accessed June 2024. https://sites.utexas.edu/gentrificationproject/a-snapshot-of-the-study-2/.

University of Texas School of Law and Community and Regional Planning Program. "The Uprooted Project: Vulnerability Map." Accessed June 2024. https://sites.utexas.edu/gentrificationproject/vulnerability-map/.

US Census Bureau. "American Community Survey, Demographic and Housing Estimates, 2022." https://data.census.gov/table/ACSDP5Y2022.DP05?q=dp05&g=160XX00US4805000.

US Census Bureau. "American Community Survey, Demographic and Housing Estimates, 2012 and 2022." https://www.census.gov/programs-surveys/acs.

US Congress. Chips and Science Act, H.R. 4346, 117th Cong. (2021-2022). https://www.congress.gov/bill/117th-congress/house-bill/4346/text.

US Economic Development Administration. "Biden-Harris Administration Designates 31 Tech Hubs Across America." October 23, 2023. https://www.eda

.gov/news/press-release/2023/10/23/biden-harris-administration-designates-31-tech-hubs-across-america.

Urban Displacement Project. "Austin Gentrification and Displacement Measures: About the Study." Accessed June 2024. https://austin.maps.arcgis.com/apps/MapSeries/index.html?appid=2287ef7c16dc476ca0c7d4a10ae690ce.

Way, Heather, Elizabeth Mueller, and Jake Wegmann. "Uprooted: Residential Displacement in Austin's Gentrifying Neighborhoods and What Can Be Done About It." University of Texas at Austin Center for Sustainable Development in the School of Architecture and the Entrepreneurship and Community Development Clinic in the School of Law, 2018. https://sites.utexas.edu/gentrificationproject/files/2019/10/AustinUprooted.pdf.

WP Engine. "WP Engine Careers." Accessed June 2024. https://wpengine.careers/.

Zillow Research. "Zillow Home Value Index (ZHVI)." Accessed April 2024. https://www.zillow.com/research/data/.

CHAPTER SEVEN

Alexander, Leigh. "Why It's Time to Retire 'Disruption', Silicon Valley's Emptiest Buzzword." *The Guardian*, January 11, 2016. https://www.theguardian.com/technology/2016/jan/11/disruption-silicon-valleys-buzzword.

Austin Chronicle. "Critics Poll 2000." *Austin Chronicle*, January 5, 2001. https://www.austinchronicle.com/music/2001-01-05/80040/.

Bradley, Ryan. "Time to Retire the Word 'Disrupt.'" *Fortune*, July 12, 2013. http://fortune.com/2013/07/12/time-to-retire-the-word-disrupt/.

Buchele, Mose. "The Origin of Austin as 'The Live Music Capital of the World,' Take Two." KUT News, March 12, 2019. https://www.kut.org/post/origin-austin-live-music-capital-world-take-two.

Calore, Michael. "Twitter Is Ruling SXSW." *Wired*, March 9, 2007. https://www.wired.com/2007/03/twitter-is-ruling-sxsw/.

Carroll, Jim. "Go South by Southwest, Young Techie." *Irish Times*, March 21, 2012. https://www.irishtimes.com/culture/tv-radio-web/go-south-by-southwest-young-techie-1.485806.

City Council of Austin. "Austin City Council Minutes." August 29, 1991. http://www.austintexas.gov/edims/document.cfm?id=24484.

Collins, Meghan. "Napster Files for Bankruptcy." CNN Money, June 3, 2002. https://money.cnn.com/2002/06/03/news/companies/napster_bankrupt/.

Coppola, Sarah. "East Lawn of Auditorium Shores to Be Named for Vic Mathias." *Austin American-Statesman*, October 17, 2014. https://www.statesman.com/article/20141017/NEWS/310179653.

Engelking, Susan. "Austin's Opportunity Economy: A Model for Collaborative Technology Development." *Annals of the New York Academy of Sciences* 798, no. 1, December 1996. https://doi.org/10.1111/j.1749-6632.1996.tb24854.x.

Gammage III, Earnest, ed., "Austin Music: Into the Future." April 1985. Earnest Gammage Papers, AR.2006.041, Austin History Center, Austin Public Library.

Gibson, David V., and John Sibley Butler. "Sustaining the Technopolis: High-Technology Development in Austin, Texas 1988–2012." IC² Institute, February 2013. https://repositories.lib.utexas.edu/bitstream/handle/2152/19862/ic2-wp-2013-02-01.pdf?sequence=2&isAllowed=y.

Gomez, Rose. "Former Essex Jct. IBM Plant Marks a Milestone." WCAX Channel 3, August 9, 2014. https://www.wcax.com/content/news/Former-Essex-Jct-IBM-plant-marks-milestone-439428613.html.

Hartenberger, Lisa, Zeynep Tufekci, and Stuart Davis, "A History of High Tech and the Technopolis in Austin." In *Inequity in the Technopolis: Race, Class, Gender, and the Digital Divide in Austin*, edited by Joseph Straubhaar, Jeremiah Spence, Zeynep Tufekci, and Roberta G. Lentz. University of Texas Press, 2012.

Hudspeth, Mark, producer, "What's in Store for Sears?" CBS News, December 16, 2018, https://www.cbsnews.com/news/the-fall-of-sears-from-worlds-leading-retailer-to-bankruptcy/.

Jacobs, Jane. *Cities and the Wealth of Nations*. Vintage, 1984.

Jervis, Rick. "How SXSW put itself on the map." *USA Today*, March 6, 2014. https://www.usatoday.com/story/tech/2014/03/06/sxsw-swenson-evolution/5922177/.

Jones, Monty. *A Civic Entrepreneur: The Life of Technology Visionary George Kozmetsky*. Briscoe Center for American History, University of Texas at Austin, 2018.

Kabanov, Dmitry. "The History of SXSW: How It All Started." HackerNoon.com, September 26, 2018. https://hackernoon.com/the-history-of-sxsw-how-it-all-started-66b9aa379ee7.

Liffreing, Ilyse. "'It Lost Its Community of Innovation': Why Agencies Are Skipping SXSW This Year." Digiday, February 15, 2018. https:/h/digiday.com/marketing/lost-community-innovation-agencies-skipping-sxsw-year/.

Maas, Jimmy. "Sears to Close Its Last Austin Department Store Locations." KUT News, October 15, 2018. https://www.kut.org/post/sears-close-its-last-austin-department-store-locations/.

Maciag, Mike. "What the Rise in Renting Means for Cities." *Governing*, April 2019. https://www.governing.com/topics/urban/gov-renters-apartments-affordable-housing-cities.html.

McGaughy, Lauren. "Growth of SXSW Makes City Confront Festival's Future." *San Antonio Express-News*, March 21, 2015. https://www.expressnews.com/news/local/article/Growth-of-SXSW-makes-city-confront-festival-s-6150541.php.

Mike Tolleson & Associates. "Mike Tolleson." Accessed April 10, 2019. http://miketolleson.com/attorneys/.

Miller, Stephen. "Founding Prodigy Chief Created Online Services for Consumers." *Wall Street Journal*, January 13, 2010. https://www.wsj.com/articles/SB126335118860527243.

The Onion. "Word 'Innovate' Said 650,000 Times at SXSW So Far." *The Onion*, March 11, 2013. https://entertainment.theonion.com/word-innovate-said-650-000-times-at-sxsw-so-far-1819574674.

Powers, Ann. "Reporter's Notebook: Who's Got the Sound? Baby Moguls and Techies." *New York Times*, March 22, 2000. https://www.nytimes.com/2000/03/22/movies/reporter-s-notebook-who-s-got-the-sound-baby-moguls-and-techies.html.

Powers, Pike. "Pike Powers, CEO, Pike Powers Group, LLC." Interview by We Are Austin Tech, July 10, 2012. Retrieved from https://www.youtube.com/watch?v=UKz3zzkF7VQ.

Robbins, Paul. "The Town That Won the Pennant." *Environmental Business*, 2003.

Shank, Barry. *Dissonant Identities: The Rock 'n' Roll Scene in Austin, Texas*. University Press of New England, 1994.

Shannon, Megan Elizabeth. "Quantifying the Impacts of Regulatory Delay on Housing Affordability and Quality in Austin, Texas." Master's report, University of Texas at Austin, May 2015. https://repositories.lib.utexas.edu/bitstream/handle/2152/32194/SHANNON-MASTERSREPORT-2015.pdf?sequence=1&isAllowed=y.

Smilor, Raymond, David V. Gibson, and George Kozmetsky, "Creating the Technopolis: High-Technology Development in Austin, Texas." *Journal of Business Venturing* 4, no. 1, January 1989. https://www.sciencedirect.com/science/article/abs/pii/0883902689900335?via%3Dihub.

South by Southwest. "History." SXSW.com. Accessed April 8, 2019. https://www.sxsw.com/about/history/.

South by Southwest. "Analysis of the Economic Benefit to the City of Austin From SXSW 2019." November 18, 2019. https://explore.sxsw.com/hubfs/2019%20SXSW%20Economic%20Impact%20Analysis%20-%2011.18.19%20OPT.pdf.

Taleb, Nassim Nicolas. *Antifragile: Things That Gain from Disorder*. Random House, 2012.

Taleb, Nassim Nicolas. *The Black Swan*. Random House, 2007.

Thompson, Stephen. "South by Southwest 2000." AV Club, March 29, 2000. https://music.avclub.com/south-by-southwest-2000-1798208041.

Tinsley, Anna M. "Warning to Texas Renters on Property Taxes: 'You're Being Eaten for Lunch.'" *Fort Worth Star-Telegram*, April 25, 2019. https://www.star-telegram.com/news/state/texas/article229334299.html?fbclid=IwAR3IpgIVdo8mzGdqe5RGIWsTX-6s5P2YbqsQp6rDAQI3Fu89EdpMgMlz65Y.

Tretter, Eliot. "Live Music, Intercity Competition, and Reputational Rents: Austin, Texas the 'Live Music Capital of the World.'" *Human Geography* 8, no. 3, January 2015. https://www.researchgate.net/publication/301225995_Live_Music_Intercity_Competition_and_Reputational_Rents_Austin_Texas_the_'Live_Music_Capital_of_the_World'.

Vujasinovic, Vuki. "It's Time to Stop Saying Everything Is Disruptive." *Forbes*, March 2, 2017. https://www.forbes.com/sites/vukivujasinovic/2017/03/02/its-time-to-stop-saying-everything-is-disruptive/#2b85f04a708d.

CHAPTER EIGHT

Herrington, Chris, executive Producer, Kaela Champlin, Producer. "Tank Farm: Organizing for Justice." City of Austin, Watershed Protection. May 12, 2021. https://storymaps.arcgis.com/stories/0d6e3273366041e48625aa05f4e21822.

CHAPTER NINE

Bai, Matt. "Thrown for a Curve in Rhode Island." *New York Times*, April 20, 2013. https://www.nytimes.com/2013/04/21/business/curt-schilling-rhode-island-and-the-fall-of-38-studios.html.

Davidson, Adam. "Can Anyone Really Create Jobs?" *New York Times*, November 3, 2011. https://www.nytimes.com/2011/11/06/magazine/job-creation-campaign-promises.html.

Funkhouser, Mark. "How to Stop the Economic Development Wars." *Governing*, November 22, 2013. https://www.governing.com/gov-institute/on-leadership/col-economic-development-incentives-federal-law-washington-state-seattle-boeing.html.

Hartenberger, Lisa, Zeynep Tufekci, and Davis, Stuart. "A History of High Tech and the Technopolis in Austin." In *Inequity in the Technopolis: Race, Class, Gender, and the Digital Divide in Austin*, edited by Joseph Straubhaar, Jeremiah Spence, Zeynep Tufekci and Roberta G. Lentz. University of Texas Press, 2012.

Herrara, Sebastian. "After Amazon closes HQ2 door, Austin shrugs and moves on." *Austin American-Statesman*, November 13, 2018. https://www.statesman.com/story/business/technology/2018/11/13/after-amazon-closes-hq2-door-austin-shrugs-and-moves-on/8383507007/.

Jensen, Nathan M. "Exit Options in Firm-Government Negotiations: An Evaluation of the Texas Chapter 313 Program." Nathan M. Jensen website, 2017. https://www.natemjensen.com/wp-content/uploads/2017/02/Jensen-Chapter-313-Policy-Brief-1.pdf.

Ma, Jason. "Top VC Kai-Fu Lee says his prediction that AI will displace 50% of jobs by 2027 is 'uncannily accurate.'" *Fortune*, May 25, 2024. https://fortune.com/2024/05/25/ai-job-displacement-forecast-50-percent-2027-kai-fu-lee-chatgpt-openai/.

NPR Marist Poll. "1/22 Employment Poll Findings." Marist Institute for Public Opinion, January 2018. https://maristpoll.marist.edu/nprmarist-poll-results-january-2018-picture-of-work/.

Parilla, Joseph, and Sifan Liu. "Examining the local value of economic development incentives: Evidence from four US cities." The Brookings Institution, March 2008. https://www.brookings.edu/articles/examining-the-local-value-of-economic-development-incentives/.

Pramuk, Jacob. "Alexandria Ocasio-Cortez and other New York Democrats pick a fight with Amazon and Jeff Bezos over HQ2 in Queens." CNBC, November 13, 2018. https://www.cnbc.com/2018/11/13/alexandria-ocasio-cortez-and-new-york-democrats-criticize-amazon-hq2.html.

Rockwell, Lilly. "50 years in, IBM still helping shape Austin's tech sector." *Austin American Statesman*, July 29, 2017. https://www.statesman.com/story/business/2017/07/29/50-years-in-ibm-still-helping-shape-austins-tech-sector/10376400007/.

Rockwell, Lilly. "Steve Adler posts decisive victory over Mike Martinez for Austin mayor." *Austin American-Statesman*, December 16, 2014. https://www.statesman.com/story/news/2014/12/17/steve-adler-posts-decisive-victory/6714349007/.

Texas Comptroller of Public Accounts. "Chapter 313: Trading Tax Limitations for Development." Comptroller's website, Fiscal Notes, Publication no. 96-369, November 2020. https://comptroller.texas.gov/transparency/open-data/

Thompson, Derek. "Amazon's HQ2 Spectacle Isn't Just Shameful—It Should Be Illegal." *The Atlantic*, November 12, 2018. https://www.theatlantic.com/ideas/archive/2018/11/amazons-hq2-spectacle-should-be-illegal/575539/.

Truppner, Mark. "Biden: We've Created Over 2 Million Jobs." MyMotherLod.com, June 7, 2021. https://www.mymotherlode.com/news/local/1773860/biden-weve-created-over-2-million-jobs.html.

CHAPTER TEN

University of Texas at Austin. "University of Texas at Austin's brand message is 'What Starts Here Changes the World.'" *UT News*, March 8, 2006. https://news.utexas.edu/2006/03/08/university-of-texas-at-austins-brand-message-is-what-starts-here-changes-the-world/.

Wheeler, J. Craig. Forward by Neal DeGrasse Tyson. *The Path to Singularity: How Technology Will Challenge the Future of Humanity*. Globe Pequot, November 2024.

Index

abatements, tax, 75, 169–75, 177–79
Abbott, Greg, 120
academic spin-offs, 84–86, 96
ACC (Austin Community College), 103–4, 125
ACL (Austin City Limits Music Festival), 67, 140, 157
Adler, Steve, 122, 165, 174, 181
Advanced Micro Devices, 15, 96
AE (Angelou Economics), 17
affordable housing, 109, 117, 119, 120–21, 123, 124, 131, 152–53, 161, 162, 164, 173, 188
African American Leadership Institute, 123
agglomeration economies, 105–6
AI (artificial intelligence), 151, 170, 175, 182, 190
Aielli, John, 7–8, 31, 32–34
air pollution, 45, 138, 161, 186
Alexander, Christopher, 187
Altounian, David, 80
AMAC (Austin Music Advisory Committee), 139–41
Amazon, 11, 43, 49, 75, 149, 172–74, 179, 182
AMD, 77, 84
Anderson, Marcellus "Andy," 113
angel investors, 48, 88, 91, 92–93, 101, 152
Angelou, Angelos, 17, 112
Angelou Economics (AE), 17
Ann and Roy Butler Hike-and-Bike Trail, 37, 158
anticapitalism sentiment, 47–48, 50, 53, 54–55, 57–58
Anti-Displacment Task Force, 123
antigrowth sentiment, 19, 21–23, 39–44, 117, 152
Apple, 77, 92, 96, 201n38
Applied Materials, 201n38
Aqua Fest, 96
aquifers, 35, 38
ARA (Austin Revitalization Authority), 119, 123
Aragona, Joe, 89
Arlington, Virginia, 173
Armadillo World Headquarters, 7, 21, 25, 33, 67, 140, 152, 168
Armstrong, Lance, 67
Army Futures Command, 185
artificial intelligence (AI), 151, 170, 175, 182, 190
ATI (Austin Technology Incubator), 19, 23, 54, 65, 100, 114
Atlanta, Georgia, 119, 155
AT&T, 125
Austin, Stephen F., 4
Austin, Texas: geography and landscape of, 1, 2, 16, 22; site selection as capital, 1–4; technopolis vision, 12, 14, 18, 23; weirdness and openness of, 7–11. See also culture; East and Central East Austin; tech entrepreneurial ecosystem; urban planning; water
Austin Area Economic Development Foundation, 14

Austin Area Urban League, 123
Austin Chamber of Commerce, 18, 96, 100, 112, 113, 137–41, 187
Austin City Limits (TV series), 140, 145
Austin City Limits Music Festival (ACL), 67, 140, 157
Austin Community College (ACC), 103–4, 125
Austin Creeks (1976 booklet), 158
Austin Dam, 36
Austin Music Advisory Committee (AMAC), 139–41
Austin Planning Commission, 113
Austin Revitalization Authority (ARA), 119, 123
Austin Technology Incubator (ATI), 19, 23, 54, 65, 100, 114
Austin Tomorrow, 161, 162
Austin Urban Technology Movement (AUTMHQ), 124–25, 133
Austin Ventures, 89–91, 93, 102, 202n49
Austin-Bergstrom International Airport, 166, 203n69
Austria, 20–21
Austron, 201n34
automation, workplace, 170, 175

Baer, Josh, 94, 95
Baireuther, Kathleen, 55
Balcones Canyonland Preserve, 157
Balcones Research Center, University of Texas, 96
banks, venture, 91, 102, 202n49
Barbaro, Nick, 141
Barchas, Isaac, 65
Barton, William "Uncle Billy," 1
Barton Creek, 24, 27, 35, 38, 39–40, 43, 46, 159–60
Barton Creek Greenbelt, 116–17, 155, 157, 181
Barton Creek Planned Unit Development (PUD), 39–40
Barton Springs, 1, 33, 35, 37–39, 45–46, 117, 152, 155
Base Realignment and Closure Commission, 166
Bazaarvoice, 89
Bean Path, 132
Bedichek, Roy, 38
Bend, Oregon, 68
Bergstrom Air Force Base, 166
Bezos, Jeff, 149, 172
Biden, Joe, 169, 193
Bioware, 201n38
Bishop, Bill, 60
Bizzard, 201n38
Black, Louis, 141
Black, Sinclair, 38–39, 65, 159, 165, 187, 189
Black chamber (Greater Austin Black Chamber of Commerce), 112–13, 114
Black Citizens Task Force, 113
Black communities: cultural identity, 107, 111, 118–19, 123; entrepreneurship, 109, 124, 132–33; gentrification and displacement, 24–25, 43–44, 46, 108, 116–19, 120–21, 188; gentrification and displacement, initiatives to rectify, 122–25, 161; population statistics, 108, 118, 120; segregation, 111, 121, 160; tech/STEM participation, 109, 110, 124–25; violent unrest in, 52, 66; wealth gap, 109, 122, 126–27
Black Lives Matter movement, 66, 153
Bloomberg, Michael, 59
BookPeople, 8, 49
Boston, Massachusetts, 15, 80, 102, 123
Boulder, Colorado, 44
Bradley, Gary, 39
branding and slogans, 8–9, 10, 21, 23, 29, 121, 139, 141, 145

Broken Spoke, 30
Bryant, John Hope, 132
Burlington, Vermont, 69–74
Burnette, Colette Pierce, 122
Burton, Diane M., 199n14
Bush, George W., 40, 116
business incubators, 79, 88, 93, 95, 100, 101
Butler, Ann and Roy, 158

California, 15, 44, 52, 59, 72, 78, 79, 80, 99, 102–3, 105–6, 114
call centers, 179
Capital City African American Chamber of Commerce (CCAACC, later Greater Austin Black Chamber of Commerce), 112–13, 114
Capital Factory, 89, 91, 92, 93–94
capital(ism): access to, 48–49, 54, 55–57, 59; and community investment, 57, 65; criticism of, 47–48, 50, 53, 54–55, 57–58; defined, 48; as essential to growth, 49–50, 51–52, 57; and open societies, 51, 53, 64–65; and social equity, 25, 44–45, 51–53, 60
Carinthia, Austria, 20–21
Carmel, California, 44
Carnegie Mellon University, 89
Caro, Robert, 22
Carr, Norris, 112
Cash, Johnny, 142
Catellus Development Corporation, 166
The Catfish Station (now Mr. Catfish & More), 118, 119
CBS, 149
CCAACC (Capital City African American Chamber of Commerce, later Greater Austin Black Chamber of Commerce), 112–13, 114
Central East Austin. See East and Central East Austin
Central Texas Angel Network, 93
Chafee, Lincoln, 179
Chamber of Commerce, Austin, 18, 96, 100, 112, 113, 137–41, 187
Chapter 313 program, 178
Chapter 380 agreements, 98
Chattahoochee River, 155
Chicago, Illinois, 172
CHIPS and Science Act (2022), 125
Choose New Jersey, 119
Christensen, Clayton, 135, 136
Christian, Elizabeth, 17
Christie, Chris, 119
Circle C community, 39
Cisco Systems, 13
city planning. See urban planning
Clardy, Jim, 198n3
Cleveland, Ohio, 72
Clinton, Bill, 13, 50
closed societies, 64, 65, 150
cluster growth, 71
Cochran, Leslie, 8, 168
Code2College, 124
CodeNEXT, 163–64, 165
collaborative networks and partnerships: attracting high-tech firms through, 95–98, 100, 104–5, 116; and community reinvestment, 57, 65; and environmental preservation, 158–60; and innovation, 136; and knowledge sharing, 22, 113; and technology transfer, 13–14, 65
Colorado River, 1, 22, 30, 35, 36, 158
Comanche people, 1, 2
commuting and transportation concerns, 39, 45, 162, 164, 167, 186–87
Compaq, 201n38
Comprehensive Plan for the Development of Town Lake, 158–59
Comprehensive Watersheds Ordinance, 27

constructive capitalism, 25, 51–52, 53, 54
Continuum, 201n34
Cooke, Lee, 112, 113
Coronado, Julia, 174
corporations: attracting high-tech firms, 14–16, 78, 86, 95–105, 114; distrust of, 47–49; and fallacy of traditional job creation model, 177, 182; and gig economy, 170, 175–76, 177, 183; incentive packages, 75, 98–99, 169–75, 177–79; as incubating firms, 79–80; tech spin-offs, 88–90, 97
cost of living, 33, 44, 45, 114, 118–19, 120–21, 131. See also housing affordability
counterculture, 7–9, 21–23, 32, 47
COVID-19 pandemic, 71, 88, 92, 175, 176, 186, 188, 193
coworking spaces, 93–95
creative capitalism, 25
creative class and talent: access to capital, 48–49, 54, 55–57, 58–59; and cluster growth, 71; and social equity, 44, 45, 60, 129–30, 168. See also tech entrepreneurial ecosystem
creative destruction, 136
creativity. See innovation and creativity
creeks and rivers. See water; specific bodies of water
Crenshaw, Roberta, 36–37, 158
critical mass of entrepreneurs, 80, 91, 92, 94–95, 101
Cruz, Paul, 122
Crystal Semiconductors, 198n3
culture: attraction of Austin's, 7–8, 56; Black cultural identity, 107, 111, 118–19, 123; counterculture, 7–9, 21–23, 32, 47; music scene, 7, 10, 12, 21, 25, 33, 56, 118, 139, 141, 152, 157, 168. See also open societies and openness
Cyversity, 130

Dallas, Texas, 78, 153, 174
dams, 34–37, 57, 158
Data General, 96
Daugherty, Gordon, 94
Davidson, Adam, 178
Davis, Marc, 93
DeAngelis, Ken, 89
DECA (Diversity and Ethnic Chambers Alliance), 123
Defense Research Laboratory (DRL), University of Texas, 84–85
DEI (diversity, equity, and inclusion) initiatives, 65–66, 124–25, 193
Delaware, 87, 201n41
Dell, Michael, 11, 49, 56, 65, 114, 189
Dell Technologies, 11, 49, 77, 86, 114
Denver, Colorado, 123
desegregation, 111
Detroit, Michigan, 173, 175
displacement: and corporate site selection, 170, 173; and gentrification, 24–25, 43–44, 46, 108, 110, 116–19, 120–21, 188
disruption: in music industry, 140–44; overuse of term, 135; risks of, 136, 148; withstanding, 150–51. See also innovation and creativity
disruptive innovations, 136
diversity, equity, and inclusion (DEI) initiatives, 65–66, 124–25, 193
Diversity and Ethnic Chambers Alliance (DECA), 123
diversity and inclusion: in Austin chamber, 113; DEI initiatives, 65–66, 124–25, 193; and exclusionary

impulse, 66, 67, 68, 73–74; in open societies, 65–66. See also social equity
Dobie, J. Frank, 38
Dochen, Sandy, 17
Domain development, 145, 166
"Don't Mess with Texas" campaign, 29
dot-com crash (2000), 89, 93
Dow Chemical, 85
downtown residential development, 164–65
Driskill Hotel, 67, 145
DRL (Defense Research Laboratory), University of Texas, 84–85
Dropbox, 98
Drucker, Peter, 15, 57
Dunn, Laura, 45

Eagle Signal, 96
East and Central East Austin: Black cultural identity in, 107, 111, 118–19, 123; as desired development zone, 46, 117, 161; gentrification and displacement in, 43–44, 46, 108, 110, 116–19, 120–21, 188; gentrification and displacement in, initiatives to rectify, 122–25, 161; housing affordability in, 109, 117, 119, 120–21, 123, 124; master plan (1928), 110–11, 160; population statistics, 108, 118, 120
East Austin Strategy Team, 161
eBay, 98
Eberly, Angelina, 4, 6
economic development: criticism of field, 58, 122; talent framework, 55–56. See also capital(ism); job creation; tech entrepreneurial ecosystem; urban planning
Edwards Aquifer, 35, 38, 117
egalitarianism, 51
Eklektikos (public radio show), 7, 33
Emerging Technology Fund (ETF), 98, 100
Emerson, 147
employment. See job creation
Engelking, Susan, 138
entrepreneurial recycling, 79, 80, 82–83, 88, 91, 101
entrepreneurs/entrepreneurship: access to capital, 48–49, 54, 55–57; Black, 109, 124, 132–33; critical mass of, 80, 91, 92, 94–95, 101; network density, 65, 80, 82, 92; urban vs. market, 35, 46. See also tech entrepreneurial ecosystem
environment/environmentalism: "clean" industry focus, 138; as factor in Austin's future success, 190; growth concerns, 24, 26–27, 116–17, 161; and protection of minority communities, 128–29; public parkland development and preservation, 37, 40, 42, 156–60, 181; undesirable consequences of, 42–44; water preservation concerns, 37–41, 45, 117, 152, 157–60
Envision Central Texas (ECT), 40, 161–62, 163, 165, 166
Equidad ATX, 123
equity. See social equity
Erard, Michael, 35
ETF (Emerging Technology Fund), 98, 100
ethnicity. See race and ethnicity
exclusionary impulse, 66, 67, 68, 73–74
experimentation. See innovation and creativity

Fabbio, Bob, 91, 93
Facebook, 98

Fassiotto, Magali, 81
federal funding, 84, 125
FeedMagnet, 94
Festival Beach, 159
flooding, 38, 158, 159
Florida, Richard, 44, 45, 55–57, 58, 59, 60, 64, 121, 160
Floyd, George, 65, 153, 187
food deserts, 123–24, 126
Ford, Jason, 94
Foreign Corrupt Practices Act (1977), 179
Fort Worth, Texas, 78, 170
Foursquare, 143
Francis, Scott, 94
Franke, David, 89
freelance workers, 170, 175–76, 177, 183
Freeport-McMoRan, 39
Fregonese Calthorpe Associates (FCA), 162, 164
Friedman, Milton, 47
Funkhouser, Mark, 179

Galaxy Microsystems, 201n34
Gammage, Ernest, 139, 140, 141
garbage disposals, 146–48
Gardner, Booth, 17
gender equity, 66, 126
General Electric Company, 85
General Magic, 80
gentrification, 24–25, 43–44, 46, 108, 110, 116–19, 120–21, 188
geography and landscape, of Austin, 1, 2, 16, 22
Georgetown, Texas, 109
Gibson, David, 16, 21, 22, 24, 30, 60, 97, 105, 151–52
gig economy, 170, 175–76, 177, 183
Gilbert, Dan, 173
Glaeser, Edward, 81
Google, 13, 77, 80, 124, 201n38
Gordian, Carmelo, 93
grant and loan incentives, 96, 98–99, 100, 101, 104
Great Recession (2008), 92
Greater Houston Partnership, 119
Greider, William, 46
growth: capital as essential to, 49–50, 51–52, 57; “smart,” 13, 46. See also technology growth; urban planning
GSD&M, 10
Guzman, Jorge, 201n41

Harrison, Bill, 92
Harrison, Richard, 83
Harvard University, 89
HBCUs, 107, 124, 125
H-E-B, 124
Hewlett Packard, 96, 201n38
Highland Lakes, 22, 36, 189
Highlight, 143
high-tech firms, attracting, 14–16, 78, 86, 95–105, 114
Hill, Homer, 118–19
Hippie Hollow, 34
hippies, 7, 21, 34
Hispanic communities: gentrification and displacement, 24–25, 43–44, 110, 118, 188; gentrification and displacement, initiatives to rectify, 123, 124; population statistics, 110; racial wealth gap, 127
Holiday House, 197n1 (ch 1)
Holloway, Amy, 17
Home Options for Mobility and Equity (HOME) initiative, 167
home ownership, 109, 153
HomeAway, 20, 89, 91
Hood River, Oregon, 69
Hood River Brewing Company, 41, 69

housing affordability, 109, 117, 119, 120–21, 123, 124, 131, 152–53, 161, 162, 164, 173, 188
housing developments, 123, 152–53, 167
Houston, Sam, 2, 4
Houston, Texas, 1–2, 4, 78, 119, 153
Hsieh, Tony, 165, 180
"human capital" slogan, 121
humanism, 51
Humphrey, David C., 180
Huston-Tillotson University, 107, 122, 124
Hyams, Chris, 91, 92

I-35, 111, 159, 162, 167, 187
IBM, 14, 70–71, 75, 77, 84, 86, 88, 96, 105, 125, 138, 149, 180
IC² (Institute of Constructive Capitalism), 12, 14, 16, 20, 23, 49, 51–54, 100, 136
IEDC (International Economic Development Council), 122
Imagine Austin, 162–63, 181
immigrants, and xenophobia, 66
Imperial Bank, 91, 102, 202n49
incentives: corporate, 75, 169–75, 177–79; loans and grants, 96, 98–99, 100, 101, 104
inclusion. See diversity and inclusion
income, household, 109, 127
income equality, 24, 25. See also social equity
incubating firms, 79–80, 81–83, 85
incubators: business, 79, 88, 93, 95, 100, 101; networked, 93–95, 101
Indeed, 77, 88, 89, 92
independent contractors, 170, 175–76, 177, 183
Indigenous people, 1, 2, 37
industry clusters, 71
inequity. See social equity
information technology, 18
initial public offerings (IPOs), 54
Inman, Bobby R., 15, 105
innovation and creativity: capital as essential to, 49–50, 53–54, 58–59; civic, 152–53; disruptive, 136; as essential to tech sector, 136–37; failures in, 149–50; Kozmetsky's vision for, 136–37, 150, 189; openness as essential to, 9, 10–11, 14, 150–51; overuse of term, 135; resistance to, 146–49; in SXSW origin story, 137–42. See also disruption
InSinkErator, 147, 148
Institute of Constructive Capitalism (IC²), 12, 14, 16, 20, 23, 49, 51–54, 100, 136
institutional betrayal, 55
integrated analytical framework, 83
Intel, 86, 201n38
intellectual property: and knowledge economy, 15; ownership and protection of, 51, 53; and technology transfer, 13
International Economic Development Council (IEDC), 122
internet, and music industry, 140, 141, 142–43
Interstate 35, 111, 159, 162, 167, 187
investment, by angel investors and venture capitalists, 10, 23, 48, 59, 88, 89–91, 92–93, 101, 136, 152, 202n49
Isenberg, Daniel, 83, 101

Jackson Tech District, 132
Jacobs, Jane, 44, 56, 149–50, 187
Japan, 15
Jennings, Waylon, 168

Jensen, Nathan, 98, 178
Jim Crow-era policies, 24
J. J. Pickle Research Campus, 14
job creation: and AI, 151, 170, 175, 182, 190; Austin's model of, 180–81; corporate incentives, 169–75, 177–79; rethinking model of, 175–77, 182–84; and unemployment rates, 109, 169, 180
job relocation, 178
Jobs, Steve, 32
Johnson, Lady Bird, 158
Johnson, Lyndon B., 36
Jones, Anson, 4
Jones, Monty, 25, 50, 54, 150
Judge, Mike, 142

Kaham, Roy, 88
Katz, Don, 149
"Keep Austin Weird" slogan, 8–9
Kerr, William, 81
Kessler, Ron, 17
Kilcrease, Laura, 20, 93
King, Martin Luther, Jr., 66
King, Rodney, 66
knowledge economy, 15
Kocurek, Neal, 17
Kozmetsky, George: background, 12, 50; on capital, 49–50; on collaborative partnerships, 13–14, 22; donations, 38, 65; innovative vision, 136–37, 150, 189; Richard Florida on, 57; and SEMATECH, 71; social equity concerns, 24, 25–26, 45, 52–53, 58, 60, 66; startup experience, 12, 99–100, 114; on technology transfer, 13–14; technopolis vision, 12, 19, 151–52
Krantzman, Phyllis, 140, 141

Lady Bird Lake, 35, 37, 157–58, 160, 161
Lake Travis, 33–34, 35
Lamar, Mirabeau, 1–4, 5
Lamb Research, 201n38
land development codes, 163–64, 167
landscape and geography, of Austin, 1, 2, 16, 22
Las Vegas, Nevada, 165
Latino communities. See Hispanic communities
Lee, Kai Fu, 175
libertarianism, 58
Liemandt, Joe, 89
light-rail extensions, 167, 186
Linklater, Richard, 142
Litton Industries, 99
"Live Music Capital of the World" slogan, 10, 139, 141
LiveOak, 202n49
living wage, 33, 124
loan and grant incentives, 96, 98–99, 100, 101, 104
Long, Walter E., 36
Longhorn Dam, 37, 158
Lord, David, 139, 141
Los Angeles, California, 52, 140

Mackey, John, 10–11, 49
Malecki, Ed, 82
Malick, Terrence, 45
Las Manitas, 67
Martin, Trayvon, 153
Martin Prosperity Institute, 121
Marx, Karl, 47, 50
Mathias, Vic, 112, 137–38
Maximum Integrated Circuits, 201n38
Mayfield Park and Nature Preserve, 157
McBee's Research Applications, 201n34
MCC (Microelectronics and Computer Technology Corporation), 14–16, 18, 23, 57, 86, 96–97, 102, 104, 105, 114, 115

McCall, Tom, 68
McClure, Tim, 10, 29
McDaniel Strategy Ecosystems, 121
McKinsey Institute for Black Economic Mobility, 124, 127, 131
McLuhan, Marshall, 13, 197n2 (ch 1)
Measure Austin, 132
Meerkat, 143
Mellow Johnny's, 67–68
Melster Engineering, 201n34
microchip manufacturing, 15, 20, 70, 96, 114, 116
Microelectronics and Computer Technology Corporation (MCC), 14–16, 18, 23, 57, 86, 96–97, 102, 104, 105, 114, 115
Microelectronics Research Center (MRC), University of Texas, 17
Microsoft Corporation, 89, 104, 125
Mike D, 149
MIT, 84, 89
Mitchell, Eric, 112
Mitsubishi Corporation, 42
Modine, 146
Moffett, Jim Bob, 39
Moodie, Gordon, 180
Moore's Law, 136
Mopac Boulevard, 39, 162
Moretti, Enrico, 198n7
Motorola, 14, 15, 80, 86, 96, 105
Mr. Catfish & More (formerly The Catfish Station), 118, 119
MRC (Microelectronics Research Center), University of Texas, 17
MRI Systems Corporation, 85–86
Mueller development, 145, 165–66
music industry, 139–44, 149
music scene, 7, 10, 12, 21, 25, 33, 56, 118, 139, 141, 152, 157, 168
Musk, Elon, 143, 189
NAACP, 123
Naisbitt, John, 19, 22, 27
Napster, 142–43, 149
NASCAR, 171
Nashville, Tennessee, 69, 140
National Bar Association, 113
National Coalition of Black Meeting Professionals (NCBMP), 113
National Instruments, 77, 84, 85, 86
Native Americans, 1, 2, 37
natural resources, economies built on, 52–53, 57. See also water
Nelson, Willie, 7, 142, 168
Nest, 80
network density, 65, 80, 82, 92
networked incubators, 93–95, 101
New Jersey, 119–20
New York City, 102, 141, 173
Nike, 5
Nokia, 201n38
North Carolina, 15, 59, 114
Northwest Independent School District (NWISD), 170–71
Not In My Backyard (NIMBY) collective, 23, 117
Nova Graphics International, 201n34
NXP Semiconductors, 124

Obama, Barack, 169
Ocasio-Cortez, Alexandria, 173–74
Occupy Wall Street (2011), 47, 48, 54
Office of Equity, 122
Olympic Peninsula, Washington, 42
open societies and openness: and capital, 51, 53, 64–65; vs. closed societies, 64, 65, 150; and collaboration, 65, 150; as concept, 9, 64; and creativity, 9, 10–11, 14; diversity and inclusion, 65–66; vs. exclusionary impulse, 66, 67, 68, 73–74; and innovation, 9, 10–11, 14, 150–51;

open societies and openness (*cont.*)
threats to, 67–68; uniqueness of Austin's, 11, 167–68
Operation Hope, 132
opportunity economy, 140, 141
Oracle, 77, 92, 104
Oregon, 8, 13, 41, 68, 69
Oregon Resource and Technology Development Corporation (ORTDC), 13, 41
Oregon State University, 13
Orum, Anthony, 22, 23, 30, 34–35, 36, 46, 50, 152
outsourcing, 179, 183

Palo Alto, California, 203n64
Pasternak, Boris, 191
Paxton, Ken, 167
People Organized in Defense of Earth and Her Resources (PODER), 161
Perry, Rick, 98, 100, 116, 178
Pervasive Software, 20
Philadelphia, Pennsylvania, 123
Pickle, J. J., 14
Pinson Associates, 201n34
place. See quality of place
PODER (People Organized in Defense of Earth and Her Resources), 161
pollution, 22, 38, 39, 45, 138, 155, 161, 186
Popper, Karl, 9, 64, 67, 150
population statistics: in Austin, 18, 108, 110, 188; in Burlington, 69, 73–74
Porter, Bruce, 89
Porter, Michael, 71, 139
Portland, Oregon, 8, 41, 68, 123, 156
Powers, Pike, 11, 18–19, 96, 100, 115, 138
preservation. See environment/environmentalism
Princeton University, 89
process-view perspective, 82
Prodigy, 149
Project Connect, 167
property taxes, 153
property values, 117, 153, 161
public parkland development and preservation, 37, 40, 42, 156–60, 181
public service funding, 170, 177–78

Qualcomm, 201n38
quality of life, defined, 63–64
quality of place: attraction of Austin's, 16, 18–19, 34, 41, 72, 114, 138, 180; challenges of measuring, 3, 64; defined, 63; diversity and inclusion in, 131; and social equity, 123. See also open societies and openness
Queens, New York, 173
Quicken Loans, 173

race and ethnicity: exclusion/segregation based on, 51, 66, 111, 121, 160; wealth gap, 109, 122, 126–27; wealth gap, practical solutions to close, 128–33. See also Black communities; Hispanic communities; Indigenous people; social equity
Racine, Wisconsin, 146
racing industry, 170–71
Radian Corporation, 14, 85, 201n34
Rainey Street, 145
R&D consortia, attracting, 14–16, 96–97, 103–4, 114
Rather, Robin, 27, 40, 43–44, 46
Rawlings, Mike, 174
RCA, 15
Reagan, Ronald, 169
recycling, entrepreneurial, 79, 80, 82–83, 88, 91, 101
Redford, Robert, 45
religion, exclusion based on, 51, 66
remote work, 176, 177, 186, 188

renting, 153, 173
Research Triangle, North Carolina, 15, 114
Rhode Island, 179
Richards, Ann, 17, 40, 115–16
Richardson, Texas, 116
rivers and creeks. See water; specific bodies of water
Robbins, Paul, 138
Roberts, Jon, 116, 121, 125
Roberts, Velma, 113
Rogers, Everett, 15–16, 21, 22, 97, 105
Round Rock, Texas, 8, 109
Route 128 tech corridor, Boston, 15, 80
runaway capitalism, 57–58
Russia, 51, 53, 66
Rust Capital, 89
Ryan, Rebecca, 64, 70

salary and living wage, 33, 124
Samsung, 201n38
Samsung Semiconductor, 16–18, 115
San Antonio, Texas, 78, 116
San Francisco, California, 59, 72, 102–3, 123
San Jose, California, 59, 102–3
Sanders, Bernie, 55
Saudi Arabia, 53
Save Our Springs Alliance (SOS), 27, 39, 40, 43, 46, 159–60
S. C. Johnson, 146
Schilling, Curt, 179
Schumacher, E. F., 26, 32, 44, 50, 58, 136
Schumpeter, Joseph, 136
Scott, Jeffrey, 198n3
Sears, 149
Seattle, Washington, 17, 42, 69, 102, 188
segregation, racial, 111, 121, 160
SEMATECH (Semiconductor Manufacturing & Technology Institute), 16, 57, 71, 86, 96–97, 102, 103–4, 114, 115
semiconductor manufacturing, 16–17, 20, 79, 86, 96, 104
Sephus, Nashlie, 132
SGE, 201n34
SGI (Smart Growth Initiative), 117
Shank, Barry, 138
Shatner, William, 172
Silicon Labs, 77, 86, 91, 198n3, 201n38
Silicon Valley, 13, 21, 48, 54, 65, 80, 86, 89, 99, 102, 114, 136
Silicon Valley Bank, 91, 102, 202n49
Silicon X branding, 21, 23
Six Square (Central East Austin district), 111
Six Square (community organization), 123
Sixth Street, 118, 144, 145
slogans and branding, 8–9, 10, 21, 23, 29, 121, 139, 141, 145
Smart Growth Initiative (SGI), 117
Smilor, Raymond, 24, 151–52
Smith, Bruton, 171
Smith, Gregory, 119
social compact, 60, 182, 193
social equity: and capital, 25, 44–45, 51–53, 60; and creative class, 44, 45, 60, 129–30, 168; as factor in Austin's future success, 190; gentrification, 24–25, 43–44, 46, 108, 110, 116–19, 120–21, 188; housing affordability, 109, 117, 119, 120–21, 123, 124, 131, 152–53, 161, 162, 164, 173, 188; initiatives to bridge gaps in, 122–26, 128–33, 167; and technology growth, 24–27
socialism, 47, 48, 55, 58
Software, Frontera, 92
software spin-offs, 85–86
soil pollution, 161
Sooch, Nav, 198n3

Sørensen, Jasper, 81
SOS (Save Our Springs Alliance), 27, 39, 40, 43, 46, 159–60
South by Southwest. See SXSW
Speedway Motorsports, 170–71
Spelce, Neal, 17
Spiegel, Ben, 83
spin-offs: academic, 84–86, 96; defined, 198n9; tech firms, 88–90, 97
St. Louis, Missouri, 72
Stacy, William H., 36
Stanford Research Institute (SRI), 18, 136–37, 140
Stanford University, 13, 54, 65, 84, 89
startups: Austin's rankings for, 5, 23–24, 77; Black-owned, 124; capital for, 48–49, 54; failed, 80, 82; support infrastructure, 92–93; and SXSW, 143. See also spin-offs; tech entrepreneurial ecosystem
Startups for Black Founders fund (Google), 124
Stellman, Tom, 121
Stern, Scott, 201n41
Streetman, Ben, 17–18, 20
suburban development, 164, 166
Sun (company), 13
Sun Valley, Idaho, 44
sustainability. See environment/environmentalism
Swearingen, William Scott, Jr., 40–41
Swenson, Roland, 141, 144
SXSW (South by Southwest): buzzwords at, 135–36; creativity at, 145–46; criticism of, 144; innovations highlighted at, 142–43; origin story, 137–42; real estate agents at, 67; as synonymous with Austin's identity, 5, 12, 24, 71, 120, 145

Taleb, Nassim Nicholas, 151
talent. See creative class and talent
Tang, Eric, 118
tank farms, 161
Tarantino, Quentin, 67, 142
Task Force on Institutional Racism and Systemic Inequities, 122–23
taxes: on city land use, 40; corporate incentives, 75, 169–75, 177–79; property, 153
tech entrepreneurial ecosystem: attracting high-tech firms, best practices, 102–5; attracting high-tech firms, collaborative networks, 95–98, 100, 104–5; attracting high-tech firms, monetary incentives, 96, 98–99, 100, 101, 104; entrepreneurial recycling as driver of, 82–83; incubating firms as driver of, 81–82; integrated analytical framework, 83; phase 1, nascent, 79–80, 84–86; phase 2, growth, 80, 86–91; phase 3, self-sustaining, 80–81, 91–95
technology growth: and antigrowth sentiment, 19, 21–23, 39–44, 117, 152; context of Austin's, 12–20 (see also tech entrepreneurial ecosystem); and environment, 24, 26–27; and social equity, 24–27
technology transfer, 13–14, 65
technopolis, vision of Austin as, 12, 14, 18, 23
TEF (Texas Enterprise Fund), 98
Teledyne, 12, 100
1099 economy, 170, 175–76, 177, 183
Tesla, 77, 123, 124, 189
Texas A&M University, 104
Texas Archives War (1842), 4
Texas Economic Development Corporation, 120
Texas Enterprise Fund (TEF), 98
Texas Instruments, 14, 84, 86, 116
Texas Motor Speedway, 170–71
Texas Research International, 201n34

Texas Strategic Economic Development Plan, 71
38 Studios, 179
Thompson, Derek, 177
Thrall, Calvin, 98
3M, 77, 86, 105, 114
3Ts of economic development, 55–56
TIP Strategies, 43, 55, 63, 121, 160, 191
Tivoli, 77, 88–89, 91, 92
Tokyo Electron, 201n38
tolerance. See open societies and openness
Tolleson, Mike, 140, 141
Tonkawa people, 2, 37
tourism and travel industry, 112, 114–15, 116, 139
Toyota, 116
Tracor (Texas Research Associates), 14, 84–85, 201n34
traffic and transportation concerns, 39, 45, 162, 164, 167, 186–87
transfer of technology, 13–14, 65
Tretter, Eliot, 140–41
Trilogy, 77, 88, 89
Triton Ventures, 93
Trump, Donald, 169, 193
Turner, Dorothy, 112–13
Twin Disc, 146
Twitter (now X), 143

unemployment rates, 109, 169, 180
The Unforeseen (documentary film), 45–46
University of Texas: alumni retention, 11, 70; Austin Technology Incubator (ATI), 19, 23, 54, 65, 100, 114; Balcones Research Center, 96; Defense Research Laboratory (DRL), 84–85; high-tech research emphasis, 16, 19, 79, 104; IC² (Institute of Constructive Capitalism), 12, 14, 16, 20, 23, 49, 51–54, 100, 136; Microelectronics Research Center (MRC), 17; School of Architecture, 38; as source for startups, 5, 14, 84–86, 96
University of Vermont, 69–70, 71–72
Urban Music Fest (now Urban Cultural Festival), 118
urban planning: dams, 35–37, 57; environmental preservation concerns, 37–45, 116–17, 156–60, 181; and gentrification, 24–25, 43–44, 46, 108, 110, 116–19, 120–21, 188; growth management, 45–46, 161–67; and housing affordability, 109, 117, 119, 120–21, 123, 124, 131, 152–53, 161, 162, 164, 173, 188; "smart" growth, 13, 46; traffic and transportation concerns, 39, 45, 162, 164, 167, 186–87; water preservation concerns, 37–41, 45, 117, 152, 157–60
Urdy, Charles, 112

Vast.com, 89
venture banks, 91, 102, 202n49
venture capital(ists), 10, 23, 48, 59, 88, 89, 91, 93, 101, 136, 202n49
Vermont, 69–75
Victory Grill, 111
vision(s)/vision statements: of Austin as technopolis, 12, 14, 18, 23; of Austin's future, 185–91; competing, 23, 24–27; as concept, 4–6; crafting, 6–7

Walker, Jerry Jeff, 7
Waller, Edwin, 16, 36
Waller Creek, 160
Ward, Michael, 133
Washington (state), 17, 41–42
Wassenich, Red, 8
water: Aqua Fest, 96; dams, 34–37, 57, 158; pollution, 22, 38, 39, 45, 138, 155, 161; preservation concerns, 37–41, 45, 117, 152, 157–60;

water (*cont.*)
as prized resource in Austin, 1, 16, 22, 155, 189–90; and river commerce, 30–31; "something of the water" singularity, 31, 34, 46
Waterloo (now Austin), 1–4
Waterloo Greenway, 160
Waterloo Records, 8
Watson, Kirk, 117
Watts Uprising (1965), 52, 66
Webb, Walter Prescott, 38
Weed Instrument, 201n34
weirdness, 7–11, 27
Welland, David, 198n3
West, Glenn, 86, 97, 103, 105–6, 112
white-collar workers, 57
whitetrification, 118
Whole Earth Catalog, 32
Whole Foods, 10–11, 49
Williams, Evan, 143
Wirtz, Alvin, 22
women, and gender equity, 66, 126
Wood, Bill, 88, 89
Wooldridge, Alexander Penn, 35–36
work. See job creation
work-from-home model, 176
workplace automation, 170, 175
Wozniak, Steve, 32
WP Engine, 89, 124
Wyatt, Tommy, 112
Wynn, Will, 164, 165, 180

X (formerly Twitter), 143
xenophobia, 66
Xplore Technologies, 201n38

Yagjian, Marc, 92, 94
Yahoo, 13

Zilker, Andrew Jackson, 157
Zilker Park, 37, 157, 158
zoning, 44, 49, 111, 116–17, 163, 181
Zycor, 201n34